Markets and Marketing

An Orientation

Lee E. Preston

Melvin H. Baker Professor of American Enterprise
State University of New York at Buffalo

Scott, Foresman and Company

For Katherine, James, and Mary Jane

Library of Congress Catalog Card No.: 71-104319

Copyright © 1970 by Scott, Foresman and Company, Glenview, Illinois

Philippines Copyright 1970 by Scott, Foresman and Company

All Rights Reserved

Printed in the United States of America

Regional Offices of Scott, Foresman and Company are located in Atlanta, Dallas, Glenview, Palo Alto, Oakland, N. J., and London, England

About This Book

This book is intended to provide a basis for understanding the character and role of marketing activity in the economy and in the firm. It offers an orientation, not a comprehensive description or a handbook of current marketing practices. In writing it, I have assumed that readers are already familiar with some aspects of marketing from personal experience, and that they observe marketing developments taking place all around them. The book attempts to provide a framework for collecting and sorting out these random experiences and observations, and a basis for systematically gathering new ones, so that significant elements can be identified and analyzed and inferences and implications brought out.

A scientific or analytical approach to any problem or subject consists of three elements: **description, explanation,** and **prediction.** Thus the task of the analyst or manager confronted with a problem in marketing is, first, to describe it; then to explain the forces at work and their interactions; and, finally, to predict the results of various actions, both those that he might initiate and those that might be initiated by others. This is both a neat conception and a useful guide to practical study and problem solving. However, the three analytical steps are inherently interrelated, and each step requires a fundamental understanding of the others.

If we set out to describe marketing activity without any notion of the kind of explanation or prediction we might want to make, we will become lost and exhausted in the accumulation of meaningless detail. An efficient description focuses on the key factors needed for explanation. Similarly, a useful explanation provides the basis for prediction, either of what will happen under changed circumstances or of developments over time.

An overview of the entire process is required before we can determine *what* we need to predict or *how* we should attempt to build an explanation. Marketing data are accumulating very rapidly, and formal models of individual parts and pieces of the marketing process are being generated by practitioners and scholars. The problem facing users of these materials is to determine what *kind* of model of what *part* of the process would be most useful in dealing with some particular problem; what data would be relevant or irrelevant; and the validity of the resulting explanation and predictions. To answer these questions, the user requires both an acquaintance with the available data and models and some conception of the *complete* process about which his materials suggest numerous partial insights.

The current teaching literature in marketing is heavily oriented to the presentation of numerous partial models and, to a somewhat lesser extent, toward implementing them with data, all of which are primarily focused on marketing situations common in the United States and other highly developed countries. It has seemed to me that the usefulness of this excellent material for students and practitioners alike is somewhat reduced by its general neglect of the characteristics of the larger context of marketing activity within which the partial analyses are embedded. Therefore, one aim of this book is to restore the **market** itself—the arena of competition and exchange—to a central place within marketing teaching and analysis. And an additional but closely related aim is to provide a vehicle for teaching and study that treats current marketing problems and practices in the United States as examples of more general situations, not as unique phenomena that constitute the entire subject matter of the field.

In order to accomplish these goals, three important concepts seem to require substantial emphasis. One of these is the concept of the **marketing system** as an interlinked and dynamic network of firms, agencies, industries, and regions. The idea heavily stressed in the management science literature—that the firm is a system of interlinked activities—needs to be tied to this larger conception so that we see the whole marketing process as composed of systems and subsystems with multiple interrelationships. Second, and closely related, is the concept of **market reaction**—that is, the sequential response of other marketing decision-making units to actions taken unilaterally by any of them and to disturbances arising from other sources. Finally, the concept of **historical evolution and dynamic change** links the long-term development of the system with the actions and reactions of individual decision-making units and groups within the system or process.

Can these ideas be put across by didactic writing and teaching? Or can they be understood only by each individual's accumulation of experience and analysis of specific situations over time? On this point I must confess some doubts, and some sympathy with the view, traditionally associated with the use of the case method of instruction, that "wisdom can't be taught." However, it seems to me that students and practitioners are more likely to understand ideas—and to use and modify them on the basis of their own maturing experiences—if the ideas are at least exposed to view. Such is the motivation behind this book.

In writing this book, I have assumed that its readers will have had some exposure to basic economic and behavioral concepts and some training in analytical thinking. Within these broad limitations, the book has been designed so that its principal points will be accessible to the beginning student and to the marketing practitioner. For more sophisticated students, the book might serve as an introduction to a course that uses one of the more advanced marketing management texts or a survey of significant readings, models, and/or cases. Its role in this usage would be to provide a comprehensive frame of reference so that the sequence of detailed topics could be placed in an integrated perspective.

One final point. Every word in this short book was written to be read, and much of it has been read and reread by students and faculty colleagues over a considerable period of time. I have tried to eliminate digression and details readily available elsewhere or from the reader's own knowledge, and thus to keep the main points and key relationships at the forefront. At the same time, I have tried to make the book accessible to a wide audience—a basic introduction for beginners and, hopefully, a source of new insights for more sophisticated readers.

This little book is the fruit of eleven years of teaching and research at the School of Business Administration, University of California, Berkeley. During these years I have benefited beyond measure from contact with two senior colleagues, E. T. Grether and David A. Revzan, and with many other faculty associates—Norman R. Collins, F. E. Balderston, Richard H. Holton, Louis P. Bucklin, John G. Myers, and Francesco M. Nicosia. Visitors and friends from other institutions, particularly G. David Hughes, Leon E. Richartz, and Reed Moyer, have also contributed importantly to the development of my own understanding of marketing activities and problems. Each of these individuals will probably find some idea appearing here to which he might justly lay claim; each may also find some lingering error that he has attempted to eradicate. Several generations of students, both at Berkeley and elsewhere, have used parts of these materials and permitted me to learn something from their reactions. For the help of all of these colleagues and students I am grateful; none of them can be held responsible for the final results.

Preparation of the book in its final stages was facilitated by support from the Institute of Business and Economic Research, which permitted Mr. Gert Assmus to spend many invaluable hours checking data and references and noting points requiring clarification and revision. The manuscript itself was produced by Mrs. Ellen D. McGibbon; this, I fear, is the last of many projects in which I shall enjoy the benefit of her tireless cooperation and perfect skill.

Buffalo, New York   Lee E. Preston
January, 1970

Contents

1

Markets and Marketing

What Is a Market?

A **market** is an exchange relationship among buyers and sellers. Whether we think of the traditional **marketplace** for local fresh produce and handicrafts, or the **market** for consumer goods in a metropolitan area, or the national and international **market** for steel, chemicals, or industrial equipment, the essential nature of a market remains the same.

Within a market, two activities take place: **communication** and **exchange.** Buyers and sellers communicate to acquaint each other with the products and services available and desired, and with their willingness and ability to trade, which includes prices and quantities. Then, when both buyer and seller are able and willing, they effect a transaction or exchange. Money or a promise to pay is presented, a service is performed, merchandise changes hands, or a promise of delivery or performance is made.

These activities of communication and exchange are undertaken by the individual buyers and sellers in order to accomplish their own purposes. The interaction of numerous buyers and sellers, however, yields other results that are attributable to the market as a whole, not to any of the individual participants as such. Important among these results are **allocation** and **valuation**. Through a market exchange, available supplies are allocated among possible purchasers, and available demand is allocated among possible sellers. Note that the allocation of demand is just as significant as the allocation of supply, and that firms and industries grow or decline as a result of their ability to attract shares of total demand. Market exchange also serves to establish the value of goods and services. Although sellers might wish to receive more and buyers might prefer to pay less, the exchange price at which transactions take place becomes the **market value** of the goods and services exchanged. This market value may therefore be compared to alternative uses of the time and materials involved, and may be referred to by buyers and sellers, and by others not directly involved in the market, for their own decision-making and accounting purposes. (See Entenberg and Boness, 1964, pp. 43–52, and Steiner, 1968, pp. 575–581.)

Market and Nonmarket Transactions

Markets are not the only means by which goods and services are transferred among individuals and organizations. Such transfers are also made, usually on an informal basis, within households and other similar groups in the normal course of their existence, and between groups in the form of charity (Belshaw, 1965). Large and important transfers of goods and services among producers and users may also be effected by administrative action or political decision, as well as by markets. An administrative transfer occurs, for example, when a firm producing both raw materials and final products transfers some of its raw materials to its manufacturing plant for processing. Although the firm may choose to consider the value of the raw materials in an outside market when it makes such a decision, and may use such market prices for accounting purposes, it need not do so. The same kind of transfers are made within units of government and other organizations, and the administrative criteria may or may not include references to market values.

Political decisions are also used as a substitute for or supplement to the actions of the market. By popular vote, or by decision of government agencies, certain goods or services may be provided to the general public and their cost apportioned among the citizenry by means of taxes and assessments. Further, political actions may shift whole classes of problems from private to public decision making. For example, activities aimed at providing police protection, education, or medical care may be placed under public control by the collective action of the citizens or their representatives. Public authorities, such as local governments, school districts, and agencies of state and national governments, are then created to exercise this control. These authorities may rely primarily on administrative procedures in carrying out their day-to-day operations. For example, school district administrators will probably determine pay scales and assign teachers to schools, rather than give each school principal a budget and allow him to negotiate directly for the services of teachers in the open market. However, public authorities in the United States will deal primarily in markets when they come to buy property, construct facilities, select equipment, and determine standards for hiring personnel. Thus, like large integrated firms, public agencies are embedded in the market economy and subject to market constraints in their external dealings.

Political decisions also supplement or limit market activities in quite another way. Even in societies where markets are the principal mechanisms for coordinating supply and demand and for effecting the transfer of goods and services among economic units, political authority may be used to condition the way in which markets function or to limit their activity. Simple examples are legal protection of the validity of contracts, legal standards of liability and fraud, and statutory requirements for engaging in business. More complicated issues are raised by public control over product quality, such as the purity of foods and cosmetics, the effects of drugs, or the safety of automobiles. Very significant limitations on the operation of markets may arise when access to a type of business is controlled by restrictive licenses or grants or monopoly, or where prices or sales volumes are subject to specific regulations.

The substitution of administrative and political transfers for market transactions can be readily observed both in the United States and in other countries. Indeed, this substitution is a necessary implication of the relative growth of large private and public economic units within the economy. However, both the scope of the public sector and the extent of public control over private market activity are relatively limited in the United States, compared to other countries of the world. In most other countries, much larger segments of economic activity (such as common-carrier transportation and telephone, telegraph, and broadcast communications) are assigned to public agencies; and more rigorous control is exercised over private markets. In almost all countries, a substantial amount of public control is exercised over international market transactions, even when all the parties involved are private individuals and firms.

An Essential Distinction

When we describe a particular transfer of goods and services as resulting primarily from market, administrative, or political decision processes, we are not necessarily praising or condemning the result. All three approaches seem to have certain advantages and certain defects in particular circumstances. Even the most market-oriented economies do not handle all economic decisions by means of the market mechanism. Many large and far-reaching programs in such economies are governed by political and administrative procedures: national defense, regional development, and public services, for example. At the same time, even heavily centralized and controlled economies continue to have recourse to markets for certain types of exchanges and transfers, and it appears that an increasing use of markets tends to accompany increasing prosperity in the "command" economies of the Soviet Union and Eastern Europe (see, e.g., Grossman, 1967).

The peculiar advantages of markets lie in their flexibility and variety and in the scope they provide for individual decision making. In a market transaction, we are reasonably sure that the buyer does not pay more, nor the seller receive less, than each believes the merchandise or service is worth to him. Further, if all potential buyers and sellers cannot be satisfied, the market mechanism tends to permit the more willing traders (high-price buyer and low-price seller) to be satisfied, while the less willing (low-price buyer and high-price seller) are excluded. No nonmarket exchange system automatically provides this explicit test of relative value.

However, neither the character and quality of goods and services nor their specific allocation among buyers and sellers, achieved by markets, need conform to particular standards of welfare, equity, performance, or taste. Different individuals will have different opinions as to the desirability of the product and price results in various markets, and the community as a whole may choose to intervene in order to alter specific results of market activity. Particular problems of broad public concern arise when market results are strongly affected by substantial inequities in the distribution of income or ownership, unequal bargaining power between buyers and sellers, or lack of information.

This book is principally concerned with the way markets work in a large, complex economy that is based on private ownership; thus we give primary attention to the character and importance of marketing activities by private firms and individuals. Although, by implication at least, this analysis also identifies some of the problems that have to be handled if administrative or political decision systems are substituted for the market mechanism, it does not consider the problem of choosing or mixing market and nonmarket mechanisms from the viewpoint of society as a whole. These decisions usually involve broad social and cultural issues that are far beyond our immediate scope. However, we do have occasion to note specific instances (e.g., vertical integration) in which a buying or selling firm may choose to alter its operations, so as to increase or decrease its use of markets, and to shift decision making between market and administrative mechanisms.

What Is Marketing?

Although in even the most primitive societies, goods and services are produced and exchanged, and values established, markets are not natural phenomena. They do not come into being and operate simply because of "a certain propensity in human nature . . . to truck, barter, and exchange one thing for another," as Adam Smith put it (1937, p. 3). On the contrary, markets of any significant size and continuity require complicated and deliberate activities on the part of many individuals and economic units—households, firms, associations, and government bodies. In short, markets require marketing.

Marketing is the complex of activities that brings markets into being and causes them to operate. Marketing thus includes the immediate market activities of communication and exchange. It also includes the important activities that necessarily precede and follow the market transactions themselves, such as activities of potential sellers aimed at finding out what kinds of products and services potential buyers might want and activities of buyers aimed at identifying their own requirements and possible ways of meeting them. It also includes important auxiliary or supportive activities, such as transportation, financing, and storage. Thus the network of marketing activities associated with any particular market reaches out to include many actions and decisions on the part of the potential sellers and buyers (in addition to the immediate act of exchange) and to encompass the actions of many economic units that are not direct participants in the market.[1]

Although emphasis on definitions always runs the risk of substituting jargon for understanding, it may be useful to relate our use of the terms **market** and **marketing** to some other uses in common speech. Frequently, when we speak of the "market" for some product or service, we are referring only to the conditions of demand: "The market for X is expanding rapidly" or "There is no market for Y at the present time." There is nothing confusing about such statements, and they may be appropriate even in the technical sense. That is, if the demand for X is increasing and the supply of X is increasing in response, it may be precisely true that the **market**—the whole set of possible exchange relationships—is expanding rapidly.

We also speak of a salesman marketing a product and of housewife doing her marketing before preparing a meal. In the first case, we probably mean that he is attempting to sell the product, and in the second that she is selecting and buying her groceries. Again, both these uses may be strictly correct, and, what is more important, they emphasize two very significant points. (1) Marketing involves many different activities and actors; thus the housewife and the salesman might be involved in the marketing of the same merchandise, and many other kinds of economic units might also be involved with them. (2) Buying is just as much a part of the marketing process as selling; therefore marketing must not be thought of as a one-directional flow of merchandise and promotional messages from sellers to buyers.

A Schematic Model

Our basic conception of a market and marketing is illustrated schematically in figure 1–1. On the selling side of the market, the ability of the firm to produce or procure merchandise or services is combined with an analysis of potential demand to guide product development and promotion. The result is a **market offer**—a willingness to make a certain type of merchandise or service available to some potential

---

1. For a collection of definitions of marketing, see Bell (1966), pp. 4–5.

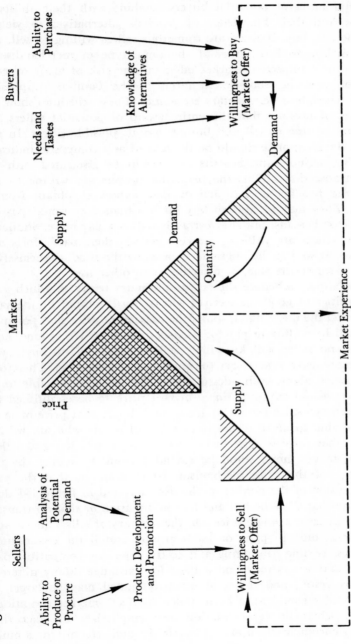

Figure 1–1   Marketing: A Schematic Model

buyers under some exchange conditions. On the buying side, the needs and tastes of potential buyers combine with their ability to purchase and their knowledge of purchase alternatives to yield a willingness to buy. If there are numerous sellers willing to sell, and buyers willing to buy, units of the same type of merchandise or product, their respective market offers—at the risk of great oversimplification—may be depicted in terms of the familiar supply-and-demand schedules of elementary economics. These schedules show the quantities of product that the entire group of potential sellers and buyers are willing to sell and buy at various possible prices. In this context, the term **price** should be thought of as a composite indicator of all the sacrifices and benefits that might be associated with the market transactions. Thus the price that buyers are willing to pay reflects the benefits or satisfactions they expect to obtain from a product. They may be able to buy for less than they would pay for the expected benefits, but they certainly will not pay more. Similarly, the price sellers are willing to accept reflects their past efforts and their costs, as well as the alternatives of using the product themselves, holding it for future sale, or directing it to other uses.

The supply schedule shows the **minimum** terms on which various quantities of goods or services will be forthcoming; the demand schedule, on the other hand, shows the **maximum** price that potential buyers will be willing to pay for various quantities. We assume, however, that no seller will knowingly sell for less, and no buyer will buy for more, than is necessary to complete his transaction. Therefore, if information about both sides of the market is fully available to all parties, we would expect a single market price to be established for all transactions. All buyers who are willing to pay that price or more would be able to make transactions with all sellers who are willing to accept that price or less. Buyers who wish to pay less and sellers who wish to get more would be excluded from the market by the "rationing" of the price mechanism. Note, however, that the general conception of the market mechanism depicted in figure 1-1 does *not* require that there be full and free information *or* that all transactions take place at a single price. On the contrary, if sellers and buyers communicate only in pairs or small groups, and if the communication process is time consuming and costly, then any compatible pair of buyers and sellers may find a basis for exchange. Many different prices may result, and the total quantity traded may be larger or smaller than it would have been under "perfect" market conditions.

This schematic representation also emphasizes the fact that **marketing** encompasses an array of activities and circumstances much broader than, and logically prior to, the appearance of potential sellers and buyers who are willing to trade. In consumer goods markets, the potential sellers may be thought of as the primary active units, developing products and promotion programs in anticipation of demand. In industrial and institutional goods markets, buyers are often equally active in determining their own needs, developing performance requirements and cost-effectiveness evaluations. The individual marketing decision-making systems of the buying and selling units receive information from, and contribute reactions to, the market as a whole.

Thus the marketing units learn from market experience—including the experience of not being able to buy or sell on the terms determined in advance—and adapt their behavior accordingly. As a result, market conditions and marketing behavior change over time. A buyer satisfies his needs and exhausts his ability to pay, or finds his past purchase decisions unsatisfactory, and therefore withdraws from the market; or he develops a desire for the product, or a technology requiring its regular use, and therefore comes to want it more intensely (i.e., at a higher price or in larger quantities). Similarly, a seller learns that certain types of merchandise remain unsold, that other types are moving more rapidly than anticipated, and that some potential buyers are as yet unaware of his market offering, and he revises his behavior accordingly. Hence the marketing process should not be conceived primarily in terms of a beginning, middle, and end but rather as a continuous, recurring process of action and reaction.

Figure 1–1 illustrates only a single market in which some participants are clearly potential buyers and others potential sellers. The actual market economy consists of a diverse array of such markets, with buyers and sellers and products and prices interrelated in complex and changing ways. Actual market choices are made from an array of products and services, and are differentiated from each other in quality, location, convenience, and timing. Both buyers and sellers find some (but not necessarily the *same*) products reasonably close substitutes for one another; other items may not be substitutable in use but only in terms of relative shares of total purchases or sales. Markets become **segmented** according to special buyer needs or supply conditions. In the reverse process, separate markets become merged into one as a result of changes in tastes, information, and product availability.

The final complication, and the basis of a fundamental economic interlinkage, is the fact that most economic units function both as buyers and as sellers, and their purchase behavior in one market affects their sales behavior in another, and vice versa. Business firms, in particular, must be thought of as engaged in an endless process of buying and reselling, although the items bought and sold may be so different in physical and functional characteristics as to appear unrelated in the eyes of an outside observer. The importance of resale values, even after a very substantial change in physical form, may cause the purchasing behavior of buyers in any particular market to be primarily a reflection of the needs and tastes of *their* potential customers. Correspondingly, the sales offers of any particular group of sellers may be importantly determined by the sales offers, actual or anticipated, of *their* sources of supply, and so on. This means that the marketing process does not involve a single group of sellers and buyers who affect one market exchange but, rather, a complex network of reseller-buyers who may change the form and location of merchandise, perform a wide variety of services, and both stimulate and adapt to changes in ultimate supply and final demand conditions.

Enterprise Structure and Marketing Functions

We shall define the term **enterprise** to mean any economic unit, other than a consuming household, engaged in the production and marketing of goods or services. Private business firms, cooperatives, and public agencies that provide goods and services for sale are thus included; public regulatory agencies and units of government are, of course, excluded. The producing and marketing sectors of an economy can be described in terms of the number and types of enterprises involved, the relationships among the enterprise units, and the relationships between the enterprises and the consuming households. Any individual enterprise can, in turn, be described in terms of four salient characteristics: (1) products and services produced and marketed, (2) geographic and economic location, (3) form of ownership and management, and (4) functions performed. These terms are familiar from common usage, but their use in describing and analyzing marketing activities requires a few explanatory comments.

Products and Services

The location, functions, size, and organizational structure of an enterprise are determined to a considerable extent by the particular characteristics of the products and services it produces and markets. Enterprises that are engaged primarily in physical production activity (changing the **form** of materials) will be substantially different in most respects from enterprises engaged primarily in performing services or in buying and reselling. Even among enterprises engaged in the production and marketing of goods, substantial differences in location, function, and organizational structure arise as a result of differences in (1) stages of processing of the materials involved, (2) their physical characteristics (e.g., bulky or small, heavy or light, durable or perishable, etc.), and (3) their economic characteristics (high cost or low cost). In addition, enterprises engaged primarily in the production of services differ substantially, depending upon whether the services are specifically linked with goods (as in retailing) or necessarily associated with the service-receiving individuals (as in barber shops). Enterprises that perform other services, such as legal and financial services, may be entirely free from the constraints of dealing with particular merchandise units or providing face-to-face contact with customers.

Enterprises differ not only with respect to their particular products and services but also with respect to the degree of specialization or diversification among products and services. Some enterprises are highly specialized; others offer a broad range of choice, or combinations of products and services, many of which may be produced and purchased simultaneously. Highly specialized enterprises frequently have much in common, even if they are highly specialized in providing very different products and services; and diversified enterprises may exhibit similar cost and organizational characteristics, although their specific combinations of products and services differ substantially.

Geographic and Economic Location

The location of an enterprise includes not only its geographic place of operation but also its economic location and communication outreach. Significant geographic location characteristics include (1) the number of places of operation and their relationship to each other; (2) basic locational attributes, such as rural or urban, central-city or suburban, and proximity to natural resources, productive factors, or final users; as well as (3) the specific geographic site in relation to political boundaries (i.e., country, state, county, city, and street). Economic and communication dimensions of location include transportation modes and costs to relevant contact points for supply and demand, centrality or remoteness with respect to other locations or

clusters of activity, and the convenience and geographic range of communication. Clearly, then, we are interested in location not simply to
locate enterprises on a map but to understand why particular types
of activity are located in places with particular characteristics and
to analyze the relationship of one location to another.

Two kinds of location patterns are of particular importance in
marketing analysis. One of these is the **flow** pattern, in which a collection of physical materials flows from an original supply source,
through one or more locations in which some processing or other
intermediate activity takes place, and finally to a location for end use.
Marketing, transportation, and communication activities will grow
up around this flow, and various enterprises will become linked along
it as well. A second locational pattern is **central-peripheral,** in which
an activity that originates at some central point is extended through
a surrounding area to a peripheral boundary. The central-peripheral
pattern describes a major wholesale center serving surrounding retail
centers, a port serving a hinterland, a retail store serving a neighbor-
hood, and so forth. Actual locational arrangements interweave these
two basic patterns, and others as well, in adapting to the "pull" of
supply and use centers, the pressure of costs, and the appearance of
new locational alternatives. Location is such a paramount feature
of marketing activity that it requires extensive and detailed consideration, and we have therefore sharply limited the discussion of locational aspects of marketing in this book, leaving them for more comprehensive treatment elsewhere (e.g., Berry, 1967).

Ownership and Management

The pattern of ownership and management is an enterprise characteristic of primary importance, and the careful study of such patterns is
a task of great complexity. For our purposes, only a few essential
points need be made. The great population of businesses in the United
States may be broadly separated into two groups: those that are small
and owner-managed and those that are large and professionally managed. Owner-managed units are principally proprietorships and part-
nerships, although many small units adopt the corporate form for
legal and tax purposes. Large and professionally managed enterprises
typically take the corporate form. Cooperatives are a third type of
organization, and are particularly important in some areas of marketing. The members of cooperatives are also the owners, and they co-

operate in order to have certain activities carried out through a central management for the benefit of the members themselves.

Government enterprises are not commonly engaged in production and marketing in the United States, although there are a number of significant exceptions, such as postal and electric power services. Such enterprises are very important in many other countries, where they may either operate alongside private businesses or enjoy complete monopoly in the production and sale of certain types of merchandise (gasoline, matches, sugar, and salt are typical examples). Even where government ownership is relatively limited, the impact of its public policies and directives on managerial activity and decisions may be quite substantial. Thus a relevant aspect of ownership and management is the extent to which the activities of enterprise managers are directed or constrained by external authority.

Functions Performed

The final salient characteristic of an enterprise is the particular group of functional activities it performs. Common observation and official reports alike describe enterprises as primarily engaged in agricultural production, mining, construction, manufacturing, wholesaling, retailing, and so forth. These are gross functional categories and they suggest the principal types of activity in which an enterprise is engaged. Within each of these principal categories, additional functional breakdowns might be suggested as a basis for description and analysis. Particularly within marketing, the large number of different types of activities that take place, as well as the varied patterns of specialization and combination that are observed, suggest that a more detailed functional analysis would be fruitful. Such analysis, which has long been a prominent feature of marketing literature, has generally been made in terms of **marketing functions.**

Marketing functions. Every major contributor to the literature has suggested a somewhat different set of categories to describe the functional activities involved in marketing. The longest list, containing 120 functional elements, is that of Ryan (1935, pp. 205–24). The shortest, perhaps, is the Clark and Clark (1942) list of "exchange," "physical supply," and "facilitating" functions. This diversity suggests that, instead of there being a single correct approach or various incorrect approaches to the analysis of functional activity within marketing, different analysts adapt different approaches for different purposes.[2]

The purpose of identifying marketing functions in the present context is to permit a functional description of marketing activity that is sufficient to explain differences in the number, size, location, and profitability of different marketing enterprises. For this purpose, marketing functions should be identified so that we can both group activities that have similar cost structures and separate and distinguish between activities that have different cost structures. A minimum list of the functions that seem to meet this general criterion is the following:

1. **Transportation:** Physical movement in space, together with all auxiliary activities associated with such movement.

2. **Storage:** The holding of commodities and merchandise over time, including the time involved in production and transportation.

3. **Financing:** Providing both ownership for physical materials during the marketing process and credit that permits ownership transfers and bridges the time gap between expenses and receipts.

4. **Risk bearing:** Closely associated with financing, risk bearing has the additional dimensions of insurance, return privilege and liability, and the use of futures markets and other risk-shifting mechanisms.

5. **Communication-negotiation:** Personal and impersonal contacts intended to acquaint buyers and sellers with the range of market alternatives, conditions of sale, and other informative or persuasive points.

6. **Development of the trading mechanism, standard descriptive terminology, and contracting terms:** Collective action, either by government or among traders themselves, is generally required in order to provide a basis for the regular and orderly conduct of marketing operations, legally binding contracts, and quality norms.

7. **Exchange:** Actual buying and selling—the consummation of transactions made possible by the foregoing functions.

Three important features of this and any similar list of marketing functions should be noted. First, the functions are inherently interconnected. Transportation and storage can be both joint and substitute activities: merchandise is inevitably "stored" in transit; on the other hand, transportation can be substituted for large-scale local

2. For additional discussion of marketing functions, see McGarry (1950), pp. 263–79, and Bucklin (1966), pp. 10–15.

storage as a means of filling orders. Financing inevitably involves risk bearing, although risks can be shifted through insurance and other arrangements that provide no financing. Retail display is a form of storage that also provides a direct communication function. And so on.

Second, one indication of the differences in fundamental characteristics among these functions is the existence of marketing enterprises and organizations that are primarily specialized in one function alone. Advertising agencies perform the communication function; organized commodities exchanges provide a regular trading mechanism; public warehouses provide storage; and so on.

The third and most important point is that any such list of marketing functions, based upon distinctive cost patterns, omits the salient activity of **market making.** Any enterprise that is engaged in marketing may take the initiative in seeking out and developing market contacts. Any enterprise may, under other circumstances, remain passive, responding to market alternatives but not initiating them.

An active role in market making may be associated with production activities, with wholesaling or retailing, or with an auxiliary function, such as transportation or advertising. We cannot readily anticipate, on the basis of cost and functional activity data alone, just where the primary source of initiative will lie in a particular sequence of marketing relationships, or how the role of marketing making will change over time. This unpredictability is not, however, a reflection of analytical inadequacy; it is, rather, a basic characteristic of the marketing process itself. The importance of variety and adaptation in marketing is so great, and the opportunities for differentiation are so numerous, that any analysis based exclusively on a specific classification of marketing functions and their costs cannot tell the whole story. Market making is an additional function, based on various combinations of imagination, favorable economic position, entrepreneurial vigor, and luck. Without this vital function there may be some physical distribution and exchange, but there will be little marketing—in the sense that term is used in modern business management and in this book.

Marketing and distribution. We noted above that markets require marketing, and the reverse proposition is also true: Marketing, in the sense discussed here, requires markets. The transfer of goods and services from producers to users can be handled by non-market means, and many of the same functions will of necessity be performed, but **marketing,** including the market making function, need not take place. It is therefore useful to define the term **distribution** as the **allocation and transfer of goods and services among producers and users.**

Distribution by one means or another is an essential intermediate step between production and consumption in all economies beyond the subsistence household stage of development. Marketing is an important means of distribution—the primary means in a private ownership economy, and a significant auxiliary means in most others. Marketing involves more than distribution, however. The critical differences between marketing and distribution are the relative importance of the two-way flow of negotiation and communication between potential buyers and sellers, the critical role of risk and finance, and the dependence of the entire marketing process on individual sources of initiative and market making throughout the system.

Marketing as a Field of Study

The preceding comments describe marketing in very general terms as a social and economic process involving a varied collection of activities. Since all of the activities are interrelated in some way, it is possible to study marketing (1) by starting with any one activity and tracing its connection with others, (2) by starting at one stage in the marketing process and following the contacts between this stage and preceding and succeeding supply-and-demand levels, or (3) by analyzing the marketing activity of particular firms, industries, geographic areas, or buyer groups. All of these approaches to the study of marketing, and many variants of each approach, are to be found in the modern professional and academic literature.

Among these varied approaches and viewpoints, however, three principal orientations to marketing as a field of study seem to be generally recognized as essential: (1) marketing organization and operations seen as a complex action system involving many actors and many goals, (2) marketing management as an activity of the business enterprise, and (3) buyer behavior as an independent phenomenon. The first of these is sometimes referred to as a macrosystemic approach, meaning that emphasis is placed on the marketing system as a whole or on large segments of the system identified by industry, product, or type of marketing activity. Historical studies and analyses related to public policy—for example, whether a particular type of marketing activity should be encouraged, prohibited, or taxed—would also follow this orientation. Clearly, this broad viewpoint is essential to a comprehensive understanding of marketing as a means of accomplishing important functions for society as a whole. It is also essential to understanding the conditions facing an individual buying or selling unit within the larger system.

The study of marketing management in the business enterprise begins with identification of the place of the firm within the system, but it places primary emphasis on the tools of management decision making and the scope of managerial activity. Thus we consider the marketing goals of the firm—profits, sales, market share—and the way in which these goals can be achieved through the use of the firm's "marketing mix"—its products, prices, promotional program, and distribution channels. Most commercial marketing research reflects this management orientation, and the purpose of such research is to gather material that will be useful for managerial decision making and action.

The study of buying behavior has been approached from both the macrosystemic and the managerial viewpoints, but buying behavior has in recent years been increasingly regarded as a separate area of study. This change is primarily due to developments in the methodology of the behavioral sciences and resultant increases in knowledge and understanding of behavioral phenomena. The background of information and the collection of research techniques necessary to study the determinants of buying behavior—cultural factors, social contacts, habits, information sources, and so forth—have become somewhat distinct from the knowledge and the professional tools used in analyzing aggregate marketing trends or managing marketing activities within the firm. The results of the analysis of buying behavior may, of course, be used to explain the organization and operation of the marketing system as a whole or to guide decision making in the firm.

Summary

A market is an exchange relationship among buyers and sellers. Within a market, communication and exchange activities take place and goods and services are allocated and valued. Nonmarket means for accomplishing these same tasks include informal allocations within households and administrative and political allocations within larger segments of society.

Marketing is the complex of activities that brings markets into being and causes them to operate. Marketing includes not only communication and exchange activities but also the necessary preceding and succeeding activities surrounding market transactions, as well as specialized auxiliary functions. An economic unit on the selling side of a market joins its ability to produce or procure goods and services with an analysis of potential demand to determine product development and promotional strategies. The result is a market offer, which reflects the willingness of the seller to sell various products and services under various conditions. On the buying side, needs and tastes and purchase ability, plus knowledge of market alternatives, conjoin to yield the market offer of buyers. The interaction of the two groups of able and willing traders constitutes the operation of markets.

An economic unit that is engaged in marketing may be described in terms of its products and services, geographic and economic location, form of ownership and management, and functional activity. Marketing agencies may be specialized or diversified in each of these respects. The identification and analysis of significant marketing functions has been a major topic in the traditional literature; and we have identified seven distinct functions on the basis of differences among their cost structures and the importance of agencies that are specialized in each function. However, because no single classification of functional activities can be appropriate for all purposes, the key function of market making—taking initiative in the development of marketing contacts and opportunities—cannot be analyzed in terms of activity costs and specialization alone.

References

Bell, Martin L. *Marketing: Concepts and Strategy*. Houghton Mifflin, 1966.

Belshaw, Cyril S. *Traditional Exchange and Modern Markets*. Prentice-Hall, 1965.

Berry, Brian J. L. *Geography of Market Centers and Retail Distribution*. Prentice-Hall, 1967.

Bucklin, Louis P. *A Theory of Distribution Channel Structure*. University of California, Berkeley, Institute of Business and Economic Research, 1966.

Clark, Fred E., and Carrie P. Clark. *Principles of Marketing*, 3rd ed. Macmillan, 1942.

Cox, Reavis, and Wroe Alderson, eds. *Theory in Marketing*. Irwin, 1950.

Entenberg, Robert D., and A. James Boness. "On the Idea of a Market." *Journal of Industrial Economics,* Vol. 12, November 1964.

Grossman, Gregory. *Economic Systems*. Prentice-Hall, 1967.

McGarry, Edmund D. "Some Functions of Marketing Reconsidered." In *Theory in Marketing,* eds. Reavis Cox and Wroe Alderson. Irwin, 1950.

Ryan, Franklin W. "Fundamental Elements of Market Distribution." *Harvard Business Review,* Vol. 13, January 1935.

Smith, Adam. *An Inquiry into the Nature and Causes of the Wealth of Nations,* ed. Edward Cannan. Random House, 1937.

Steiner, Peter O. "Markets and Industries." *International Encyclopedia of the Social Sciences,* Vol. 9. The Free Press, 1968.

Part I

Organization and Coordination in the Marketing System

2

Scale, Productivity,
and Efficiency in Marketing

The Scale of Marketing Activity

Marketing accounts for both a substantial part of economic activity and a substantial use of productive resources in all developed countries. In the United States, approximately one-third of all nonfarm business firms are engaged in some form of retail and wholesale trade, and most of the other firms engage in marketing activities to a significant extent. Employment in the distributive trades, plus estimated marketing employment in primarily manufacturing companies, amounts to about one-fourth of all nonagricultural employment.[1] Value added by distribution—that is, the increase in final price that is due specifically to marketing operations—has been estimated at about 45 percent of the value of all final goods (Cox, *et al.,* 1965, p. 159).

The scale of marketing activity tends to increase with the process of economic development and increasing income. For example, employment in retail and wholesale trade has increased from 6 percent of our national labor force in 1870 to more than 20 percent in 1968. An international comparison (figure 2–1), based on data for the years

---

1. Computed from Census Bureau figures (1968).

Figure 2–1   Relationship of Gross Domestic Product per Capita and Percentage of Commercial Employment in the Total Labor Force (C/LF Ratio) (Preston, 1968)

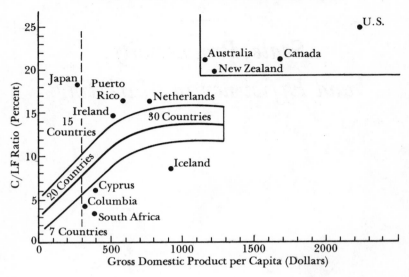

around 1960, shows that commercial employment as a percent of the total labor force tends to increase steadily, along with increases in gross domestic product (GDP) per capita up to levels of about $500, then to rise at a slower rate and to level off at about 14 or 15 percent in economies with about $1000 GDP per capita. This relationship is by no means uniform, but variations from it are widest among the poorest countries, whose data are most suspect. The sharp contrast provided by the four "born free" countries—Australia, New Zealand, the United States, and Canada—with their very high levels of income and commercial employment, is evident from the figure (see Preston, 1968).

This general tendency for marketing to absorb relatively more resources as economies become wealthier may be traced to several different sources, one of which is the sheer size and variety of wealthy economies. As development proceeds, there is an increase in the number of different goods and services that require marketing, which may also involve a shift in the composition of production and purchasing toward lines that require relatively more marketing effort. For example, the introduction of durable home appliances and highly technical industrial equipment requires more marketing activity than expanded consumption of staple foods and raw materials. A second factor that might contribute to the trend is a change of tastes that favors marketing—including desires for added convenience, advertising, packaging, and so forth. In addition, marketing services may well be considered "superior goods," that is, expenditure categories that tend to absorb larger proportions of rising incomes, such as education, medical care, and the fine arts. A third factor may be the geographic shifts in population and population density that accompany economic development. Cities are marketing centers, and rising per capita incomes historically have been accompanied by urbanization and thus by the development of new geographic concentrations of marketing activity.

Aggregate Productivity in Marketing

In addition to the qualitative factors that underlie the relative growth of marketing activities over time, there is a critical question concerning marketing costs. Are marketing activities subject to a substantially lower rate of productivity increase and cost reduction, over time, than other sectors of the economy, particularly agriculture and manufacturing? This is a significant analytical question, for the following reasons: If productivity increases more rapidly in one sector of the economy than in another, and if both sectors are equally competitive, costs and prices may be expected to fall in the more progressive sector and to rise in the less progressive sector.[2] When such relative cost and price changes take place, the allocation of expenditures and resources between the two sectors will change, with the pattern of change depending upon the elasticities of demand.[3] The two extreme possibilities are as follows.

1. If demand for the output of the less progressive sector is elastic, relative to demand for the output of the more progressive sector, the less progressive sector will gradually decline in size. In effect, the lack of productivity increase and the relatively rising costs will have priced the output of this sector out of the market.

2. If demand for the output of the less progressive sector is inelastic, relative to demand in the other sector, the less productive sector will maintain its size (or even grow), costs and prices in this sector will rise, and this sector will absorb larger and larger shares of total resources.

2. This analysis is based upon Baumol (1967).
3. For an explanation of the elasticity concept, see the appendix to chapter 7.

There is a significant body of opinion that precisely these types of differences in productivity trends and demand elasticities between marketing and nonmarketing sectors of the economy offer an important explanation for the tendency of the marketing sector to grow over time, relative to other sectors, and to be relatively larger in wealthy countries than in poor countries. Most empirical studies of this question have focused on labor productivity. Barger's analysis for the eighty-year period 1869–1949 indicated that man-hour output in retail and wholesale trade had risen at an average annual rate of about 1.0 percent per year, whereas man-hour output in commodity production and construction had risen about 2.6 percent per year (Barger, 1955, p. 40). An analysis of more recent data shows a difference of approximately the same magnitude between rates of labor productivity change in all goods-producing and all service-producing industries for the period 1929–1961 (see table 2–1). In terms of differences in total factor productivity as compared to the total economy, retail and wholesale

Table 2–1   Average Annual Rates of Change in Productivity Indicators, 1929–61 (Fuchs, 1964)

Industry	Output per Man	Output per Man-Hour
All industries	+ 1.62%	+ 2.26%
Goods	+ 2.44	+ 2.92
Services	+ 0.70	+ 1.57

	Output per Unit of Total Factor Input (Expressed as a Difference from Total Economy)
Agriculture, forestry, fisheries	+ 0.35%
Manufacturing	− 0.08
Transportation	+ 2.05
Communication, public utilities	+ 2.39
Wholesale, retail trade	− 0.53
Finance, insurance, real estate, services	+ 0.35

trade lagged at an average annual rate of about 0.5 percent per year (Fuchs, 1964, p. 15).[4]

These results should be taken as tentative and indicative, rather than definitive, for a number of reasons. To begin with, the data are open to question, and even complete data on wholesaling and retailing would not encompass the full scope of activity in marketing. In addition, there is considerable conceptual difficulty in measuring the value of marketing output. For example, an increase in customer service or in the variety of merchandise available may, indeed, result in increases in both the cost and the value of marketing activity; however, price increases due to monopolistic practices or mutually offsetting competitive expenditures may not. Further, there may have been substantial increases in marketing services, such as convenience, that may not have involved rising costs or prices and are not, therefore, measured by the usual statistical procedures. Finally, there are very great differences in the measured rates of productivity change even within rather similar types of marketing activity. For example, data for eight service and ten retail trades (table 2–2) show rates of change in output per man for 1939–1963 that range from negative values up to more than 3 percent per year. These data also show a positive association between rates of productivity change and rates of output growth among the activities. Activities with more rapidly increasing productivity trends tend to have expanded their output more rapidly than activities with less productivity improvement. We cannot, of course, easily infer the causal mechanism that is involved here. Do the activities grow because they become more productive or do they become more productive because they grow; or are both growth and productivity improvement the results of some other, as yet unidentified, phenomenon?

These questions are not solely of intellectual interest; their answers suggest important implications for marketing management. In an economy characterized by rapid technological progress and increasing labor productivity, are less progressive activities doomed to extinction? If so, the critical managerial task is to develop new and more productive marketing technology. On the other hand, if rapid growth in total output is the key to productivity increase, then increasing demand is the principal task, and cost reductions may be expected to follow rather directly. For example, percentage operating costs decline

---

4. For a comprehensive review of many of the issues involved in this analysis, see Fuchs (1969). Of particular interest in this connection is Schwartzman (1969).

Table 2-2   Average Annual Percentage Rates of Change, Output per Man, and Related Variables, 18 Selected Industries, 1939–63 (Fuchs and Wilburn, 1967, pp. 15–16)

Industry	Real Output per Man	Real Output	Employment	Compensation per Man
Services				
Auto repair	3.32	7.14	3.82	5.06
Barber shops	0.60	0.60	0.00	5.67
Beauty shops	1.69	4.08	2.39	5.37
Dry cleaning	2.47	4.41	1.94	4.75
Hotels, motels	0.49	2.20	1.71	5.35
Laundries	1.42	2.36	0.94	4.78
Motion picture theaters	− 2.83	− 3.28	− 0.45	2.98
Shoe repair	1.16	− 2.07	− 3.23	4.77
Retail Trades				
Apparel stores	0.99	1.87	2.86	4.17
Automobile dealers	2.09	4.82	2.73	5.19
Drugstores	2.68	4.71	2.03	5.29
Eating, drinking places	− 0.18	2.30	2.48	5.31
Food stores	2.44	3.62	1.18	5.32
Furniture, appliances	2.88	5.37	2.49	4.88
Gasoline stations	3.25	5.25	2.00	5.08
General merchandise	1.40	3.53	2.13	4.38
Lumber dealers	1.21	3.07	1.86	4.99
Other	2.09	4.11	2.02	4.63
Summary				
8 services, total	1.14	2.68	1.54	5.07
10 retail trade categories, total	1.63	3.67	2.04	4.90

in supermarkets, in comparison to smaller stores, *because* the size of individual customer purchases increases; direct labor and merchandise costs, and physical labor efficiency, remain about the same regardless of store size. Finally, is it possible that the demand for marketing services is so inelastic that the sector will continue to grow, in spite of rising costs, relative to other sectors of the economy? Some portions of marketing activity seem to fit each of these descriptions, and thus the critical challenge for marketing management differs substantially from one area and industry to another.

Three Concepts of Marketing Efficiency

The preceding data on rates of change in labor productivity focus on one aspect of efficiency in marketing, which may be called **technical efficiency.** An activity of a firm, an industry, or the total economy is technically efficient when it is performed in a least-cost manner, as determined by the existing state of technology and available resources. Activities that require larger inputs per unit of comparable output (larger costs per dollar of product value or sales, for example) are less efficient than activities that require lower inputs per comparable output unit. This is a standard extension of the concept of physical production or transformation efficiency, carried over from the physical sciences and engineering. However, if we are concerned whether marketing activities are more or less efficient than other activities of a firm or the economy, and whether marketing efficiency is increasing or decreasing over time, two other efficiency concepts are worth considering. One of these is **exchange efficiency,** which has been defined as "how well the quantity available . . . leaves the hands of persons who value the commodity least and ends up in the hands of persons who value it most" (Sosnick, 1964, p. 88). The second concept will be referred to as **innovative efficiency,** which is defined as the selection both of the marketing tasks to be performed and of the ways of doing them. Each of these concepts merits brief discussion.

Technical Efficiency

Technical efficiency is defined as accomplishing a particular task by the least-cost means. The familiar notions of cost accounting and cost analysis emphasize this efficiency concept. And the concept of technical efficiency carries the important implication that, if each enterprise seeks to conduct its operations so that each task is carried out as cheaply as possible, then, under competitive conditions, more efficient enterprises will grow while less efficient ones decline. As applied to marketing activities, the pressure toward technical efficiency should lead to two results: (1) marketing functions will be performed by individual enterprises in combinations that lead to the lowest minimum costs for the entire collection of functions, and (2) marketing activities in the economy as a whole will be performed by the appropriate number of enterprises, each with the appropriate combination of functions, so as to lead to least-cost results for the marketing sector as a whole.

These propositions have been developed into a formal conceptual framework by Bucklin (1966), and other writers have used them as guides for managerial analysis in the firm (see Berg, 1962). The principal attempt to examine technical economies in marketing in a sample of firms and industries is Bain's (1956) study of seventeen major industries, each of which was dominated by relatively few large firms. Bain asked, first, whether the observed high level of concentration was accounted for by economies of scale in production and, second, whether concentration beyond that required for production economies was accounted for by economies in marketing. He found that all the largest firms in these industries were larger than they had to be to obtain all the economies of large-scale production, and that marketing economies might be substantial in about half (eight) of the cases. Bain focused only on evidence of the *presence* of economies in marketing associated with large-scale promotion and mass physical distribution; he did not attempt to measure the *amount* of such economies in specific detail.

Exchange Efficiency

Exchange efficiency refers to the efficiency of the trading process itself, and, in the economic theory of exchange, "perfect" competition has generally been accepted as the criterion of such efficiency. Under perfectly competitive conditions, the free interplay of suppliers and demanders leads to the establishment of a unique market price, such that the marginal costs of suppliers are balanced against the marginal benefits of buyers, and no market participant can be made better off without making another worse off. This conception, important as it is, ignores the organizational and information-communication characteristics of markets. Yet these characteristics are by no means the same everywhere, and differences among markets in these respects give rise to differences in the level and stability of prices, costs, sales volume, profits, and other significant results of market operations.

Sosnick (1964, esp. pp. 112–16) suggested that these aspects of marketing activity be analyzed in terms of exchange efficiency, and Preston and Collins (1966) subsequently identified three specific dimensions of exchange efficiency for empirical investigation:

1. **Stability.** A market is stable if, over time, it operates with sufficient continuity that buyers and sellers can come together, complete their exchanges, and adapt their behavior to anticipated market alternatives. Transaction terms, prices, and trading volumes are flexible, neither completely erratic nor rigid. Stigler (1964, p. 127) has suggested **resilience** to describe the desirable blend of market stability properties, including supply-and-demand adaptation, over time.

2. **Revenues of market participants.** An appropriate efficiency criterion for a marketing firm or a total marketing channel would be a maximum level of total net revenues or profits. If, on the other hand, one wishes to take the viewpoint of final buyers, or of one marketing system versus another, this criterion might be reversed: Let the marketers get as little as possible and let the customers or primary suppliers obtain maximum benefits. For example, agricultural analysts focus on "the farmer's share" and international economists focus on the division among countries of the "gains from trade." These concepts of shares and gains are simply divisions of market revenues among participants. In order to identify a particular revenue division as preferable to another, one must first specify some goal or criterion—outside the market—as the basis for making the distinction. The important point is that there is no natural or unique division of market benefits, even in theory; and experimental results suggest that the distribution of trading gains is strongly affected by organizational and informational factors.[5] Therefore any particular distribution of revenues and costs among participants might be specified as a potentially significant aspect of exchange efficiency.

3. **Realization of potential transactions.** The economic model of perfect competition depicts a completely centralized market in which all transactions take place at one and the same market price. However, because actual markets tend to be decentralized and partially

5. V. L. Smith (1964) found that, in an experimental market, average transaction prices were lower when sellers initiated price offers than when buyers took the initiative. This finding, which reverses the usual assumption that the one who takes the initiative has the advantage, seems to arise from the openness of price-offer information in the experiment and the large amount of information that was consequently available to the noninitiating side of the market.

segmented, transactions may take place between any pair of trading parties who present compatible bids and offers and who lack either the ability or the inclination to search for better deals. The volume of transactions in a decentralized market might be larger or smaller than it it would have been under centralized market conditions (but with the same basic cost and demand conditions), and the average transaction price might be higher or lower. Early experimental results by Chamberlain (1948) suggested that, if there were no other change in perfect competition conditions, decentralization might result in the trading of larger quantities at lower prices. More recent experiments by Smith (1962) suggest that decentralized trading initially results in market outcomes that are different from those of centralized trading where both have the same schedules of cost and demand. However, the differences go in both directions; and, if the experiments are repeated so that learning can occur among the market participants, fewer and smaller differences are observed.

Innovative Efficiency

Both technical efficiency and exchange efficiency, as defined above, take the products and services involved in marketing as given quantities. They do not examine the more basic question: Are the products and services demanded and supplied, and the marketing activities that accompany them, the most appropriate that could have come into being under the circumstances? Although this question can be raised at the moral or ethical level, it most commonly occurs in both the firm and the household in the routine course of choosing among alternative products for production or introduction and for alternative consumption patterns and life styles. The term **innovative efficiency** is suggested to describe the effectiveness of the marketing unit, firm, or system in making these choices among both existing and potential alternatives. The often-repeated statement that "marketing is the delivery of a standard of living" (Mazur, 1947, p. 138) stresses this aspect of marketing activity, as does Cox's comment (1965):

> By the test of acceptance in the open market, distribution generally comes off very well indeed. Businessmen do not hesitate to spend huge sums in marketing their wares, and consumers show no great reluctance to pay the resultant charges embodied in what they buy (p. 3).

Marketing activity is not simply a response to the pressure of outside forces, nor the execution of exchanges based upon given and fixed supply-and-demand conditions. On the contrary, a major purpose of marketing activity is to widen the range of available choice and to stimulate demand for (and supply of) various quantities, qualities, and assortments of merchandise and services. Thus the specific tasks to be performed by marketing agencies are in part determined by the agencies themselves—and by the interaction of competitive units, or buyers and sellers—in the marketing process. This means that the job of marketing—in the firm, the marketing channel, and the entire economic system—includes not only the performance of specific tasks so as to link specific supply sources with specific users, it also includes the selection of the tasks themselves and the development of new sources, uses, and means of marketing contact.

Two important objectives of innovative change in marketing are (1) increased **consumer efficiency;** that is, making marketing activity in some way easier for final users, and (2) **psychological transformation** of goods and services, so that available market alternatives are seen from new perspectives. Downs' (1961) concept of consumer efficiency suggests that the household buyer seeks to minimize not only the money cost of particular purchases but also the total cost of shopping itself, including the time involved in reaching a shopping location and making selections within that location and the effort and frustration attendant to these activities. He stresses the importance of these efficiency goals (which may be thought of as **technical efficiency** for the buyer) in explaining recent changes in retailing. The notion of psychological transformation, originated by Avril and popularized in English by McAnally (1963) emphasizes the symbolic significance that specific goods and services have for potential buyers, and attributes this symbolism largely to marketing activity. Thus unimpressive materials are transformed into recognized products that have well-known performance characteristics, and perhaps additional social or psychological significance as well, as a result of branding, advertising, packaging, display, and selling effort.

Implications of Efficiency Analysis

These efficiency concepts are useful for marketing analysis in two different ways. First, they provide a basis for understanding *why* things are as they are and, perhaps more importantly, the likely directions and speed of change. Second, the search for greater efficiency is in a sense the principal guide for managerial action and public policy, and identifying the possible sources of efficiency improvement is an essential aspect of the search process.

The relationship between these two points is worth emphasizing. The *reason* why an analysis of efficiency sources provides a guide to likely changes is that managers of both private and public activities are motivated to shift from less efficient to more efficient methods and activities. If such motivation were absent, the general notion that economic activities will adapt themselves in the direction of decreased costs or increased satisfactions would be an inaccurate guide to future developments. Even when pressures for efficiency are strongest, however, it is not to be expected that the process of efficiency-increasing change will ever lead to its logical end, a "nirvana" in which all possible favorable adaptations have been made. On the contrary, the dimensions of efficiency are too numerous and changes in the external environment are too frequent and far reaching to permit such an equilibrium condition to develop.

Under some circumstances, several aspects of marketing efficiency may be increased at once; in other cases, an improvement in one direction involves a reduction of efficiency in another direction. An example of efficiency improvement in several directions at once might be the introduction of vending machines, which not only release human labor from low-value activities but make products available at places and times that would otherwise be impossible. Obvious conflicts occur, however, between the economies that are available through standardization and the satisfactions that are gained from variety. The technical tasks of production, transportation, storage, and exchange can generally be carried out most cheaply with merchandise that is highly standardized. However, opportunities to attract additional customers, to make greater sales, and to obtain wider profit margins frequently involve variety in merchandise, communications techniques, and distribution systems. Thus the gains available from responding to innovative opportunities may well offset the losses involved in technical or exchange efficiency. Further, because innovations may take many forms, firms and marketing channels that perform very similar marketing functions may engage in very different activities, with different costs and results. In such circumstances it may be impossible to say that one way of performing the functions is "more efficient" than the other, since the ways in which they are performed, and therefore their overall impact, differ substantially.

A classic example of these difficulties in efficiency comparisons is the frequently cited contrast between the cost of marketing in the United States and in the Soviet Union. There is some evidence that total retail and wholesale margins—costs plus profits—on consumer goods in the United States average about 40 to 50 percent of final goods prices, whereas similar distribution costs and turnover taxes average about 20 to 30 percent in the Soviet Union (Goldman, 1962). Does this indicate that Soviet marketing is more efficient than American marketing? It is very doubtful that this question can be satisfactorily answered. It may be true that the distribution system in the Soviet Union conveys a particular collection of consumer goods into the hands of final users more cheaply than our distribution system. However, any such difference is due in part to differences in services and locational convenience between the two systems. Another important source of cost differences is the variety of merchandise available through each system and the speed with which demand requirements can be met by suppliers. Differences may also be due to the structure of costs—that is, to the relative importance of labor, capital, and other resources and their prices in the two systems. For example, sales per retail worker are not clearly higher in the Soviet Union than in the United States. If actual amounts of labor and capital per unit of sale are about the same in the two systems, the apparent cost differences may be due to higher real wages in the United States or to an inadequate accounting of the cost of capital in the Soviet Union. On the other hand, it may be that larger amounts of capital and other resources per dollar of sales are used in the United States, and the cost of these factors may account for the difference. The point is that without taking account both of the differences in the tasks performed and of the possible differences in cost structures, it is impossible to say that either system is more efficient than the other. Each is doing somewhat different things in different environments, and each system may have achieved a high level of technical, exchange, and innovative efficiency with respect to its own economic and social setting.

Summary

Marketing activities tend to be both more extensive and more clearly specialized in economies with high levels of development and income than in less developed and poorer countries. This tendency is due in part to the greater variety of merchandise and the greater consumption of services that usually accompany economic development, and also to differences in productivity trends between marketing and other types of economic activity.

On the basis of the available evidence, it appears that the distributive trades (retailing and wholesaling) have been subject to slower rates of productivity increase than manufacturing, transportation, communication, and agriculture. However, there have been great differences in the rates of productivity change among individual kinds of marketing activity, and productivity increases in other parts of the economy have made a substantial impact on the overall efficiency and cost of marketing.

The traditional type of productivity analysis, which underlies the above statements, is based primarily on physical input-output relationships. Such an analysis focuses on the **technical efficiency** with which particular operations are carried out. However, two additional types of efficiency are significant in appraising marketing activities: **exchange efficiency,** the efficiency of the market mechanism in transferring goods and services among potential buyers and sellers, and **innovative efficiency,** the efficiency with which combinations of products, services, and marketing activities are developed and changed over time.

The performance of a marketing system with respect to each type of efficiency must be appraised in somewhat different terms, and it frequently seems that the several efficiency goals are in conflict. For example, actual marketing costs per transaction may be reduced if some potential transactions are not made and if the variety of products and services, or the rate of change in such variety over time, is curtailed. If so, technical efficiency may be increased if exchange and innovative efficiency are reduced or held constant. For this reason it is difficult to describe one area of marketing activity as more efficient than another in any comprehensive sense. However, the concept of efficiency analysis is useful both for identifying critical differences among the performance characteristics of different marketing arrangements and for appraising alternative means of improving performance within individual parts of a marketing system.

References

Bain, Joe S. "Advantages of the Large Firm: Production, Distribution, and Sales Promotion." *Journal of Marketing*, Vol. 20, No. 4, April 1956.

Barger, Harold. *Distribution's Place in the American Economy since 1869*. Princeton University Press, 1955.

Baumol, W. J. "Macroeconomics of Unbalanced Growth." *American Economic Review*, Vol. 57, June 1967.

Berg, Thomas L. "Designing the Distribution System." In *The Social Responsibilities of Marketing*, ed. William D. Stevens. American Marketing Association, 1962.

Bucklin, Louis P. *A Theory of Distribution Channel Structure*. University of California, Berkeley, Institute of Business and Economic Research, 1966.

Chamberlain, Edward H. "An Experimental Imperfect Market." *Journal of Political Economy*, Vol. 56, No. 2, April 1948.

Cox, Reavis, Charles S. Goodman, and Thomas C. Fichandler. *Distribution in a High-Level Economy*. Prentice-Hall, 1965.

Downs, Anthony. "A Theory of Consumer Efficiency." *Journal of Retailing*, Vol. 37, No. 1, Spring 1961.

Fuchs, Victor R. *Productivity Trends in the Goods and Services Sectors, 1929–1961*. Occasional Paper No. 89, National Bureau of Economic Research. Columbia University Press, 1964.

——, ed. *Production and Productivity in the Service Industries*. Studies in Income and Wealth, No. 34, National Bureau of Economic Research, 1969.

——, and J. A. Wilburn. *Productivity Differences within the Service Sector*. Occasional Paper No. 102, National Bureau of Economic Research, 1967.

Goldman, Marshall I. "Cost and Efficiency of Distribution in the Soviet Union." *Quarterly Journal Economics*, Vol. 16, No. 3, August 1962.

McAnally, A. P. "The Measurement of Retail Productivity." *Journal of Industrial Economics*, Vol. 11, No. 2, April 1963.

Mazur, Paul. "Does Distribution Cost Enough?" *Fortune*, November 1947.

Preston, Lee E. "The Commercial Sector and Economic Development." In *Markets and Marketing in Developing Economies*, eds. Reed Moyer and Stanley C. Hollander. Irwin, 1968.

————, and Norman R. Collins. "The Analysis of Market Efficiency." *Journal of Marketing Research,* Vol. 3, No. 2, May 1966.

Schwartzman, David. "The Growth of Sales per Man-Hour in Retail Trade, 1929–1963." In Fuchs, *op. cit.*

Smith, Vernon L. "Effect of Market Organization on Competitive Equilibrium." *Quarterly Journal of Economics,* Vol. 78, No. 2, May 1964.

————. "An Experimental Study of Competitive Market Behavior." *Journal of Political Economy,* Vol. 70, No. 2, April 1962.

Sosnick, Stephen H. "Operational Criteria for Evaluating Market Performance." In *Market Structure Research,* ed. Paul L. Farris. Iowa State University Press, 1964.

Stigler, George J. "Public Regulation of the Securities Markets." *Journal of Business,* Vol. 37, No. 2, April 1964.

U.S. Bureau of the Census. *Statistical Abstract of the United States, 1968.* U.S. Government Printing Office, 1968.

3

Patterns of Marketing Organization

Marketing activity involves the functioning of a complex operating system with many constituent parts. Any such system may be described in terms of three main characteristics: (1) the type and number of its operating units, (2) the way in which these units are arranged and coordinated, and (3) the operations they perform and the final results they achieve. In some simple systems these three characteristics may be uniquely related: specific results can be achieved only if specific units are arranged and operated in a particular way. However, it is usually the case that many different types and numbers of marketing units—different numbers of firms, communications contacts, hours of labor time, and so on—can be arranged and coordinated in many different ways to accomplish the same or similar tasks. Therefore it is important to discover how various sets of characteristics are related to specific results and how decision-making units (firms, households, organizations) might choose among the alternative marketing arrangements available. In this chapter we try to suggest both the variety of organizational arrangements that may be used to accomplish particular marketing tasks and some of the reasons for this variety and for changes in organizational patterns over time.

Variety in Marketing Organizations

It is almost impossible even to indicate the variety of operating units that are engaged in marketing activities in a highly developed private-ownership economy. Revzan (1961) has suggested that one of the performance attributes of the marketing system is "the maximization of alternatives" (p. 17), a particularly apt phrase to describe the process of continually increasing variety. A true maximum is, of course, never attained, both because the environment of market opportunities changes continuously and because new ways of solving old problems are continually being developed. For example, the 1967 *U.S. Census of Business* lists 38 different kinds of retail stores, grouped into ten principal categories, plus three kinds of nonstore retailers (mail order, vending machine, and direct personal selling). Each of these may be organized in the proprietorship, partnership, or corporate form and as single-unit or multiple-unit (chain) organizations. Wholesaling operations are divided into five major operating types and twenty-five individual categories. Merchant wholesalers alone are classified among twenty-two kinds of business, and manufacturers' sales branches and offices among twenty different product groupings. In order to be reduced to its present vast but manageable proportions, this category system requires the lumping together of many kinds of marketing units that are almost totally dissimilar with respect to product assortment, specific functional activities, size, market location, and other key variables. And necessarily omitted from this enumeration are the marketing activities of central-office executives, primary producers (such as farmers, financial intermediaries, and industrial and institutional purchasers), and many other participants in the marketing process. The number and variety of units engaged in marketing in a developed economy literally boggles the mind.

Two Examples

Even within a single industry and product environment, many different organizational forms may operate to perform the same broad tasks. Consider, as examples, the variety of units engaged in wholesale distribution of food and industrial equipment in the United States at the present time.

Food wholesaling. Wholesale marketing of foods involves selecting and assembling food products from various sources and distributing these products among retail outlets. In the United States this important marketing activity is performed by (among others):

1. Full-function wholesalers—independent firms that purchase on their own account, promote and sell the merchandise through their own sales force, provide delivery and credit services, and perform numerous auxiliary marketing tasks. Historically, firms of this type have been important centers of marketing initiative, seeking out new suppliers and customers and bringing supply and demand together.

2. Cash-and-carry wholesalers—independent firms or co-operatives that purchase on their own account but provide, primarily, location-storage services for a limited assortment of merchandise. The contact and purchasing initiative shifts to the buyer, who is attracted to the wholesaler principally because of the lower prices made possible by reduced services.

3. Chain-store warehouses—links in a system of corporate management activities that includes a number of retail outlets, and frequently manufacturing facilities as well. Initiative rests with a management group that oversees the entire marketing process, from supply sources to final consumer sales. Although operating economies may be achieved, increased managerial complexity and inflexibility may appear.

4. Manufacturers' sales branches—wholesale outlets established and operated by firms engaged primarily in food processing and dealing primarily in the products of the individual manufacturing firm. These agencies, which may be the sole intermediaries between processors and retailers, perform the entire wholesaling function, or they may supply other wholesale outlets that, in turn, supply retailers.

Industrial equipment wholesaling. The sale of industrial equipment and machinery generally involves a considerable amount of direct, personal contact between representatives of the seller and the buyer so that the particular needs of the latter can be understood and the particular pieces of equipment can be selected or developed to meet such needs. Some of the marketing arrangements that are used to perform this function involve:

1. Industrial distributors—independent wholesale firms that carry a wide line of merchandise and operate as technical specialists in the industrial fields they serve. These firms may carry similar types of merchandise of different brands and technical specifications, and may also provide after-sales service or engineering assistance to customers.

2. Manufacturers' representatives—independent sales organizations that handle the lines of only a few manufacturers, and usually not more than one line of any particular type of equipment. These firms typically operate on a commission basis but spread the cost of sales calls over a number of noncompetitive products.

3. Manufacturers' sales forces—employees of manufacturing companies who contact potential customers for the purpose of selling their firms' products exclusively. Usually paid on a combination salary-and-commission basis, these men focus their specialized knowledge and selling effort on merchandise from a single source.

The foregoing examples are intended to suggest the variety of ways in which the same broad type of marketing operations may be conducted. They also suggest the difficulty of identifying one firm or type of marketing arrangement as superior to another in any general sense. For example, cash-and-carry grocery wholesalers have lower operating expenses in relation to their sales than full-function wholesalers. (In fact, according to the 1958 Census of Business, operating expenses were 6.0 percent of sales for the former and 8.4 percent of sales for the latter.) But this difference in costs is primarily due to differences in the functions performed. The costs of performing one of the functions—say, warehousing—might be higher or lower for either type of firm, or the same for both types of firms, and a particular retailer might find that *his own* total cost of procuring merchandise is higher or lower because of dealing with either type of distributor. In response to differences in buying costs, convenience, and variety of products and services, as well as for other reasons, retailers prefer to purchase from one type of wholesale outlet rather than from another. Thus the various types of outlets will also have different revenue functions and cost-revenue relationships. Many different organizational forms can therefore yield "satisfactory" results, both in terms of profitability and in terms of discharging specific functional roles.

Marketing Channels and Networks

A particularly important feature of a marketing organization is the number and sequence of specific activities that occur between initial production and final consumption and the number and size of firms and other market decision-making units that perform these activities. This organizational sequence, for any particular good or service, is

commonly referred to as the **marketing channel.**[1] The fundamental
activity in the marketing channel is the physical flow of merchandise
from the production unit through its transportation, storage, and exchange facilities to its final users. In addition to the physical flow
channel, however, a "flow" of finance and ownership, communication
and negotiation, and other activities is necessary to accomplish the
physical flow movement itself. Even when all these activities are performed under the ownership or control of a single organization or
firm, the marketing-channel concept remains useful as a way of describing the production and marketing tasks that the organization
performs.

Some marketing problems require the analysis of long marketing
channels that extend from the raw material stage, proceed through
processing activities, and end in purchase by final users. Other problems involve shorter channels, which include only some portion of
these activities. The appropriate channel concept in any particular
instance depends both on the physical and economic changes involved
and on the problem under analysis. The wheat-flour-bread sequence,
for example, is a flow of physical merchandise and market contact that
extends from farmers to flour mills to baking companies to household
and institutional consumers. At various stages this sequence of contacts
involves organized central markets, government control activities, and
special transportation and storage arrangements, as well as exchanges
among independent buying and selling units. The flow of transactions
is facilitated by agents and brokers, who specialize in communication
and negotiation for the benefit of buyers and sellers, and by advertising
agencies. For many analytical and managerial purposes we might be
concerned only with the wheat-flour portion of this channel, or only
with the flour-bread portion, or only with bread marketing. For other
purposes—for example, long-term trends in food supplies, quality and
prices, or factors that affect farm income—we might be concerned with
the entire sequence of events, and might consider substantial changes
in the form of the product in a comprehensive view of channel
activity.

The comprehensive view of marketing channels is reflected in
the idea, originally suggested by Alderson (1957, pp. 199–211), that
marketing converts "conglomerations" of resources into "assortments."
In his terms, a **conglomeration** is a varied collection of physical and
chemical substances and their properties as they occur in nature or at

1. For an extensive discussion and review of the pertinent literature, see
McCammon and Little (1965).

random. An **assortment** is a collection of goods and services that are related on the side of demand. Alderson described the conversion process as consisting of four stages:

1. Sorting out: separating the conglomerate resources into their components
2. Accumulating or assembling: building up collections of similar items
3. Allocating: dividing a collection of similar items among various users
4. Assorting or forming assortments: bringing together collections of merchandise and services that meet demand requirements

This sequence of events may occur not once but many times as goods pass from raw materials to their final uses, and substantial amounts of processing activity (i.e., changes in the *form* of goods) may take place along the way. In an extreme interpretation, manufacturing activities become only "incidents" in the long flow of marketing contacts. (This is the reverse of the engineering or production orientation that treats marketing as only an "incident" in the production process.)

Alderson's scheme is illustrated in figure 3–1, where the four steps in the conversion process are shown as the successive building up and breaking down of homogeneous (like) and heterogeneous (unlike) resources. The marketing channel that connects the conglomerate resource with a particular demand use—which might be described as the channel for component D in use 4—is shown as a double line.

An example of such a long and complex channel is the production and marketing sequence linking cattle, hides, and leather goods. Cattle on the hoof represent a conglomerate resource in Alderson's terms, including the components of meat, hides, tallow, bones, and so forth. In the slaughtering process the components are, in effect, "sorted out" of the conglomerate, and then each component flows into its own marketing and processing sequence. Hides from many different sources and of different kinds and qualities are purchased for tanning; and leather, as well as synthetic and plastic "leather" products, is purchased and sold competitively in many markets. These markets thus assemble and then allocate supplies of like or similar items among various uses and outlets, such as industrial belting, shoe manufacturing, luggage and other leather goods, export, and so forth. In each of these uses leather will be combined with other kinds of materials to form an assortment of materials, possibly joined in a single product, that is appropriate for purchase and use. If the final product is, for example, shoes, another stage of assorting takes place in which appropriate combinations of sizes and styles are brought together for distribution in particular markets. Still another assortment is formed when shoes are combined with other merchandise items—socks, shoe polish, clothing, and so forth—to form a collection that will be attractive to final purchasers.

Figure 3–1 also illustrates the important point that marketing

Figure 3–1   Marketing Channels and Networks

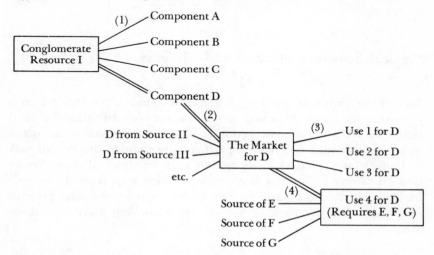

channels are only individual and somewhat artificial sequences of contact within more complex marketing networks.[2] Therefore, many significant questions cannot be investigated unless we consider larger network segments, including portions of many different marketing channels. For example, if there were a substantial increase in the demand for component *A* of the conglomerate resource in our diagram, this might result in a *decrease* in the quantity of *D* available (if the production process could be altered to yield more *A* and less *D,* as in the case of gasoline and fuel oil refining) or in an *increase* in the quantity of *D* if it is generated as a by-product. Either type of change in the quantity of *D* might have substantial effects on its price in the markets, on its availability for various uses, and thus on the demand for materials that complement or substitute for D in these uses.

All of this simply means that the marketing channel should not be thought of as a deep canyon with sheer walls but rather as a stream that runs into other streams and lakes and frequently changes its course and boundaries. The marketing channel is a useful concept for describing a particular sequence of marketing activities. Just as important as the sequence of activities in any particular channel, however, are its links with other channels and with the larger marketing system as a whole.

Vertical Structure of Costs and Margins

Each of the separate enterprises and functional units engaged in a particular marketing channel makes its own contribution to total channel activity. This contribution results in costs, which are incurred to accomplish each enterprise's particular portion of the overall task and which are reflected in its revenues. If we think of a marketing channel of several business firms, each of which buys from the preceding and sells to the succeeding firm in the channel, the sales price of each unit of output from each firm may be broken down into three components:

1. Initial purchase cost of merchandise from the preceding firm in the channel
2. Cost of the operations performed within the individual firm
3. Margin or profit earned from performing this channel activity

The initial purchase cost for firms at each channel level is the same as the sales price received by firms at the preceding channel level, and so forth. These vertical price, cost, and margin relationships are diagrammed in figure 3–2, which shows the components of final value of a single unit of output that originates in firms at Channel Level 1, passes through firms at Channel Level 2, and is sold by firms at Channel Level 3 to final buyers. The principal costs of firms at Levels 2 and 3 should be thought of as costs of performing marketing functions.

The figure shows that firms at Level 1 (initial producers or suppliers) incur basic materials' cost, plus their own operating or processing costs, and gain an additional margin when they sell their output to marketing intermediaries. The difference between their gross revenue (sales) and the cost of purchased materials corresponds approximately

Figure 3–2   Vertical Structure of Costs and Margins

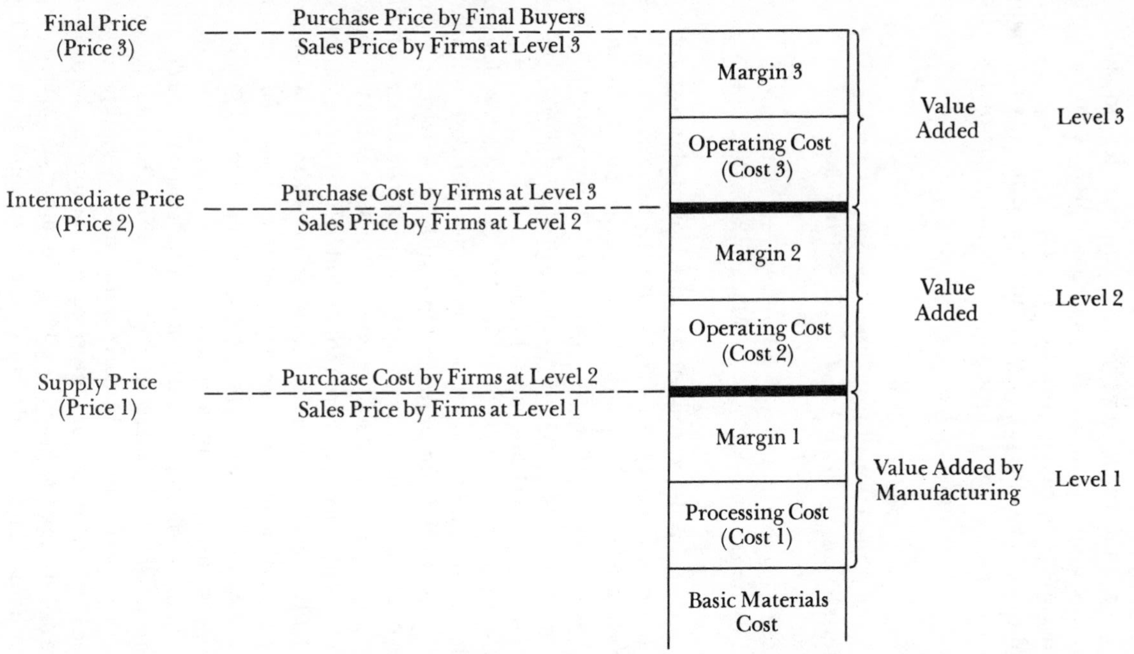

Final Price
(Price 3)

Purchase Price by Final Buyers
Sales Price by Firms at Level 3

Intermediate Price
(Price 2)

Purchase Cost by Firms at Level 3
Sales Price by Firms at Level 2

Supply Price
(Price 1)

Purchase Cost by Firms at Level 2
Sales Price by Firms at Level 1

Margin 3

Operating Cost
(Cost 3)

Margin 2

Operating Cost
(Cost 2)

Margin 1

Processing Cost
(Cost 1)

Basic Materials
Cost

Value
Added

Level 3

Value
Added

Level 2

Value Added by
Manufacturing

Level 1

to the statistical concept of **value added by manufacturing.** Intermediary firms at Channel 2 purchase merchandise at the suppliers' price, perform their own operating (marketing) activities and incur the corresponding costs, and resell at a price that includes an additional profit margin for themselves. Firms at Level 3 purchase from intermediaries, incur costs, and make sales to final buyers.

A number of key concepts for the analysis of marketing channels and systems can be specified quite easily on the basis of this simple model:

Total value of final goods = Price 3
Total volume of transactions throughout the system =
  Basic materials' cost + Price 1 + Price 2 + Price 3
Total marketing costs = Cost 2 + Cost 3
Total marketing profit margins = Margin 2 + Margin 3
Value added by marketing = Cost 2 + Margin 2 + Cost 3 + Margin 3

Note that we have simplified this model in terms of the cost and price of one unit (more accurately, an *average* unit) of merchandise passing through the channel. A more complete descriptive model would show a complex network in which each type of firm is linked with several other types, each having different selling prices and costs associated with a variety of products and customers.

The simplified framework of figure 3–2 is useful for describing any particular sequence of marketing transactions in cost and margin terms. It is also useful in examining, and possibly anticipating, changes that will occur at one channel level as a result of changes at another. For example, an increase in costs at one channel level *may* simply be passed forward as an increase in purchase and selling prices at all subsequent levels. However, such a cost increase *may also* be transformed into larger or smaller increases—or even into *decreases* in costs and margins for some channel participants, depending upon their decision-making processes and bargaining power.

As an example of the diversity of results that may occur in response to any particular change in costs, consider the results of the five simulation experiments summarized in table 3–1. These experiments were made in a large computerized simulation model in which individual firms at three channel levels (as in figure 3–2) were represented by mathematical relationships (see Preston and Collins, 1966). Three of the simulation experiments involved changes in Cost 1, and two of the experiments involved changes in Cost 3. The results of this

Table 3–1   Impact on Prices and Margins of Changes in Costs: Results of Simulation Experiments in a Hypothetical Three-Stage Marketing System (Adapted from Preston and Collins, 1966, p. 51)

Experimental Condition	Experiment 1	2	3	4	5
Initial Cost Change					
Cost 1	+ 100	+ 200	− 100	none	none
Cost 3	none	none	none	+ 100	+ 200
Resultant Changes in Price and Margin (Average)					
Price 1	+ 61	+ 70	− 56	− 47	− 98
Price 2	+ 46	+ 68	− 65	− 66	− 93
Price 3	+ 142	+ 184	− 82	+ 48	+ 186
Margin 2	− 15	− 2	− 9	− 19	+ 5

model show that firms at Channel Level 1 (suppliers) tended to absorb a substantial portion of their cost increases; but when price increases were passed up through the channel, final prices tended to rise by multiples of the initial change in Price 1. To put it in more concrete terms, competition among suppliers tended to limit their own price increases, even when costs had risen. However, weakness of competition and the pattern of price setting among retailers permitted them to raise prices substantially whenever cost increases occurred. In experiment 3, however, cost decreases for suppliers were not fully passed along through the channel. When costs increased for firms at Level 3 (retailers), in experiments 4 and 5, these firms tended to pass these increases *backward,* by paying lower prices to preceding channel levels, as well as forward to final buyers.

The characteristics of the firms and markets simulated in these experiments are, of course, highly simplified and abstract, and may not correspond to those of any actual marketing channel. Hence these experimental results may not yield predictions of the price and margin changes that might be anticipated in a particular actual situation. However, these results suggest both the variety of changes that may take place in actual markets and the fundamental linkage of cost, margin, and price structures of firms at successive channel levels.

Sources of Organizational Variety and Change

In addition to the immense variety of enterprises and organizational arrangements within the marketing system, common experience provides evidence of organizational **change:** the decline of existing kinds of business activity and the rise of new ones. Thus variety and change are two aspects of **diversity** in marketing systems. Different means of accomplishing similar tasks are used at the same time (variety) and different means are substituted for one another over time (change). Since changes do not occur everywhere at once, the process of change itself involves variety: new activities come into being even while older ones continue. Hence Revzan's emphasis on "the maximization of alternatives."

The diversity of organizational forms within the marketing system may be traced to three broad sources: [3]

1. Intrinsic heterogeneity—fundamental diversity among both potential supply and potential demand sources, and differences in location, size, and other characteristics between units on opposite sides of any potential market transaction
2. The structure of marketing costs and cost changes
3. Patterns of bargaining power and coordination within the marketing system

The first two sources of diversity are discussed in the remaining sections of this chapter. The third source of diversity is more fully considered in chapter 4, which deals with coordinating mechanisms in marketing.

Heterogeneity

Sources of potential supply of the same or similar goods and services are not all alike. Farms, mines, and factories exist at different places as a result of different natural and historical circumstances, including historic marketing opportunities and arrangements. Production units in the same industries operate at different scales of activity, use different methods, and respond differently to the same marketing developments. Similarly, final buyers of both industrial-institutional and

---

3. A similar analysis is suggested by Balderston (1958).

household consumption goods differ greatly among themselves in size, specific needs, and purchasing ability. In addition, potential buying units and selling units are separated in space, and the production and the use of goods and services take place at different rates over time.

Marketing activities arise, in part, in order to bring these diverse activities into balance, to transmit information so that producing and using units can adapt to each others' requirements, and to transport, store, and make goods and services available in such a way that supply and use activities can be planned and carried out over time. Because the supplying and the using units differ greatly among themselves, the forms of marketing organization that operate between them are extremely diverse. Further, independent changes occur to economic units at either end of the marketing process, and within the marketing sector as well, and this leads to increased organizational variety. Finally, potential supply and purchasing units respond in various ways to new marketing alternatives, so that similar marketing innovations fail in some areas and succeed in others. The result of all this is the great diversity of marketing units and organizational arrangements that we observe in the economy.

Cost and Cost Changes

In an enterprise economy the force of competition and the search for profit gives rise to continuous pressure for cost reduction, both in individual enterprises and throughout the economic system. Thus, within a single marketing channel, we would expect competition and profit seeking to lead, over time, to changes in channel arrangements that would tend to reduce marketing costs in individual enterprises and in the channel as a whole. For example, the number of establishments and enterprises, and their size and location, should tend toward levels that are consistent with minimum costs. Also, marketing functions should be performed by enterprises in such combinations that the lowest cost for the entire group of functions is achieved. This need not, of course, be the same as the lowest cost for each separate functional activity.

In the previous chapter we referred to some evidence of economies of scale in marketing and its implications for the size and number of firms in particular industries. Here we note that very different organizational changes may lead to similar cost changes, under different circumstances. For example, the cost of wholesaling might be reduced either by coordinating bulk distribution with manufacturing or by coordinating it with retailing. On the other hand, wholesale marketing activities, as a whole, may be performed at lower costs when functional specialization occurs—with negotiations handled through a broker, with storage and merchandise movement through public warehouses and carriers, and so forth. Thus marketing costs may be reduced through integration in one industry or marketing channel and through *dis*integration and specialization in another.

The structure of costs and cost changes does not tell the whole story, however, because cost changes are passed into the marketing system through changes in prices and margins. The various possibilities of price and margin change in response to cost changes, within a stable organizational structure, are suggested by the simulation results in table 3–1. When behavioral and organizational changes also occur, the range of possible outcomes becomes almost unlimited. Changes in margins and prices that result from an operating cost change at any particular channel level may lead to changes in organizational forms and functions throughout the system, so that a new set of relationships emerges. Of particular importance are cost changes that simultaneously change the importance or the bargaining power of enterprises at one channel level relative to those at another.

Examples of these phenomena are changes that increase the relative size of enterprises at one channel level, or that permit one group of units to perform a critical decision-making activity. When such changes occur, the enterprises whose positions are strengthened may be able to bargain for larger shares of the total channel margin, at the expense of preceding or succeeding channel units. If, for example, retail outlets become dependent on large intermediaries for procurement functions—functions that may well be more cheaply performed by large, centralized units—they may find themselves in a weak bargaining position with respect to prices and margins in the future.

Summary

Patterns of marketing organization in a highly developed economy are complex and varied. Innumerable specialized tasks must be performed, and basically similar tasks may be organized and carried out in many different ways. The variety of both the tasks themselves and the ways of performing them has been described as "the maximization of alternatives."

The sequence of the agencies and activities that are involved in marketing any particular flow of goods and services from their original source to their final use is termed the **marketing channel**. Every such channel is part of a larger network of marketing contacts, which includes auxiliary merchandise and service inputs, jointly produced outputs, and marketing activities that are competitive with or complementary to those of the channel itself. Actual marketing channels, and the descriptions or simulations of marketing channels that are used for planning and analysis, may be long or short, simple or complex. Also, the appropriate channel and network concept for any particular marketing situation depends upon the specific circumstances and the type of problem under consideration. The Alderson scheme of sorting-assembling-allocating-assorting is a useful guide in the analysis of marketing channel structures.

The final market value and price of any unit or flow of goods and services can be described in terms of the accumulation of costs and profit margins by the successive units in the marketing channel. This vertical structure of costs and margins constitutes a framework for analyzing the implications of organizational and behavioral change within the marketing system. Thus cost changes at one level of the channel may result in price and profit margin changes at both the preceding and succeeding levels. Similarly, vertical integration—the joining of previously separate channel levels—may result not only in the combination of margins and costs at the several levels but also in changes in their total amounts.

The variety of marketing organizational forms and the continuous pressures for adaptation and change arise from three principal sources: (1) the fundamental diversity among enterprises, households, and public agencies within the economy; (2) the structure of costs and cost changes; and (3) patterns of bargaining power and coordination within the system, which is the subject of the following chapter.

References

Alderson, Wroe. *Marketing Behavior and Executive Action*. Irwin, 1957.

Balderston, F. E. "Theories of Marketing Structure and Channels." In *Proceedings of the Conference of Marketing Teachers from Far Western States*. University of California, Berkeley, 1958.

McCammon, Bert C., and Robert W. Little. "Marketing Channels:

Analytical Systems and Approaches." In *Science and Marketing,* ed. George Schwartz. Wiley, 1965.

Preston, Lee E., and Norman R. Collins. *Studies in a Simulated Market.* University of California, Berkeley, Institute of Business and Economic Research, 1966.

Revzan, David A. *Wholesaling in Marketing Organization.* Wiley, 1961.

Stern, Louis W., and Jay W. Brown. "Distribution Channels: A Social Systems Approach." In *Distribution Channels: Behavioral Dimensions,* ed. Louis W. Stern. Houghton Mifflin, 1969.

4

Coordinating Mechanisms in Marketing

The diversity of marketing units, and the number and diversity of the marketing tasks they perform, give rise to the need for coordinating mechanisms among them. Such coordinating mechanisms accumulate and transmit information; they may also include decision-making systems and decision criteria. Indeed, the amount of information and its processing, and the locus of decision making, are critical characteristics of the coordinating mechanisms. In marketing, as in many other areas of social interaction, three principal coordinating mechanisms can be identified: **competition, cooperation,** and **control.**[1] Within any complex network of marketing activities, all three means of coordination are to be found, but for purposes of explanation and analysis we shall consider each means separately.

Competition

Competition is the principal coordinating mechanism in a market economy. Control and cooperation are exceptions—although very im-

1. This trichotomy was suggested by Baligh and Richartz (1967). I have departed somewhat from their terminology and substituted "control" for "coordination."

portant and widespread exceptions—to this basic process. Competition means rivalry. Contestants striving for the same prize, politicians seeking the same office, firms seeking the same customers—these are familiar forms of competition. In a market economy, competition between and among buyers and sellers is the primary force that determines the range of products and services available, the exchange ratios (prices) among them, and the efficiency with which marketing tasks are performed. Rival sellers offer more attractive products, greater services, more convenience, or lower prices in their attempts to make sales. Buyers choose among the available alternatives and set forth counteroffers and product specifications of their own. As a result, less desired products are passed over in favor of more desired ones, and higher-cost ways of accomplishing particular tasks are replaced by lower-cost methods. Thus—ideally—innovative, exchange, and technical efficiency are achieved.

It sometimes appears, however, that competitive activities tend to frustrate the achievement of efficiency goals and to increase rather than decrease marketing costs. We can gain some understanding of this apparent paradox by considering in more detail some important dimensions, forms, and costs of competition in marketing.

Dimensions of Competition

Horizontal competition. The familiar economic concept of competition is the rivalry of economic units in pursuit of the same goal. Obvious examples are sellers of the same product attempting to make sales to the same customers and buyers bidding for the same scarce supplies or resources. This type of rivalry is described as **horizontal** competition because the competitive units operate at the same stage of the production-marketing process. Thus we speak of competition among potato farmers, among clothing manufacturers, among drugstores, among buyers of farm products, among firms bidding on government contracts, and so forth. In each instance we think of a group of sellers who attempt to sell something to a common group of possible buyers or of a group of buyers who attempt to obtain supplies from a common group of sellers.

The fundamental notion of horizontal competition, which is taken from basic economic analysis, is that the rivalry of numerous competitive buyers and sellers in a single market will serve to establish a single market price. All sellers will receive that price, all buyers will pay it; and buyers and sellers who are unwilling to trade at that price will be excluded from the market. This conception is appropriate when there are, in fact, a sufficient number of similar buyers and sellers on each side of the market and when products and services are sufficiently standardized. However, the application of this concept in marketing analysis requires its expansion to cover situations in which the number of buying and selling units may not be great and in which both the economic units and their product-service offerings and requirements may be dissimilar in important respects.

Number of competitors. Horizontal competition *may* arise whenever two or more economic units attempt to perform the same functions, provide the same services, make the same sales or purchases, or otherwise engage in rivalry for the same market goals. However, the likelihood that vigorous competitive behavior will, in fact, arise varies considerably from one market situation to another. Most analysts agree that the likelihood of active horizontal rivalry among economic units depends to a great extent upon their numbers and their mutual similarity or dissimilarity. The reason for this consensus is that if only a few economic units pursue the same goal, their own best interests may be better served by joining together to accomplish the mutual goal, or by acting as if they were a single unit, and then dividing the resulting gains among themselves. The smaller the number of potentially competitive units, and the greater their mutual similarity, the easier it should be to act as one.

In the extreme cases, when only two or three potentially rival units exist, a certain amount of mutually acceptable behavior is inevitable. For example, if two similar firms attempt to sell a very similar product to the same group of buyers, they will inevitably be led to quote the same price. Any competitive price reduction offered by one seller will, of necessity, be matched by the offer of the other, unless he is willing to abandon the market altogether. If all of the potential sellers foresee this, each knows that any competitive price reduction will be matched by the other sellers, and none has an incentive to compete in this way. When, therefore, the number of possible competitors is small, the likelihood of certain types of competitive behavior arising among them may be considerably reduced, although they may engage in active rivalry in other ways.[2]

Similarity and diversity. The likelihood of active and direct competition is also affected by the degree of similarity or dissimilarity

2. A very readable review of classical oligopoly theory may be found in Fellner (1960).

among the possibly competitive economic units and their product-service offerings and requirements. Although the basic economic model of horizontal competition assumes that the competitive economic units are similar, their *dis*similarity may, in fact, be an important source of competitive pressures in actual market situations. Differences in costs among competitive firms lead them not only to outbid each other in direct competition but, perhaps equally important, lead them to develop their products and modify their marketing activities in different ways, so that they offer a range of differentiated alternatives to customers or suppliers. Similarly, differences in firm size, resources, and management goals may lead to competitive differences in market behavior. Finally, differences among product-service characteristics, and among the tastes and requirements of customers, may permit the development of structures of different, but competitively related, prices and products. The result is that horizontal competition among somewhat dissimilar enterprises, products, and services may serve to establish stable patterns among related prices and other marketing variables rather than bring the products and prices of rival sellers into uniformity.

A familiar example of competitive diversity is the variation in gasoline prices between major and minor brand outlets and between regular and premium grades. Most automobiles can be operated on all these types of gasoline—indeed the actual differences among them are not clearly known to most buyers—and all types are clearly presented as competitive alternatives in the market. However, the response of buyers is such as to maintain a fairly stable difference between prices: 2 to 3 cents per gallon between major and minor brands and between regular and premium. If the price differences become much greater, buyers shift to the lower-priced types; if the prices differ by less than 2 cents, buyers shift to the higher-priced types. As a result, changes in the price of regular grade gasoline at minor-brand outlets may have a substantial effect on the price of premium gasoline at major-brand outlets, even though both the two prices and the two products may be substantially different.

Direct and potential competition.   The notion that there may be price and quality differences within a competitive market suggests another critical aspect of horizontal competition: the *closeness* of competitive pressures. We may think of an individual seller as being surrounded by a small circle of direct competitors, then by a larger group of secondary competitors, and finally by an incompletely identified group of potential competitors who might become active under certain conditions.

The direct competitors are those enterprises that presently offer a similar product or service to the same general group of potential buyers.

Secondary competitors may be separated somewhat by location, differences in product quality, methods of distribution, or other marketing variables. The presence of the secondary competitors serves to limit the range of marketing activity—the geographic market area, price range, or product variation—of the entire group of direct competitors.

Beyond the secondary competitors are the potential competitors —enterprises that might enter the market through geographic expansion, changes in their own product lines, or adoption of new distribution channels, if it were in their own interests to do so.

The corresponding gradations of competitive contact on the buying side may be less obvious, but they are no less important. Rival bidders in an auction market provide an obvious example of direct competition in buying. Secondary and potential competitors include alternative users of raw materials, business locations, and other scarce resources that are subject to active buying competition.

Vertical competition.   In contrast to the concept of horizontal competition among enterprises at the same level of the production-marketing process, **vertical competition** involves the rivalry of successive selling and buying units over their respective shares of the total trading margin.[3] A seller will wish to sell each unit of output at something more than its cost, and a buyer will wish to purchase the product or service for something less than its total value to him for use or resale. The cost on the supply side and the use or resale value on the demand side set the limits to the total margin available from the transaction—the difference between the total benefits obtained (by the buyer) and the total costs incurred (by the seller). If the buyer pays less than the equivalent total benefit he will obtain from his use or resale of the product or service, the difference will be his share of the trading margin. If the seller sells for more than his costs, the difference is his share. Together, these two shares entirely exhaust the

---

3. For a further discussion of vertical competition, see Mallen (1964). This term was first introduced by Palamountain (1955).

margin. (This fundamental relationship was illustrated in figure 3–2 and in the related text discussion.)

The actual shares of the total trading margin obtained by buyers and sellers in vertical competition are determined by the availability of alternatives to each of them and by their mutual bargaining. If a buyer has only the choice between (1) meeting a particular need by making a particular purchase from a particular seller or (2) not meeting the need at all—and if the seller knows this is the case and can take advantage of it—the buyer will probably have to pay a price very close to the total value of the purchase to him. That is, the seller will be in a strong bargaining position, the buyer in a weak position, and the price will almost equal the value (or cost) of the harm or inconvenience the buyer would suffer by not making the purchase. Note, however, that the buyer will not, without coercion, pay more than this value; that is, he will not pay more than the purchase is worth *to him,* since he always has the choice of doing without it. The seller, however, obtains the major share of the total trading margin.

On the other hand, if there are several rival sellers, each eager to supply the buyer with his requirements, the buyer may be able to play them off, one against the other, or they may openly engage in horizontal competition among themselves. The availability of such alternatives shifts the bargaining power in favor of the buyer, with the result that the seller who finally makes the sale will obtain a price only slightly, if any, greater than his costs. Thus the seller will obtain a very small share, and the buyer a correspondingly large share, of the total trading margin.

The operation of vertical competition is seen most clearly when small numbers of potential buyers and sellers bargain directly for the use of large amounts of scarce resources. An example of this is the lease, sale, or construction of industrial facilities. Every metropolitan area has a limited number of sites available for new industrial activity; and some of these sites will be in use, others will be idle. All of them are owned by someone, however, and thus ownership or investment costs, as well as new construction or adaptation costs, will be involved in any decision to transfer these sites to new uses. If the site is currently in productive use, the revenues gained from that use will serve as the minimum limit on the willingness of the owners to make the sites available to other uses. Potential buyers or users of industrial sites, who will make their own analyses of site values for their own uses, will have to consider the profitability of the activity to be undertaken on the site, its locational advantages in comparison with other available sites, and any additional costs they may have to incur in order to make use of it. In actual negotiations, potential suppliers (sellers or lessors) will determine their own minimum supply prices and will also make their estimates of the value of the sites to the potential users. Potential users (buyers or lessees) will estimate their own use values, the cost of alternative sites they might select, and their own estimates of the present site owners' costs and alternatives.

Note that the presence of alternatives on both sides of the market serves to narrow the bargaining range. The current site owner may have no specific and current costs associated with the site, other than property taxes; however, if he has the alternative of making the site available to a user for a specific fee, this alternative serves to limit his willingness to deal with another potential user. Similarly, the potential user will not be willing to pay the owners the *total* value of his use of the site inasmuch as alternative sites may be available to him on comparable terms. Thus **opportunity costs** and **opportunity values** —the costs and values associated with alternative choices—serve to establish limits to the willingness of buyers and sellers to trade.

When such alternatives are present, sellers need not reduce their prices to the level of their costs and buyers need not pay prices that are equal to their total use values. Instead, each may take advantage of their opportunities to sell to or buy from others. The effective limits to bargaining are often termed the **reservation prices** of buyers and sellers; that is, the prices at which they abstain from making a particular transaction, withholding their sales or purchases for another time period or shifting them to another market. These relationships are illustrated in figure 4–1.

Although vertical competition is most clearly observed and described in single buyer-seller relationships, it also operates throughout the entire production-marketing process and between groups of horizontal competitors in individual markets. If we combine the conception that was shown in figure 3–2 of a vertical structure of costs and margins with the framework of vertical competition shown in figure 4–1, we see that the actual price and margin structure of the channel is determined by the competitive forces operating at each channel level. Further, any managerial unit at any channel level may seek to increase its share of the *total* margin available *throughout* the channel, not simply at the expense of its immediately contiguous buyers and sellers. Thus, rather than bargain aggressively with its suppliers and customers over prices and margin shares, an enterprise at any level of the channel

Figure 4–1   Framework of Vertical Competition

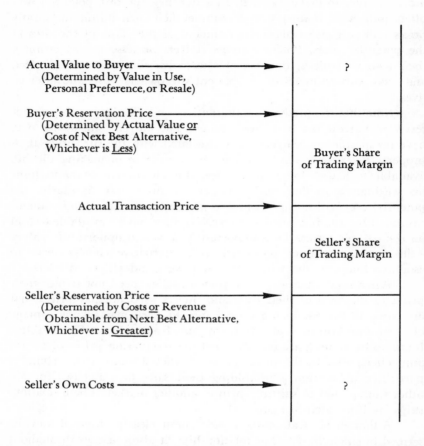

may consider bypassing them altogether, capturing their entire shares of the total margin, and dealing directly with initial producers or final buyers.

Organizational changes of this sort will, of course, require changes in functions and costs for the enterprise involved and responsive adaptation by others. However, an individual enterprise—or group of enterprises—at any channel level may be able to alter its vertical bargaining position substantially either by initiating such organizational and functional changes or simply by appearing to be able and willing to do so. Thus a major force in determining the structures of marketing channels and the entire production-marketing process is the incentive of each enterprise to adapt its organizational form and functions in ways that will strengthen its position with respect to vertical, as well as horizontal, competition.

Two familiar examples of such adaptation are (1) manufacturer integration into wholesaling, either partial (sales force only) or total, aimed at reducing the bargaining power and decreasing the margins of traditional wholesalers, and (2) intensive consumer advertising effort by producers of brand products, aimed at strengthening their bargaining position *vis-à-vis* distributors of those products at other channel levels.[4]

Horizontal-vertical competitive interaction. In the dynamics of market interaction and adaptation, forces of horizontal and vertical competition are continuously at work. In general, we expect horizontal competition among sellers to bring prices down toward costs, and thus to yield an advantage for buyers. On the other hand, horizontal competition among buyers will serve to bid prices up, toward use values, creating a vertical competitive advantage for sellers. In the perfect competition model of economic theory, horizontal competition on both sides of the market gives rise to strong vertical competitive forces as well. However, when the conditions of perfect horizontal competition are not present—that is, in the absence of numerous and similar competitive units on each side of the market—conditions of vertical competition may also be altered. Further, even when the number of buyers and sellers is rather large, it may be possible—if the market is not centralized—for high-cost sellers to seek out high-value buyers, and for low-value buyers to seek out low-cost sellers, so that transactions take place at many different prices and buyers and sellers alike trade at prices very close to their use values and costs.

Thus vertical competition may be stronger in direct bargaining situations, where horizontal competition is weaker, and strong horizontal competition on one side of a market may give rise to competitive advantages for enterprises on the opposite side.[5] These likely

---

4. A useful piece of evidence in this connection is the pattern of prices and distributors' margins on consumer goods branded and highly advertised by manufacturers as compared to similar products branded by distributors and less intensively advertised. Almost without exception, distributors obtain higher percentage margins—that is, higher shares of the total available margin—on their own brands than on manufacturers' brands. This result is consistent with the notion that branding and advertising is a source of vertical competitive advantage in the marketing channel.

5. An attempt to formalize the competitive impact of combinations of certain horizontal and vertical market structures is made by Baligh and Richartz (1967).

combinations of horizontal and vertical competitive forces are summarized in table 4–1.

Table 4–1   Strength of Horizontal and Vertical Competition

Side of Market	Dimension of Competition and Strength	
	Horizontal	Vertical
Buyers	Strong	Strong
Sellers	Strong	
Buyers	Strong	Favors sellers
Sellers	Weak	
Buyers	Weak	Favors buyers
Sellers	Strong	
Buyers	Weak	Possibly, very strong, depending on market organization and extent of direct bargaining
Sellers	Weak	

Forms of Competition

An individual economic unit engages in competitive behavior in order to increase its benefits, revenues, or profits, or to avoid a possible decrease in them. The means of achieving this goal include all the managerial activities of the enterprise, and thus the forms of competitive behavior are equally varied. Although much of the discussion and analysis of competition focuses on *price* competition, other forms of competitive activity also are of considerable importance in the modern economy. Even with respect to price competition, the critical consideration is the relationship between prices and costs, not simply with the level of prices as such.

Thus if there is a substantial difference between prices and costs for some group of suppliers, competitive activity among them might take the form of price reduction, as each attempts to gain a greater share of the market by cutting prices below the levels set by the others. Or it might take the form of improved quality, added services, advertising, or other activities that would *raise* costs. In either case, aggressive competition would bring about a closer relationship between costs and prices, but either costs or prices, or both, might change in the process.

Competition in marketing may focus on any marketing strategy variable, such as price, product quality, associated services, advertising, distribution channels, and location (among others). Further, a key aspect of marketing management is the selection of appropriate *combinations* of strategy variables to accomplish various competitive goals. These strategic aspects of marketing activity will be discussed in more detail, and primarily from the viewpoint of the individual marketing firm, in Part III. For the present, the essential point is that competitive activity can take many forms, and therefore that the conventional analysis of price competition can be—and in many instances *must* be—supplemented with a parallel analysis of competition in product development or variety, advertising, and other strategic marketing variables.

Perhaps one of the less obvious forms of competition is the development of competitive distribution channels and methods. It is difficult to categorize these activities according to a simple scale (as can be so easily done with "high" and "low" prices); however, their overall competitive impact is no less important for that reason. For example, the introduction of such new retailing techniques as mail and telephone selling and vending machines has had a substantial competitive impact on more conventional forms of retailing. Here again we note the role of variety in competition. Cigarette prices, for example, are typically higher at vending machines than at retail stores, but the difference is limited to a few cents. Market experience indicates that customers will transfer their purchases back and forth between these two types of marketing outlets in response to larger price differences.

Nonstore purchasing by mail or telephone is a more complex example. For the buyer, it offers the convenience of not having to travel to a retail store and search out the merchandise; however, it also eliminates the possibility of directly inspecting and comparing merchandise items. On the selling side, firms that conduct a regular large-scale nonstore business may obtain substantial economies of operations, as compared to conventional retailing, whereas firms that use nonstore sales only as a supplement to conventional in-store operations may find them relatively costly. The result is that prices for some nonstore retail purchases are *higher* than comparable in-store prices and prices for other purchases are *lower*. Firms that offer nonstore purchasing as a major competitive alternative to conventional retailing generally offer nonstore purchasers lower prices (compare the catalog price with the in-store price for the same items for a major retail firm that uses both marketing methods). However, firms that offer nonstore purchases only as a high-cost convenience to their regular in-store customers—that is, as a means of holding these customers in the face of other competitive developments—generally quote the same basic prices plus an additional handling charge.

Thus the same distribution methods have different roles in the competitive strategies of different firms, and, therefore, the presence of alternative distribution methods has different implications for overall competitive adaptation and development in different markets.

These examples of the relationship between distribution methods and prices suggest the importance of the total combination of marketing strategy variables in competitive activity. Changes in product quality may be desirable only if promotional activity to explain or dramatize such changes can be simultaneously undertaken. But the feasibility of making both quality and promotional changes may depend upon changes in procurement costs, prices, or distribution channels. Physical distribution and packaging are closely interconnected, and both are directly linked with the structure of the distribution channels adopted, the activities of wholesalers and other bulk purchasers, and the unit of purchase desired by final buyers.

The fact that competition may take many specific forms has led some writers to look for a comprehensive term that would encompass all of the various types of competitive activity, including not only marketing but finance, personnel, location, and other aspects of managerial decision making as well. Grether (1966, p. 32) has suggested the term **enterprise competition** for this comprehensive concept, a term that emphasizes the commitment of all the resources of an enterprise to improving its competitive position *vis-à-vis* all other enterprises throughout the economy.

Competitive Costs

The two principal criticisms of the market system as a way of organizing economic activity have been the high cost of competition and the tendency toward monopoly. There is no doubt that competitive market activity involves numerous costs that yield only doubtful specific returns, either for the firm or for society at large. Popular discussions of this topic inevitably point out the "wastes" of advertising, but it would be as relevant to point to overlapping product development efforts, duplication of distribution facilities, or the losses in property and skills due to business failures. Some of these costs can be justified as maintaining a desirable variety of available products and services, and others as testing a number of alternatives so that the chance of a successful result is increased, but many of these costs must be attributed to the competitive process itself.

Effective competition requires that rivalry take place, and rivalry itself is costly. In trying to obtain the same customers, several competitors will inevitably expend a greater total effort than a single seller who serves these same customers and uses the same marketing methods. Further, a certain amount of short-run excess capacity is essential to competitive activity. For example, when several alternative products are available but only one is selected, the remainder are for the moment in excess supply. They may eventually be sold to other customers, or shifted to another market, or disposed of at a loss, but the moment they are not chosen by the buyers they have been shown to be unnecessary to the actual transaction. The cost of maintaining a much wider array of market alternatives than can possibly be chosen by buyers during a short-term period is the cost of providing choice in the market.

Of course, discrepancies between the quantity and quality of the products and services offered and desired would arise even under monopoly conditions because marketing behavior cannot be predicted with perfect accuracy. Uncertainty gives rise to costs, whether or not competition is present. However, a monopoly firm will try to offer the range of products and services *least likely* to take sales away from each other, while still ensuring that most of its potential customers will choose one of the available alternatives rather than purchase nothing at all. By contrast, a group of competitive firms seeks to offer the products and services *most likely* to take sales and customers away from each other. They duplicate each other's marketing efforts, and the competitive activities of each firm stimulate the others to more aggressive, and perhaps costly, competitive responses. Several firms make all the necessary effort to accomplish each transaction but only one transaction is made; hence the total costs of all the firms' attempting to make an individual transaction must be greater under conditions of competition than if only one alternative (the one actually chosen) had been available.

Further, each increase in the variety of products or services offered creates an additional possibility that the special needs and tastes of a customer group will be more closely matched, and hence that the enterprise that offers the added variety will gain a competitive advantage. Thus, under competitive conditions there is the likelihood of a greater and more costly range of choice than would be provided under equally uncertain, but noncompetitive, circumstances. As a result, competition in marketing gives rise to extra costs to the economy as a whole, many of which, with the benefit of hindsight, could have been avoided.

On the other hand, fully effective competition, by taking many different forms, also yields substantial benefits, both in the short run and, even more importantly, over time. Competitive rivalry among firms brings about continuous pressure for each of them to make cost reductions within their existing cost structures. If one firm among a group of competitors obtains a cost advantage, the firm may (1) simply gain greater profits; (2) reduce prices and thereby attempt to gain a larger share of the market; or (3) increase *other* costs, such as the costs of product quality or advertising, and attempt to gain a competitive advantage thereby. Whichever alternative is chosen, the initial cost advantage remains highly desirable; and once the firm has reduced its costs and gained an advantage, others will be stimulated either to do the same or to find some other means of restoring their competitive position with respect to profitability, sales, or market share. The result is that dual pressure for cost reductions and for the use of cost-reduction opportunities in ways that yield benefits for suppliers and customers is likely to be greater and more continuous under conditions of competition than under any other form of market coordination.

Further, the cost of competitive variety is essential for introducing innovations into the market and for identifying which of several possible product and service alternatives will prove most satisfactory to potential users. Indeed, the availability of choices that will be passed over is an essential part of the competitive process. It is primarily by *rejecting* alternatives that buyers make their preferences known. Thus the cost of making the undesired alternatives available—even their promotion programs, distribution channels, and so forth, as well as the products and services themselves—is an essential cost of operating a competitive market economy over time. When such choices are eliminated, competition itself is eliminated, and some other means must be found to coordinate the forces of supply and demand. Up to the present time, capitalist and socialist economies alike have found that substitutes for competition as a means of directing economic activity have been neither cheap nor easy to establish and operate.

Cooperation

Cooperation takes place when two or more otherwise independent units act jointly to accomplish a common goal; it is the antithesis of competition. Yet a substantial degree of cooperation is necessary for the routine operation of markets, even highly competitive ones. Potential buyers and sellers must—at least—cooperate sufficiently to announce their bids and offers to each other and to reach exchange agreements. Buyers may have to cooperate among themselves to establish standardized product-quality descriptions and the like, and large groups of buyers and sellers may have to cooperate to determine the time and place of marketing activity, the meaning of contract terms, the availability of financial and other facilitating services, and many other essential bases of orderly marketing.[6]

In addition to these pervasive and subtle forms of cooperation, which are necessary for regular market activity, cooperation becomes an explicit alternative to competition when it involves formal cooperative agreements among economic units that would otherwise engage in horizontal or vertical competition.

The most prominent examples of explicit cooperation in marketing in the United States are to be found in agricultural industries. Formal agreements among agricultural producers (usually authorized by federal or state law) provide a basis for the elimination of competitive activity among the members and for their joint accomplishment of specific production or marketing tasks. Agricultural cooperatives may engage in very substantial activities with respect to production, including the introduction of efficient production methods, control of product quality, and control of total output volume, and they may also take on additional social and political functions. However, their principal focus of activity has been on marketing and associated processing, storage, and financing operations.

The basic idea is that numerous (and sometimes small) producers are able to pool their resources and their production and thus obtain economies of scale in the physical handling of their merchandise, economies of continuity in planning and conducting their operations over time, and bargaining advantages in making sales to others. These

6. For a suggestive discussion of the importance of cooperative activity in the marketing system, see Alderson (1965), especially pp. 239–58.

bargaining advantages may be quite direct or they may take the form of control over the volume of total output, the distribution of output among different markets, or the timing of production and marketing —all with the goal of increasing the revenues gained by the cooperative members over what they would otherwise be.

Aside from agriculture, the most important formal cooperative organizations are found in the grocery trades. Owners of retail food stores have joined to form retailer-owned wholesale cooperatives in order to obtain the advantages of large-scale procurement. Some established wholesale firms have formed "voluntary" retail chains, which involves, essentially, a cooperative agreement between a wholesaler and a number of retailer-customers: the retailers agree to purchase their principal requirements from the wholesaler and the wholesaler agrees to provide various price and service advantages for the retailers. Another form of cooperation in retailing is the consumer-owned cooperative, an organizational form that is more prominent in Scandinavia than in the United States. These organizations establish their own retail outlets, which then buy and resell merchandise in the same way as other retail stores. In principle, consumer cooperatives have special concern for the needs and tastes of their members. Vertical linkages of various kinds among producer, distributor, and consumer cooperatives are quite common, and generally these linkages also involve cooperative aspects as well.

Cooperative advertising is a further example of explicit cooperation that is of some importance. A firm that markets a brand product for resale through independent distribution outlets has little control over the marketing activities of these outlets with respect to the product. Therefore, to encourage the outlets to advertise the brand, the brand owner may "cooperate" by offering an advertising allowance that the reseller can use to expand his own advertising budget by including this particular brand, either alone or with others, in his advertising program. Thus cooperative advertising becomes, in part, a kind of price reduction (allowance) for encouraging resellers to advertise and sell a particular brand of merchandise. In addition, such arrangements reflect an assumption that some advertising expenditures may produce greater sales results when both the product and the point of purchase are joined in a single advertisement than when each is advertised separately.

An essential aspect of all these forms of cooperation is that the cooperators obtain some specific benefits from their endeavors. In cooperative advertising, at least in principle, both the brand manufacturer and the reseller obtain more advertising exposure than they would otherwise, and each obtains whatever additional advantage may accrue from being joined with the other in the advertising message.

In an organized cooperative, members either obtain more desirable prices for specific goods and services than they would on the open market or they receive a share of the total revenue of the cooperative over and above its costs of operation. Since such shares are distributed among members in proportion to their use of a cooperative, they amount to retroactive price adjustments. Further, members obtain proportionate shares of any benefits the cooperative management may be able to gain for its organization *vis-à-vis* other enterprises within the marketing channel.

Control

Control exists whenever one individual or organization is able to limit or specify the activities of another. Control is the primary means of coordinating activities within a managerial unit; and the basic notion of management is the direction of subordinates by superiors. There are, of course, many different styles and techniques of management, and very significant limits to the ability of managers to elicit specific types of performance from their subordinates, even within small organizations.

Control is an important means of coordination in marketing whenever one economic unit is able to direct the activities of another, whether at a single or at different marketing channel levels. Complete control—within the limits of managerial ability—may exist when several marketing establishments at the same channel level are under single ownership (as in a chain store organization), or when a supplier is owned by a distributor, or when a wholesale or retail firm is owned by a manufacturer.

The extension of control through ownership, so that formerly separate enterprises become parts of a single enterprise unit, is termed **integration.** Horizontal integration takes place when separate enterprises of the same type are drawn together; vertical integration occurs when enterprises at successive stages of a particular production-marketing process become joined. Integration may also occur through the establishment of new operating units, as well as through the acquisition of an existing enterprise by another. However, when we speak of a firm as vertically integrated we usually mean that this firm is engaged in a sequence of economic activities that are normally or frequently performed by separate business entities. No matter how an integrated enterprise comes into being, one of its essential characteristics is the ability to substitute managerial control for market competition or voluntary cooperation as the principal coordinating mechanism among its constituent units.

Complete integration by means of ownership is not the only way by which control may be substituted for other coordinating mechanisms, nor does integration by ownership imply that other coordinating mechanisms cannot be used. Many forms of partial or limited control of some enterprises by others may be established in the absence of mutual ownership among them. Contracts and agreements, licensing arrangements, and especially franchises are important means of exerting vertical control among suppliers and distributors in the U.S. marketing system. Trade association agreements and other formal relationships may also establish an element of control (or cooperation) among enterprises that normally engage in horizontal competition. On the other hand, some large divisionalized firms require their divisions to deal with each other as if they were entirely separate economic units, to consider competitive alternatives on the open market, and even to engage in direct competition with each other when possible. Examples of this practice are the competitive divisions and models of the automobile companies and the independent pricing decisions allowed some chain store managers. Thus common ownership may exist without substantial common control, at least with respect to specific marketing activities.[7]

Although some large organizations may choose to use competition and cooperation, as well as control, as means of coordination within their own operating systems, it is nevertheless true that the relative growth of large organizations serves to widen the scope for control as a coordinating mechanism throughout the economy. But this relative increase in control is not necessarily undesirable. On the contrary, it may provide benefits—not only for the specific economic units involved but also for society as a whole. Thus the control of one enterprise by another (of, say, a raw material producer by a processor) may permit substantial economies through product standardization, scheduling, inventory reduction, more efficient transportation and storage, and so forth. Similar advantages may arise from a form of horizontal control that permits operating standardization,

7. For a generalized discussion of the range of control or "power" relations in marketing, see Beier and Stern (1969).

mass promotion, and reduction in the risk of undesired variations in product quality for buyers. These extensions of control may yield cost and price reductions, or comparable quality and convenience increases, for many other buyers and sellers throughout the economy.

In addition to these extensions of private control, public control over many aspects of marketing activity has seemed so clearly desirable from time to time that special regulations and administrative bodies have been created for this purpose. Examples of significant public control in the United States pertain to product quality and safety in many lines of merchandise, limitations on the content of advertising, regulation of business locations and operating hours and methods, and so forth.[8]

It does not appear that the relative expansion of private and public control within the U.S. marketing system has thus far been sufficient to replace competition as the primary means of market coordination. In developing and analyzing specific control arrangements, however, particularly those involving very large private firms or very large segments of the economy, it is important that we consider their impact on the operation of competitive forces throughout the system as a whole. When specific control arrangements develop within a fundamentally competitive system, the arrangements themselves are tested by the pressures of competition. These pressures will not be the same as they would be in the absence of the control activity, but they nevertheless provide a check and, at least potentially, an alternative.

For example, we may judge that increased vertical or horizontal integration within an enterprise is not undesirable if integrated enterprises can compete successfully with nonintegrated enterprises. However, when there are no competitive alternatives, or when the ability of new competitive forces to assert themselves is seriously curtailed, there is no assurance that the controlled activity is operating efficiently. Again, for example, the U.S. military establishment, which is coordinated entirely by means of administrative and control techniques, is thought by some to be a model of efficiency and by others to be the outstanding example of inefficiency in our society. In the absence of a competitive alternative, it is probably impossible to determine which view is correct (although the functions of a military establishment are such that effective competition seems impossible). Fortunately, in a

---

8. For a general discussion of legal and public policy aspects of marketing see Grether (1966) and Howard (1964).

large private ownership economy there are almost no economic activities in which a substantial amount of competitive rivalry is not possible. Hence the test of competitive success can generally be maintained as a principal means of evaluating organizational, as well as marketing and technological, developments throughout the economy.

The real danger in the transfer of coordinating activity and decision making from competitive to control mechanisms is not that any specific action or decision will be worse than it would otherwise have been. Rather, the danger is that errors, once made, will be perpetuated, that a sequence of less than optimal choices will lead to the development of a less than optimal range of alternatives for future decision making, and thus that the system as a whole will lose the self-correcting feature that is the outstanding attribute of effective competition. Inasmuch as the essential task of coordinating the production, distribution, and use of goods and services has to be performed in all economies, those who abandon the competitive market mechanism are faced with the need of inventing something else to do the job.

Summary

The principal forms of coordination within the marketing system are **competition, cooperation,** and **control.**

Competition is the rivalry of separate and independent economic units that are in pursuit of the same objective. This rivalry may involve **horizontal** competition among units trying to accomplish similar transactions with the same customers or suppliers, or **vertical** competition for shares of the total profit margin available within a particular sequence of marketing exchanges.

Competitive pressures may be limited to similar products and services, and to the presentation of direct market alternatives, or they may include an array of diverse purchase and sale possibilities and the potential impact of economic units that are not currently participating in the market.

The interaction of horizontal and vertical competitive forces serves to determine the levels of prices and profit margins within any given organizational framework and cost structure. These same competitive pressures also lead to changes in organizational arrangements and costs over time.

Competitive activity may focus on any aspect of marketing activity, including price, promotion, product characteristics, and organizational arrangements.

Cooperation is a means of coordination in which two or more independent agencies act together to accomplish a common goal; and a minimum level of cooperation between buyer and seller is essential in order to effectuate any single exchange transaction. In addition, groups of buyers and sellers may formally agree to act jointly, and may even establish separate cooperative business agencies, in order to accomplish complex tasks on a continuing basis. A central problem of cooperative activity, whether formal or informal, is the division of costs and benefits among the cooperators.

Control is a means of coordination in which one economic unit operates under the explicit direction of another. Complete control of one unit by another may be based upon ownership, although there are many instances in which enterprise units under a common ownership are allowed to act independently. Conversely, control by one agency over specific aspects of marketing activity by others may be based upon law, contract, or traditional trade practices.

A significant trend within the U.S. marketing system has been the relative expansion of private and public control, at the expense of competition and cooperation, as a means of coordination. However, this expansion does not yet appear to have undermined the competitive market mechanism as the principal means of coordination throughout the economy over the long term.

References

Alderson, Wroe. *Dynamic Marketing Behavior*. Irwin, 1965.

Baligh, Helmy H., and Leon E. Richartz. *Vertical Market Structures*. Allyn & Bacon, 1967.

Beier, F. J., and L. W. Stern. "Power in the Channel of Distribution." In *Distribution Channels: Behavioral Dimensions,* ed. L. W. Stern. Houghton Mifflin, 1969.

Fellner, William. *Competition Among the Few: Oligopoly and Similar Market Structures*. A. M. Kelley, 1960 (1st ed. 1949).

Grether, E. T. *Marketing and Public Policy*. Prentice-Hall, 1966.

Howard, Marshall C. *Legal Aspects of Marketing*. McGraw-Hill, 1964.

Mallen, Bruce. "Conflict and Cooperation in Marketing Channels." In *Reflections on Progress in Marketing,* ed. George L. Smith. American Marketing Association, 1964.

Palamountain, Joseph C. *The Politics of Distribution.* Harvard University Press, 1955.

Part II

Buyer Behavior and Demand Analysis

5

The Nature of Market Demand

The Marketing Concept

The purpose of marketing activity, and the test of its success, is its satisfaction of the desires of users of goods and services. This does not mean that marketing primarily involves acts of kindly charity, nor that all the physical, social, and emotional needs of mankind can be reached through marketing. It does mean, however, that the ultimate success of a firm in an enterprise economy rests on its ability to make sales. Thus an understanding of both the marketing opportunities and the behavior of the individual firm, and the interaction of firms and industries throughout the market economy, requires comprehension of the nature and determinants of buying decisions and behavior.

Although market demand analysis has long been an important part of macroeconomics, demand studies have only recently been recognized as critical and continuing activities of the individual firm. The traditional concept of the business enterprise emphasized its physical and production activities and its financial structure. The role of marketing, comprising physical distribution and dealer-customer contact, was considered secondary. The task of marketing was simply to dispose of the given output of the firm at a reasonable profit. In contrast to this traditional viewpoint, the modern marketing-oriented firm places principal emphasis on discovering and developing market opportunities, and then on devising ways of supplying these markets at a profit.

Although the routine operating activities of the firm will be much the same in any case—and it is idle to argue which of several essential functions is the most important—the difference in basic orientation is substantial. The marketing-oriented firm emphasizes such activities as market research, promotion, and dealer-customer contact as central, not peripheral, aspects of business management. A firm that adopts the marketing concept comes to view its production of goods and services not simply as the application of physical transformation processes to resources but, rather, as **the adaptation of resources, processes, and marketing activities to the characteristics of potential buyers.**[1]

Historically, a limited form of the marketing concept has been more typical of wholesale and retail organizations. Antique retailing manuals emphasize the role of the retailer as the "purchasing agent" for his customers (in effect, his job is to buy what *they* want), and there is a hoary retailing maxim that "merchandise well bought is half sold." The traditional implementation of this guideline, however, was limited to selecting the most nearly satisfactory merchandise from the alternatives available. In its modern extension, the marketing concept leads final-goods sellers to reach back to wholesaling and production levels, and producers to reach forward toward final purchasers and users, in order to alter both the range of available alternatives and the way in which they are presented and recognized in the market.

The Basis of Market Demand

Needs and Wants

The above reference to the **characteristics of potential buyers** as the focal point of marketing analysis in the firm was precise, not casual. We refer to "buyers," not "consumers," because, even within a household, goods and services may be *purchased* by one individual for *use* by another. Further, household consumers are only one group of final-goods users, and final-consumer goods purchases may be strongly

1. For a general discussion of the marketing concept see King (1965).

affected by the activities of reseller buyers and other marketing inter-mediaries. We refer to "potential" buyers, not simply actual pur-chasers, because we are concerned with conditions under which present purchasers might choose different amounts or qualities of merchandise, and also with conditions that would lead to purchases by others who are not now active customers. If a firm or group of firms is making any sales, its products and services must be already adapted, to some extent, to the characteristics of its present customers. Its innovative effort, however, may be devoted to anticipating changes in these cus-tomers' behavior and in finding ways to reach new groups of potential buyers.

We also refer to the "characteristics" of buyers rather than to the more familiar terms "needs" and "wants." Many words have been expended in argument over whether people have been "made to want" certain items as a result of advertising, salesmanship, and other marketing efforts. Academic discussions of needs generally begin by listing certain basic physical and psychological requirements of human life, including food and drink, shelter, sex, and social relationships. Although the desire to satisfy these needs accounts for some funda-mental aspects of human behavior, the list does not go very far in ex-plaining the behavior of buyers and potential buyers in modern mar-kets because these needs are so highly generalized and are satisfied to varying degrees in so many different ways.

For the purposes of demand analysis, it is more useful to think of **needs** as **gaps between an existing state of being and a desired state.**[2] A manufacturing firm may need materials and equipment for the production process; a distributor may need supplies in order to make sales; and a household many need nourishment, health, enter-tainment, or transportation services. For most people, even those in relatively poor countries, these needs are only distantly connected with the basic requirements of survival. Even in primitive societies, only minimal food and shelter requirements may be met before "needs"

2. This short definition is consistent with the approach taken in much of the psychological literature. For example, Hall and Lindzey (1957, p. 172) quote Henry A. Murray—of whom they remark: "No other theorist has subjected the concept [of need] to so careful an analysis"—as follows: " 'A need is a construct . . . which stands for a force . . . in the brain region, a force which organizes perception, apperception, intellection, conation and action in such a way as to transform in a certain direction an existing, unsatisfying situation' " (Murray, 1938). In the mar-keting literature, Pratt (1965, p. 114) describes needs as arising from two sources: (1) physiological deprivation or disequilibrium within an individual and (2) the way in which an individual perceives or relates to his environment. "Both types of needs result in behavior directed toward goals that the individual believes will satisfy these needs."

develop for ornaments, ritual equipment, and other sources of social-psychological satisfaction. The point here is that market demand for major groups of products and services, as well as for particular items and brands, is derived from the *recognized* needs of organizations and individuals, and not—with very rare exceptions—from essential biological requirements or universally applicable standards or goals. A further point is that social-psychological needs are not new or strange phenomena invented by modern advertising. These needs are as old as human culture, although the variety of ways available for meeting them is probably greater in present-day developed countries than at any other time in the history of mankind.

If needs, then, are gaps between existing and desired states of being, wants may be defined as potential gap fillers. **Wants are the goods and services desired to meet particular needs.** This use of the terms **wants** and **needs** is broadly consistent with that of Alderson. In commenting on the contention that no needs remain to be met in the highly developed Western countries, he wrote:

> *There is no deficiency of consumer needs anywhere in the world, including the United States. Some needs appear more urgent than others, such as enough food to sustain life from day to day; but people need much more than the bare essentials of food, clothing, and shelter. They need whatever protection foresight can provide against the hazards and disasters which threaten to disrupt the preferred pattern of life. In a world of change, they need the means for adjusting and improving the pattern of life rather than being gradually overwhelmed by circumstance. The opportunities of life are so varied, the dangers which beset it so uncertain, that people will always need more things than they possess.*
>
> *It is wants that are lacking, not needs. . . . To want a product is to recognize it explicitly as a means of meeting a situation which is regarded as both probable and important. Marketing creates wants by making consumers aware of needs and by identifying specific products as means of meeting these needs. . . .*
>
> *Marketing assuredly deals with the creation of wants, but it starts with the principle that wants spring from needs and are not something alien to be set off in opposition to needs* (1957, pp. 279–280).

Wants, therefore, are more specific than needs. One *needs* transportation, but he *wants* an automobile, bicycle, scooter, or bus ticket. Sometimes, of course, it appears that needs can best be described in terms of the particular combination of qualities that is represented by some available product or service. However, it is the flow of services and satisfactions, including the satisfaction of possession, that constitutes the need. The product or the service itself is wanted to meet this need. The availability of products and services, and of information about them, contributes to both the recognition of needs and the specification of wants.[3]

For example, we may not be conscious of a gap between existing and desired situations until some means of substantially narrowing the gap comes to our attention. Then the light dawns: *"That's* what I need!" The need is recognized and simultaneously focused on a particular want that will meet it.

For the most part, however, needs are not instantaneously and permanently focused on specific wants. On the contrary, particular needs come to be focused on specific wants through a gradual process of cultural imitation, education, taste development, and broad social-psychological change.

Purchase Ability

Purchase ability transforms wants into market demand. Households and firms that have no purchase ability may have recognized needs and well-defined wants, but they will not become buyers. Indeed, market demand is generated entirely by households, firms, and agencies that are able to purchase wanted goods and services in order to meet their needs.

Purchase ability depends not only on income or wealth but also on the pressure of alternative expenditures and on the conditions of purchase. Thus we cannot say that all potential buyers with identified wants and purchase ability will become active buyers during any particular market period. We *can* say, however, that all of these potential buyers—and *only* these—*may* become active buyers. Whether they will buy, and what they will buy, depends on the market offerings of the potential sellers and the internal decision processes of the buyers themselves.

Explaining and Influencing Demand

The relationship between needs, wants, and market demand is illustrated in figure 5–1. For a major purchase decision, such as the choice of production equipment or industrial material for processing, the

3. This conception was formally introduced into economic theory by Lancaster (1966).

Figure 5–1   Needs, Wants, and Market Demand

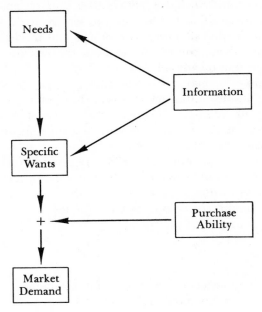

selection of a business location or a major product line for resale, or the purchase of a new residence or automobile, it may be useful to think of three very specific stages of demand evolution. Thus needs become recognized; then, as information is received and analyzed, they become focused upon particular wants. Then the costs associated with these wants are compared with the purchase ability of buyers, which generates actual demand for goods or services available in the market. Each step in such a process may be thought of as deliberate and time consuming, a conscious activity of rational potential buyers. For most types of purchase behavior, however, such distinctions are neither sharp nor necessary. A general need may be recognized and the ability to purchase available at all times, and a chance occurrence may be sufficient to identify a specific want and generate an immediate purchase.

The purpose of setting forth these relationships in a formal way is not to describe an individual purchase decision in detail but to draw attention to the three main groups of factors—needs, wants, and purchase ability—that underlie market demand. If we wish to analyze and explain market demand, we must investigate all three elements.

And if a firm wishes to stimulate or change demand, it may try to affect all of these factors, or any one of them. Thus a firm may attempt to increase the demand for its products or services by stimulating the recognition of needs it can satisfy, by converting or directing already recognized needs into wants for its own products, and by changing the purchase ability of possible buyers.

Of these three methods of increasing demand, the first—identifying needs—is by far the most difficult. The principal types of personal needs arise primarily from biological requirements, the social and cultural environment, and the style of life. Principal business and institutional needs arise from the kind of industrial, commercial, or service activity in which the organization is engaged. Needs change— old needs vanish and new ones are recognized—primarily as a result of technological and social change, education, and cultural developments. Individual firms and industries can cause new needs to be recognized, or existing needs to be felt more intensively, but the effort requires discovering buyer characteristics of which the buyers themselves are unaware, or persuading them that their known characteristics are not desirable. (The need to prevent, neutralize, or cover up natural body odors is an interesting example. Only a minority of the world's population recognizes such a need, although many more are well aware that such odors exist, and still others are apparently unaware of them entirely. The physical characteristics of mankind are similar everywhere; attitudes toward these characteristics are not.)

A much more common and relatively more feasible purpose of marketing effort is to focus recognized needs on specific wants. As needs lead to wants, potential buyers become conscious that the gaps between their existing and desired states of being can be reduced if particular gap fillers are obtained. The first step in changing needs into wants may be to determine the **kind** of product or service desired—that is, metal rather than wood for processing, a house rather than an apartment for residence. We may describe these as **generic** wants, which means that the general class (genus or genre) of product or service is identified but not the individual item. The second step is the identification of the **specific** qualities desired (performance features, style, location, etc.), and, finally, the specific item or service itself.

Marketing efforts may be aimed at making potential buyers aware of both generic and specific wants. Does this mean that marketing "makes people want things," or "makes them want things they don't need"? In our terminology, it would be more accurate to say (as above) that one purpose of promotional activity in **marketing is to** make individuals and organizations aware of needs they have previously ignored. A second purpose is to focus recognized needs on particular kinds of products and services. And a third purpose is to generate demand for specific firms, brands, or sources of supply. This last goal—generating specific demand—accounts for the largest part of total marketing promotion activity. However, the movement from needs to generic wants to specific wants is best understood as gradual and continuous, and subject to many feedback processes. Thus activities aimed at increasing demand for the products and services of individual firms may also, over time, contribute to broader want and need changes.[4]

The third way in which individual firms can influence demand is through changing the purchasing ability of potential customers. Although the basic financial circumstances of potential buyers are of course determined by economic factors that lie far beyond the control of individual sellers, an essential element in demand analysis is understanding and anticipating these circumstances and developing responses to them. Seller responses include not only the prices of goods and services to be offered for sale but also the terms of payment and the handling of additional costs that may enter into the decisions of potential buyers. Thus changes in product availability and convenience, provision of guarantees and return and repair services, and other auxiliary features that reduce the overall expenditure of money or the risk involved in the purchase and use of a product or service may be as important in expanding demand as simple price reductions or easy credit terms. All of these factors affect the ability of buyers to obtain their wants through market purchases.

Let us conclude this discussion with a not entirely trivial example of the needs-wants/market-demand relationship. I recognize a need for transportation service between my residence and my office, with occasional stops in between for errands, and I need this service at times of my own convenience. Also, I need to remain clean and dry, and to be able to carry small parcels, while being transported. If I choose to use the local bus service, I will of course be bound to its schedule and route; and I will lose time in waiting at bus stops and in relatively slow movement. I will also forgo the opportunity to stop along the way without inconvenience. This option, however, will be relatively cheap in terms of money expenditures. Or I may choose to drive myself in a private car, but I will incur great expenses of owner-

---

4. An extremely sophisticated discussion of these issues is contained in Rothenberg (1962).

ship and upkeep and will generate a new and rather terrible need—for parking space at both my residence and my place of work. I could go by taxi or hired car, but at considerable cost per trip, and only after the inconvenience of making arrangements each time or conforming to a schedule. Ideally, I would use a private car and driver, but—alas—my purchase ability is too limited for that. Thus whichever way I attempt to satisfy my general need for transportation with a particular type of transportation service, a considerable gap between existing and desired states will remain. Far from criticizing marketing effort for making me want things, I invite market innovators to provide a transportation product-service that will come closer to meeting my needs, within the limits of my ability to pay, than any alternative yet available.

Buyer Behavior: The Stimulus-Response Model

Modern analysis of buyer behavior is based primarily on a generalized form of a stimulus-response model.[5] The central element in such a model is the individual buying unit, which may be a person, household, firm, or other organization. In the analysis, the buying unit, identified in terms of its significant marketing characteristics, is said to receive stimuli, both from external forces and from its own internal processes. The buying unit's behavior and decisions are then interpreted as responses to the received stimuli. This fundamentally simple idea may be developed to any level of complexity and detail that is useful in analyzing a particular marketing problem, and it is presented here at a fairly high level of generality so that we can outline the main elements that might be included in such a model and their most significant relationships. Many more elaborate formulations of the basic model can be developed, but its appropriate detail and complexity depends upon the purpose to which it is to be put—that is, the particular aspects of buyer behavior that are to be described, explained, and predicted in the analysis.

The principal elements in a highly generalized stimulus-response model of buyer behavior are shown in figure 5–2, and we will examine

5. Detailed schematic flow charts of stimulus-response models were introduced into the marketing literature by John A. Howard; the most useful textbook development of his approach may be found in Howard (1963), chaps. 3 and 4. Another important and highly generalized framework for analysis, which puts greater emphasis on mathematical expression and empirical testing possibilities, is presented in Nicosia (1966), especially pp. 113–114 and 151–191.

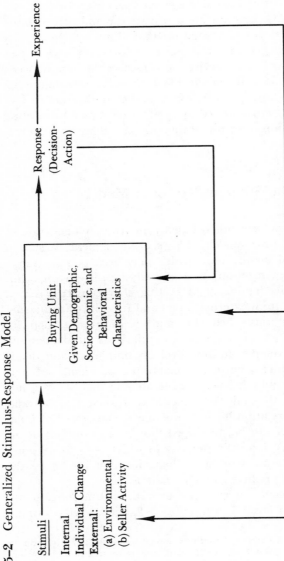

Figure 5–2 Generalized Stimulus-Response Model

each major part of the model in turn. For simplicity, the discussion will deal only with individual and household consumer buyers; a following section applies the model to industrial and organizational buyer behavior.

The Buying Unit

The individual or household buying unit is conceived as having certain basic characteristics that act as important determinants of its responses to marketing stimuli. Although any characteristic might be important for a particular demand analysis problem, three major groups of characteristics are generally regarded as particularly important.

1. Demographic characteristics: age, sex, family size, and geographic location
2. Socioeconomic characteristics: income and financial resources, social and vocational status, and established ownership and expenditure patterns
3. Behavioral characteristics: habits, attitudes, and decision-making processes

We shall not examine these characteristics in detail at this point because they are the principal subjects of analysis in the following three chapters. Here we wish only to identify them in a general way and to emphasize their central role in the structure of modern demand analysis.

Stimuli

The notion that a buying unit, possessing certain characteristics, receives a stimulus that leads it to make a particular marketing response is fundamentally simple. The identification and analysis of all the stimuli that might operate within the model is, however, a complex and difficult task. Most analysts agree that some stimuli of buying behavior are best described as **internal** to the buying unit itself while other stimuli can be clearly identified as arising from **external** forces. In addition, important stimuli arise from a change in one or more characteristics of the buying unit, but they cannot be described entirely as either external or internal; we shall term them **individual change** stimuli.

Internal stimuli. Imagine a single buying unit, say a household with a particular set of demographic, socioeconomic, and behavioral characteristics, that operates within a stable external environment. The buying behavior of such a household might be described as the result of its recognizing its needs, focusing them on specific wants, and adopting a pattern of buying behavior designed to satisfy these wants as fully as possible within the limits of its purchase ability. Such a household might, however, make different purchase decisions at different points in time in response to its own **internal** stimuli. The household may need to eat every day, but it need not purchase food every day, and it certainly need not purchase the same foods on every shopping trip. It may routinize its responses to one or another purchasing stimuli, or one of its basic characteristics may be a "taste for variety," which leads it to vary its choices deliberately to avoid routine. In addition, the household's collection of products will both accumulate and wear out. Its preferences and tastes will change on the basis of experience, and it will recognize new needs and discover that different combinations of goods and services will better satisfy them. As a result of all these processes, internal buying stimuli will arise and new buying responses will be generated, even in a buying unit with stable characteristics and operating within a stable environment.

Of course, we cannot observe such buying units with any degree of accuracy over any substantial time period; basic characteristics change and environmental influences cannot be escaped. However, in analyzing the responses of buying units to other types of stimuli it is important to take full account of forces that operate entirely within the buying unit and that have an important impact upon its actual market behavior.

Individual change stimuli.   Individual change stimuli arise from changes in the characteristics of a particular buying unit over time. Obvious and important examples are the stimuli associated with demographic changes related to marriage, family size, aging, and place of residence. Income and vocational changes, as well as changes in social contacts and relationships, also stimulate new buying behavior responses. The difference between these stimuli and the internal stimuli discussed above is that internal stimuli arise within a fixed set of characteristics and behavior patterns. Under this heading, by contrast, we call attention to stimuli that arise from **changes** in characteristics.

Admittedly, one can conceive of examples in which it would be difficult to discriminate between the two, and in such cases a fine discrimination is probably not justified for any analytical purpose. However, it seems quite clear that a purchase activity that is generated primarily by force of habit, or by a specific intention of avoiding habitual behavior, will require a different type of analysis than an activity that arises from a change in income, family size, or fundamental attitudes. It is for discriminating between these two broad types of buying stimuli that the two categories, **internal** and **individual change** stimuli, are suggested.

External stimuli. External buying stimuli arise from sources outside the individual buying unit and do not, in themselves, bring about any change in the unit's characteristics. Here we distinguish external stimuli that arise from broad developments in the buying unit's environment from stimuli arising from the efforts of sellers of goods and services to stimulate buyer responses. **Environmental stimuli** include broad social and cultural forces, and changes in traditional purchase patterns and life styles, as well as changes in the general level of economic activity, vocational and locational patterns, and so forth. (Note that environmental changes may stimulate buying responses from households that are not directly involved in them. If all my neighbors get richer, I may join them in spending more even though my own income has not increased.)

Seller activity stimuli—that is, the marketing efforts of individuals and firms—are specifically intended to generate responses from potential buyers. The relatively inconspicuous position occupied by sellers' marketing activities within the stimulus-response model should not be interpreted as indicating their unimportance. On the contrary, the purpose of the model is to enable the analyst to identify the full range of potentially important buyer characteristics and sources of buying stimuli, and *then* to evaluate the influence and relative significance of each in explaining or predicting certain types of behavior. However, it is very important that the marketing activities of sellers be seen as one among many sources of buying stimuli. The presence of other stimuli, which may either reinforce or offset the promotional activities of individual marketers, is as significant an attribute of the marketing environment as the buyer characteristics themselves.

Buyer Responses

The simplest form of the stimulus-response model ends with a buy/no-buy alternative. The given buying unit, subjected to a particular stimulus, either purchases or does not purchase a good or service. Buy/no-buy, however, is only one of many kinds of alternative responses, and even here we may distinguish between a buy/no-buy **decision** and a subsequent **action.** That is, the stimulus may produce a decision to take action at some later time, either when some other external stimulus arises (say, a change in purchase ability occurs or a particular need arises) or simply on the basis of convenience. The decision to buy may be formally taken, but the action (buying) may not occur at once, and may not occur at all if subsequent decisions intervene. In addition, the relevant response alternatives may include a wide variation in the volume or time rate of purchase, or in the particular quality combinations bought. Finally, the principal responses may be changes in attitudes or decision-making criteria, or simply in information levels and awareness, and these changes alter the effects of other stimuli or cause experience to be reinterpreted and behavior changed.

Buyer Goals and Decision Processes

In order to describe and analyze the critical aspects of the buying process, concepts and terms from a variety of disciplines have been introduced into the literature of marketing. Although many of these will be explained and used in the following chapters, as they relate to specific aspects of demand analysis, four key concepts suggest such broad implications for the interpretation and application of the generalized stimulus-response model that they require brief comment here.[6]

Maximizing

The formal economic theory of buyer behavior is based on a maximizing or optimizing concept. The idea is that the individual buying unit allocates its purchase ability in such a way as to obtain the largest or best (i.e., maximum or optimum) total of satisfactions available to it. These satisfactions may, of course, be social and psychological as well as physical and biological (economics has never questioned the importance of tastes). However, maximizing behavior involves the conscious comparison of known alternatives, in terms of their ability to satisfy specific goals, so that the best of all possible combinations of choices can be determined.

6. For a suggestive treatment of some of these same concepts, see Kotler (1965).

Satisficing

The term "satisficing" has been coined to describe choice-making behavior that does not aim at optimum or best solutions but only at satisfactory ones (see Simon, 1961). Thus a purchase alternative might be selected because it met the minimum performance level thought to be satisfactory by the buyer, even though better alternatives might have been available in the market. The notion of finding the overall maximum—the best of all alternatives—assumes both that (1) all choices can be identified and their ability to satisfy goals can be evaluated and (2) the process of information gathering and evaluation is not, in itself, expensive and time consuming. However, these assumptions are not valid for a considerable part of buying behavior. Neither the full range of products and services nor their specific performance qualities can be determined with particular accuracy. And the gathering and analysis of the available information is not necessarily pleasant. Thus buyers may be led to establish minimum criteria for reaching purchase decisions (including the decision *not* to buy) and to appraise their alternatives in terms of them.

Problem Solving

A problem-solving interpretation of buyer behavior assumes that individuals and households define their goals by finding solutions to particular problems, after which they proceed to evaluate purchase stimuli and alternatives in terms of their contributions to these solutions. This form of problem solving may incorporate either a maximizing or a satisficing approach, but its distinguishing feature is the grouping of potential buying goals, needs, or satisfactions to form **problem** categories. It may not be conceptually possible or relevant to reduce these problems to their constituent elements inasmuch as the key to problem solving is to obtain a combination of interactive features.

Problem solving also implies the existence of a number of somewhat discrete problems that may form a hierarchy but do not necessarily require simultaneous solution. For example, I may first solve my housing problem, and then solve my transportation problem. I may not explicitly consider the additional transport cost incurred by living in a lower-rent district or the way my rent bill will affect my ability to buy a car. Thus I may treat the two problems as separate problems and deal with one only after I have settled the other. On the other hand, I might try to optimize the combination of housing and transportation services available; or if I find I have a fixed sum of money available for buying a car, I may search diligently to obtain the best value for my money (maximization). It is sometimes useful to think of problem solving, or satisficing, as accounting for the distribution of expenditures *among* major need or product-service categories and maximizing as accounting for part of the choice activity *within* categories.

Deliberating

Maximizing, satisficing, and problem solving are terms that describe deliberative behavior; each of them implies taking careful thought and weighing alternatives. By contrast, a large part of observed buying behavior appears to be nondeliberative in character, with no evidence of time spent in decision making, information gathering, or making careful comparisons. Such nondeliberative behavior may be described as **habitual, random,** or **impulsive,** and each of these terms may be useful in explaining certain types of buying behavior within the stimulus-response model.

Habitual or **routine** purchase choices, although nondeliberative at a particular point in time, may reflect deliberation and a conscious evaluation of buying alternatives in some previous period. Also, such choices generally reflect at least a satisfactory level experience with previous purchases of the same merchandise and a desire to avoid the uncertainties that might arise from experimenting with alternatives.

Random selection of products or brands reflects either indifference to specific product features or a belief that the available alternatives are all alike. Both habitual and random buying behavior arise, in part, because making a choice is an activity that requires time and effort. Careful choosing may be worth the trouble, and may even be interesting with respect to large purchases of durable goods. With respect to low-price consumer goods, however, the benefits available from having made superior choices may be worth less than the trouble required to discover them.

Impulse buying, on the other hand, is the simplest form of stimulus-response behavior in marketing. A specific stimulus is received by a buying unit that possesses such characteristics that a purchase decision and action focused on a particular item result almost immediately.

Organizational Buying

The total volume of purchases by industrial users, reseller-buyers, institutions, and government agencies in a developed economy is many times the total purchase volume of final consumption goods, and the purchasing activities of household buying units are significantly affected by the behavior of organizational buyers.[7] Therefore the analysis of business and institutional buying is of considerable importance. Much of this activity, particularly that of reseller-buyers, is based upon the expected behavior of final-goods purchasers, but even here the connection is not necessarily close. The purchasing behavior of reseller-buyers is not simply a reflection and summation of the behavior of final buyers because (1) reseller-buyers lack full information of what the final buyers would choose under different circumstances and (2) the anticipated preferences of final buyers are filtered through the goal structure of the reseller-buyers. Thus if the reseller-buyers are profit-making firms, they may be expected to analyze their own buying and selling opportunities in order to obtain profits rather than to reflect the preferences of their subsequent customers. Of course, much business and institutional purchasing involves industrial equipment, supplies, and construction materials that never pass directly into final demand uses. Whether for resale or direct nonhousehold use, business and institutional buying is a separate, important, and largely independent element in the marketing system.

The principal contrast between household and organizational buying behavior is that the latter is typically more deliberative and formal. This does not mean that organizational buying is more "rational" or "wiser" than household buying, or that attitudes and preferences do not play an important role in the former. It does mean, however, that the criteria for specific purchases are more explicitly recognized and the extent to which different purchase alternatives meet the criteria is more carefully examined.

To recast the stimulus-response model to fit organizational buying, we may replace the individual or household buying unit characteristics with the following organizational characteristics:

1. Nature and function of the organization: industry and production activity, position in the marketing system, principal institutional

7. Two recent studies of organizational buying are Levitt (1965) and Robinson and Faris (1967).

purpose or responsibility, and location and geographic scope of activity

2. Economic and financial characteristics: extent and source of financial resources, profitability, or budget
3. Purchasing organization and decision criteria

The first two groups of organizational characteristics are obvious parallels of the demographic, social, and economic characteristics of households. It is the third group of characteristics—organization and criteria—that gives rise to the deliberative character of organizational buying. Households, of course, also have buying organizations and criteria, but their organization is largely informal and the criteria are rarely consciously expressed and examined. The housewife takes primary responsibility for food purchases, for example, and the husband for purchases relating to an automobile, insurance, and his own clothing and personal needs; and joint decision making will probably be involved in major expenditures, such as housing, automobiles, and high-cost appliances. Children or other household members may also have their own purchasing authority, and may contribute to decision making or exercise a veto over certain types of expenditures. The criteria to be applied in making purchase decisions may be unconsciously developed by the buyer or may be agreed upon collectively, in light of the preferences and purchase ability of the family as a whole.

In organizational buying, these arrangements become complex and formalized. Purchasing authority is distributed among different organizational units and purchasing budgets and goals are established. Internal communication systems link the users of purchased items with the actual buyers, so that changes in requirements and use experience can be taken into account. All of these arrangements must be formal and somewhat rigid, so that different individuals can perform the same tasks consistently and so that different units within the organization can have some assurance in what other units are doing. However, this formality also implies that organizational buying behavior cannot have the easy flexibility of household buying behavior and, therefore, that fairly specific knowledge of organizational purchasing practices may be a key to successful selling. For example, when organizational purchasing is concentrated in a separate purchasing department, sales effort must be directed toward that department, as well as toward the actual using units. Similarly, if decisions of magnitude are made only by top management, the marketing effort of sellers must be directed at these levels rather than at actual buyers or users.

The criteria used in organizational buying also have some special characteristics. The formal listing of performance qualities—strength, durability, weight, and so forth—and cost constraints in organizational buying correspond fairly directly to the informal consideration of quality and price in household buying. In addition, formal purchasing criteria are required because subordinate managerial units within an organization must provide higher authorities with a rationale for their activities and a basis for appraisal.

Organizational buying is also subject to a variety of explicit constraints, some of which are only indirectly related to the merit of particular purchases. Such constraints are probably most numerous and important with respect to purchases with public funds—not only purchases by governmental units but also those by publicly supported institutions, such as schools and hospitals. The additional buying criteria imposed on these organizations by public authorities may include such considerations as the location, labor practices, and size of suppliers. Thus public institutions may be constrained to favor or compelled to use local or national products, to buy only from firms that pay certain minimum wages, or to distribute their purchases in a specific way among large and small businesses. These same types of restrictions may apply, though less formally, to other organizational buying. An additional criterion that is sometimes applied to business purchasing is **reciprocity:** purchasing (wherever possible) from a firm's own customers, so that a reciprocal buying-selling relationship is established.

In spite of the complex buying organizations and formal purchasing requirements involved in organizational buying, there is considerable scope for individual preferences, habits, and attitudes in business and institutional purchasing. Continuity of relationships, reliability, and the assurance of favorable treatment in time of short supply or special need may be implicit buying criteria that are quite as important as explicit performance and cost criteria in actual buying behavior. Even old-fashioned salesmanship continues to play a role—and sometimes a large one—in stimulating and satisfying organizational demand.

Summary

Demand analysis is a central activity in the marketing-oriented enterprise because the market success of a firm rests on its ability to adapt its resources, production processes, and marketing activities to the characteristics of potential buyers. **Market demand** comes into being when the needs of potential buyers become focused on particular goods and services, and are accompanied by **purchase ability**. **Needs** can be defined as gaps between existing and desired states of being and **wants** as recognized means of filling these gaps.

Communication and informaton play critical roles in the identification of needs and wants. In order to influence market demand, a marketing agency may seek to stimulate the recognition of needs or to direct recognized needs toward particular product and service alternatives, both in terms of broad expenditure categories **(generic demand)** and in terms of individual items or brands **(specific demand)**. Alternatively, a firm may change its prices or terms of sale in order to alter the effective purchasing ability of potential buyers.

Modern analysis of buyer behavior is based primarily on a generalized form of a **stimulus-response model.** The model presented in this chapter depicts the individual buying unit (household, firm, or other organization) as possessing various (given) physical, economic, and behavior characteristics. Buying behavior stimuli are identified as (1) **internal**—those arising from the characteristics of the buying unit; (2) **individual change**—those arising from a change in these characteristics; and (3) **external**—those arising from outside developments, chiefly from changes in the general environment or the marketing activities of sellers and other agencies.

Within this broad framework of analysis, buyer behavior may be analyzed in terms of the application of either **maximizing** or **satisficing** decision criteria, and as either a comprehensive or a discrete **problem-solving** process. The distinction between **deliberative** and **nondeliberative behavior** appears to be particularly important, and may explain substantial differences in decision processes and their results among major categories of expenditures for both household and institutional purchasers.

References

Alderson, Wroe. *Market Behavior and Executive Action.* Irwin, 1957.

Hall, Calvin S., and Gardner Lindzey. *Theories of Personality.* Wiley, 1957.

Howard, John A. *Marketing Management, Analysis, and Planning.* Irwin, 1963.

King, Robert L. "The Marketing Concept." In *Science in Marketing,* ed. George Schwartz. Wiley, 1965.

Kotler, Philip. "Behavioral Models for Analyzing Buyers." *Journal of Marketing,* Vol. 29, No. 4, October 1965.

Lancaster, Kelvin J. "A New Approach to Consumer Theory." *Journal of Political Economy,* Vol. 74, No. 2, April 1966.

Levitt, Theodore. *Industrial Purchasing Behavior: A Study of Communication Effects.* Harvard University, Graduate School of Business Administration, 1965.

Murray, Henry A. *Explorations in Personality.* Oxford University Press, 1938.

Nicosia, Francesco M. *Consumer Decision Processes.* Prentice-Hall, 1966.

Pratt, Robert W., Jr. "Consumer Behavior: Some Psychological Aspects." In *Science in Marketing,* ed. George Schwartz. Wiley, 1965.

Robinson, Patrick J., and Charles W. Faris. *Industrial Buying and Creative Marketing.* Allyn & Bacon, 1967.

Rothenberg, Jerome. "Consumers' Sovereignty and the Hospitability of Freedom of Choice." *American Economic Review,* Vol. 52, No. 2, May 1962.

Simon, Herbert A. *Administrative Behavior.* Macmillan, 1961.

6

Demand Analysis: Description and Interpretation

What Is Demand Analysis?

The purpose of demand analysis is to **describe, explain,** and **predict** the behavior of potential buyers. Description is the essential first step because it is necessary that we know what features of marketing activity are to be explained; and the great bulk of the time and cost expended on routine market research is accounted for by descriptive studies. However, descriptions cannot be complete in every detail, nor would they be more useful if they were. The selection of the market features to be described reflects various tentative ideas about possible explanations and bases for prediction. For example, when a market research study for a consumer product reports data on the income and family size for purchasers and nonpurchasers of the product, it provides only a description of an observed situation. However, the selection of income and family size as relevant features for description—and not, for example, height and weight, color preferences, or the personality features and compatibility of family members—suggests that income and family size may be thought to have explanatory and predictive significance.

We explain behavior, and every other aspect of experience, by relating causes to effects. The key words in an explanation are "Why?" —which identifies the problem to be explained—and "Because"—which supplies the answer. Because we cannot trace any causal sequence to its ultimate origins, explanations of market behavior are never complete. Nor are they ever certain, because we cannot examine all possible causes, or all the ways in which a particular cause might operate.

For example, a family may purchase a new automobile *because* its income has increased. But *why* did the increase in income lead to an auto purchase instead of furniture, a vacation, or greater savings? The answer may lie in previous purchase experience, particular transportation needs, comparisons with other families in the same social environment, and so forth. And each of these possible causal factors may be traced back to *its* causes if the available time and information are sufficient. If the increase in income was associated with a job change or change in residence, these changes, rather than the change in income, may be the critical factors. By examining many families —some who only change jobs or residence and others who experience only change in income—we may get some idea as to which group of factors is paramount. Or we may learn that *both* events are required in order to explain many purchases of automobiles. We will never be entirely certain, however, that some other, uninvestigated factors were not in fact at work or that some of the explanations we rejected would not prove valid if examined from some other viewpoint.

The methods and concepts used to analyze buyer behavior and demand relationships are as numerous and varied as the marketing problems themselves, and it is essential to avoid the error of thinking that a particular approach or technique is always appropriate (or inappropriate), that some type of information is always relevant (or irrelevant). On the contrary, the variety of demand situations to be analyzed, and the variety of analytical results that may be useful for particular purposes, permit the application of the full range of available concepts and methods and the continuous development of new ones.[1]

This chapter and the following two chapters are a brief introduction to some of the principal approaches to demand analysis contained in the current marketing literature. Since most demand studies begin

---

1. For a selective inventory of major research concepts from many disciplines see Burk (1967). Among the comprehensive texts on research methods now in widespread use are Ferber and Verdoorn (1962), Boyd and Westfall (1964), Green and Tull (1966), and Wasson (1965).

with a description of the situation to be analyzed and an elementary classification and statistical summary of the data under analysis, we will begin this chapter with a discussion of problems related to the collection and use of descriptive information and the establishment of classification systems. Chapters 7 and 8 present the salient concepts of economic and econometric demand analysis and behavioral demand studies, respectively. Chapter 8 also introduces the notion that observed behavior may reflect probabilistic rather than deterministic relationships, and it examines some simple probability models and their implications.

Information and Data

The appropriate sources of information for demand analysis depend upon the type of question to be answered, the analytical method to be used, and the kind of answer desired. If we wish to predict nationwide automobile sales for next year (in number of cars), we may wish to examine past data on auto purchases, population, income, and other national economic trends. If we wish to predict the distribution of auto sales by style or price range, data on family size, purposes of car use, and preferences may be required. If we want to predict auto *use* —for example, the extent to which people within a metropolitan area will use a new public transportation system rather than drive their private cars—we will need to know traffic patterns, driving costs, and attitudes about time and convenience in various forms of transportation. If, in all these instances, we wish to get only a rough idea—say, the direction of change over time or whether differences from current levels will be small or large—limited information and analysis may suffice. If we wish to make a more specific prediction of just how much change is likely to take place, and to estimate just how accurate our prediction may be, a more elaborate analysis of a more carefully selected collection of data may be required.

Systematic analysis of market demand makes use of an incredible variety of information, ranging from general cultural and economic information to detailed purchase records, carefully collected evidence on attitudes and preferences, and experimental results. Relevant information for demand analysis is not necessarily quantitative. However, ones does not go very far into specific demand problems before it becomes necessary to get some idea of the number of potential buyers, volume of purchases, variety of uses, strength of preferences, and other pieces of information that must be expressed in quantitative terms. Therefore a large part of the actual work involved in demand analysis is the collection and interpretation of quantitative data.

Census and Sample

Information about actual and potential buyer groups is obtained from two principal types of data: **census** and **sample.** An important type of sample, particularly for consumer goods marketing studies, is a **panel.** It is essential to understand the distinctions associated with these three easily confused terms.

A **census** is a complete enumeration of a statistical population. The U.S. Bureau of the Census, like similar agencies in other countries, conducts and publishes the results of periodic censuses of the human population, as well as censuses of business, agriculture, housing, and other units of economic activity. But the term **census** is not restricted to a nationwide collection of data, and certainly not to human populations. A complete listing of a firm's customers, students in a school, or items in an inventory may also be a census if the enumerated elements in each case include *all* the units within the particular category.

By contrast, a **sample** is a collection of units chosen from a population in order to represent the whole. If we believe that all human beings are essentially similar in some respects, we might take a sample of one individual and examine him in detail, then interpret our results as characteristic of all human beings. (The one-husband one-wife sample is perhaps the most widely used, and least reliable, of all sources of market research data.) On the other hand, we may not know whether individuals are alike or not with respect to the matter under investigation, or we may believe that they are *not* alike in some critically important respects. If so, we will want to take a larger sample to see what differences appear and to take account of these differences in our analysis. The elements in a sample, like the elements in a population, may be human beings, communities, businesses, products, or any other collection of similar units.

It is not our purpose to introduce an extensive discussion of sampling procedures and statistical tests; however, since a great deal of elementary descriptive material in marketing involves the interpretation and comparison of sample results, a few comments are essential. The key problem in sampling is **representativeness,** because the purpose of gathering sample data is to obtain information about the entire population from which the sample is drawn.

In a large population with unknown characteristics, simple **random** sampling is usually thought to produce the most representative results. Random sampling requires that each unit in the population have an equal chance of being drawn into the sample. If important characteristics of the population are already known, it may be desirable to make certain that elements with different attributes are included in the sample in appropriate proportions. For **stratified** or **quota** sampling, the units in the population are grouped (say, by sex, income, location, or some other relevant attribute) and sampled randomly *within* the groups. A **judgment sample** is a collection of units that have been selected in accordance with specific criteria rather than by a random process. Statistical tests of reliability and significance are not applicable to judgment samples, but the problems these tests are intended to resolve remain. Since a great deal of market data comes from judgment samples, or from collections of facts gathered for other purposes and interpreted as sample results, the lack of a basis for estimating probable errors poses serious problems.

A **panel** is a collection of sample units that are observed repeatedly over time. As with any sample, the selected units are taken as representing the entire relevant population group. The distinguishing feature of a panel is that data are collected from the *same* units at regular intervals. Successive censuses or random samples taken at different time periods tell us how the entire population is changing over time, but panel information tells us how individual units within the population are changing. For example, the total sales of a product might be the same from one period to the next, but panel analysis might show that this overall stability in sales was the result of equal numbers of people adopting and dropping the product in each time period rather than the result of regular purchases by the same buying group. Although census and sample data may be gathered for almost any kind of observable marketing units, panel data are gathered primarily for individuals and households, and to a lesser extent for retail stores and other kinds of businesses.

Time Series and Cross Section

A **time series** is a record of the same phenomenon observed repeatedly over time. Annual estimates of the gross national product since 1929 constitute a time series; so do the compiled daily records of temperature and rainfall. Time series may be gathered on a daily, weekly, monthly, annual, or any other time basis. By contrast, collections of data describing different units or groups within a population at the same point in time are referred to as **cross-section** data. Data on birth rates in different countries, education levels among different income groups, and furniture purchases by families of different size are examples of cross-section data. Both time series and cross-section data may be obtained either by census or sampling methods. Consumer panel data frequently has a cross-sectional structure as well as a time dimension; and the term **longitudinal** is sometimes used to describe panel data to differentiate it from both aggregate time series and single-period cross sections. A single analytical study may use data of all three types, and the data may contain demographic, economic, sociological, and psychological information.

Primary and Secondary Data: Surveys

Pieces of information that are generated specifically to meet the requirements of a particular research study are generally termed the **primary data** of that study. Information that is gathered and tabulated for other purposes, including general government or industry reporting, and then is used in a particular study is termed **secondary data.** The line between the two types need not be drawn with great accuracy; the primary data of one investigation may well become secondary data in another. The key point is whether the researcher or analyst creates new data or makes use of data already available.

By far the largest part of routine market research activity consists of assembling and analyzing secondary data from government documents, public records, and company and industry sources. There are two reasons for the prominence of secondary data sources: (1) many pieces of information about the society are already known and simply need to be drawn together to be useful for the particular purposes at hand; (2) assembling secondary data is generally so much cheaper than collecting new, even if more appropriate, primary data that the latter is not justified by a comparison of costs and relative value. The great pitfall in exclusive reliance on secondary data is that such information may not have been collected and tabulated in ways that are appropriate to the problem at hand. Thus it is always necessary to subject secondary data collections to the same scrutiny one would use in planning a similar primary data collection activity before accepting them as appropriate for a particular purpose.

Primary data may be collected from many sources—detailed analysis of company records, direct observation, experiments, and so forth. Of special importance in demand research are the data collected from **surveys.** In survey research, questions of fact and opinion are directed at respondents and their answers are recorded, analyzed, and interpreted. Surveys are almost always aimed at a sample of the total population under analysis, and they are intended to obtain types of information that cannot be readily found in secondary sources. The information sought may be objective and factual, but at a fine level of detail (for example: How many shopping trips did you make last week?); or it may be subjective, involving attitudes and preferences (for example: Why did you choose this particular automobile? What is your favorite form of recreation?). In every case, survey studies aim at collecting particularly relevant pieces of information from a particularly appropriate group of respondents, according to the purpose to which the results are to be put.

Thus, as a basis for demand analysis, collecting primary data through original surveys contrasts sharply with assembling available data from published sources. The two kinds of data sources, however, are complementary. Secondary data can be used to identify key groups within the population and critical variables for primary analysis. Original observations can be used to explore the implications of relationships found in secondary data and to discriminate among possible cause-effect interpretations.

Although a detailed discussion of the problems and methods of survey research methodology and other primary data collection techniques is beyond the scope of this book, some special aspects of original data collection for behavioral research studies are mentioned in chapter 8.

Description and Analysis

Accurate description is an essential element in any investigation. Indeed, a minimum level of reliable descriptive information is necessary simply to identify a marketing problem for analysis. What are the products and services under consideration and how are they used? Who are the possible buyers and where are they located? What is their purchase ability and what other expenditures do they make? What alternative product and service choices are available? In a fully developed market, where purchase and use patterns are well established, many of these basic facts will already be known to all interested parties. In studies of new products, major product and service changes, and new buyer groups, however, considerable effort may be required simply to discover and assemble the basic market facts for further analysis.

Relevance and Accuracy

The two major problems of descriptive studies are **relevance** and **accuracy**. Since there is no limit to the number of market features that may be described or to the detail of the description, descriptive studies may easily run to undue length, on the one hand, or omit important pieces of information on the other. In the selection of market and buyer features that are worthy of description, there are no rules and no substitute for a sound, general knowledge of marketing problems, research methods, and sources of information. As noted above, descriptive studies tend to rely heavily on previously collected or secondary information sources. The question of relevance applies to these sources as well, because material that has been collected for one purpose rarely corresponds exactly to the material appropriate for a new problem. Therefore discrepancies in timing and coverage, omissions and duplications, and irrelevant classifications and details must be identified and taken into account.

Accuracy would seem to be such an obvious requirement of useful descriptive material that no further comment would be required. However, accuracy is a problem because it is expensive and because many quantitative data appear to be more accurate than they truly are. Although it is reasonable to aim for the most accurate observations attainable at any given cost in time and money, the choice between relatively inexact and low-cost information and relatively exact and expensive data can be made only in terms of the value of information. For example, rough estimates of the current population, income levels, and major expenditure patterns within any metropolitan area in the United States can be obtained from secondary sources at practically no cost. More accurate estimates in greater detail, but also from secondary sources, may be obtained by a team of professional market analysts in a few days or weeks of full-time work. Still more accurate and precise information may require the collection of new primary data from carefully designed samples of districts and households, at very considerable cost.

The choice of an appropriate level of descriptive accuracy, therefore, depends upon these cost considerations, the use to which the information is to be put, and the value of more accurate information for a particular use. If more accurate information will not change our behavior in any important respect, we are unwise to spend much money or effort to obtain it. If, on the other hand, an expenditure of $1000 for more complete and accurate information can prevent a

$10,000 error or identify a $10,000 market opportunity, the expenditure may well be justified.[2]

Spurious accuracy is characteristic of a great many secondary data and, unfortunately, of many original market research reports as well. Spurious accuracy occurs when data are presented in such a way that they appear more accurate than in fact they are. Most reported figures for economic aggregates (population, income, expenditures, and so forth) are estimates that fall within a range of probable variation from their true value; and subsequent computations from such data will be subject to at least this range of probable error. Further, when several different estimates are combined into a single statistic, the probable range of error may be increased. There is, moreover, no adequate reason for thinking that such errors "cancel out" as a matter of course. Spurious accuracy also arises when data are manipulated and reported at finer levels of detail than the data had at the outset. For example, if income data were originally collected by income classes rather than by specific dollar amounts, subsequent computations from such data are accurate only within those class limits. (In other words, if a survey obtains income levels of respondents that are accurate to the nearest $1000, the average level of income computed from the data is accurate only within a $500 range of error.)

Descriptive Classifications and Summary Statistics

Assembling descriptive data and making initial computations for analytical purposes requires a high degree of skill and precise understanding of the use to which the resulting information is to be put.[3] As a rule, the facts do not "speak for themselves." Sometimes relevant classifications and categories for data gathering and presentation may be determined in advance by the definition of the problem under study. For example, we may want to know how buying behavior differs between men and women, rural and urban households, Eastern and Western cities, and so forth. If, then, categories are established in the definition of the problem, they are obvious guides for data collection and reporting.

However, when data are gathered and reported according to predetermined classification systems, the risk of distortion and loss of information is very great. The critical behavioral differences may not

---

2. Techniques for the analysis of the value of marketing information are discussed in Green and Tull (1966), chaps. 2 and 3.
3. A useful guide for the practical descriptive statistician is Zeisel (1968).

be between men and women but between older people and younger
people, or between larger and smaller households rather than between
rural and urban households, and so forth. As an example of the
effect of classification schemes, consider the results of a survey of
cigarette smoking, which might be tabulated in either of the following
ways:

Table A		Table B	
Light smokers (less than		Light smokers (½ pack	
1 pack per day)	40%	or less per day)	20%
Heavy smokers (1 pack		Moderate smokers (more	
or more per day)	60	than ½ pack but less	
		than 1½ packs per	
		day)	50
		Heavy smokers (1½	
		packs or more per day)	30

Both tables are factually accurate and refer to the same basic
data. Table B, however, reveals not just a sharp distinction between
"heavy" and "light" smokers but the existence of a large group of
moderate smokers, with extremes on either side. Table A might be
appropriate for some purposes, but smoking behavior is much more
clearly described in table B. (Note, however, that if the figures in
table B were, say, 35 percent, 10 percent, and 55 percent, table A might
provide the *better* short description of smoking behavior.)

A similar source of descriptive inaccuracy may be found in the
choice of summary statistics—that is, the selection or computation of
one or more values from a collection of individual observations that
may be used to describe the whole. For example, if we are interested
in the retail prices of canned vegetables, we might select a sample of
stores and brands and record the unit prices for standard-size cans.
The prices will not all be the same, and we will therefore obtain a
distribution—a list of prices and a count of the number of items
marked with each price. We could summarize these data by giving
only the **range,** the highest and lowest prices, but for many purposes
this will not be sufficiently informative. To select a single summary
indicator, we may choose the **mean** (simple average), the **median,** or
the **mode,** among many other possibilities. The median is the middle
value in an ordered distribution; if we record the prices of ninety-nine
items and list them in descending order, the price of the fiftieth item
would be the median price. The mode, which is the single most fre-

quent value in a distribution, is substantially affected by the exactness of the price observations. The mode of a distribution of prices tabulated in one-cent intervals is not necessarily the same as the mode of the same distribution tabulated in five-cent intervals.

If most of the recorded prices fall within a fairly narrow interval, and if unusually high and low values are fairly evenly distributed on both sides of this interval, the mean, median, and mode will be very close to each other (if not identical), and the mean will usually be selected as the appropriate summary statistic. This is a convenient choice because the concept of an average is generally understood, and it has desirable statistical properties. However, if the extreme or unusual values tend to fall on one side of the mean—say, there are a few brands of very expensive canned goods—the mean price will be higher than the "typical" price within the entire group and the median may be a more appropriate summary figure. Finally, if a large number of the prices are the same—say, 19 cents per can—this price, the mode, may be the most accurate indicator of the *typical* price in the market.

One other point is worth making about the median and the mode as representative values: both are *observed* values in a distribution, whereas the mean may not be. The mean may contain an artificial fractional unit of doubtful significance (e.g., 2.5 persons per household), or it may be a possible but unobserved value. For example, if all prices in a list are stated in even dollars, the computed average price may be expressed in dollars and cents. Although average statistics of this type are useful for many purposes, they may not describe the *typical* values of the distribution under analysis inasmuch as there are no fractional people and a price list may have been compiled entirely in even-dollar units.

Statistical Analysis

Once the relevant market features have been identified and measured, standard statistical methods may be used to search for significant differences, correlation relationships, and other patterns of associations among the observed characteristics. Statistical techniques as such will not concern us here; however, two general points that pertain to their application are worthy of brief mention.

The statistical analysis of a collection of data is justified only if the data have been obtained and processed according to appropriate standard procedures. If data have been gathered in an irregular way, or processed (e.g., arrayed, sorted, or averaged) so as to introduce spurious regularities (or to obliterate evidence of true ones) further statistical analysis will yield numerical results of no substantive significance. Such procedures and results are sometimes referred to as GI–GO, for "garbage in–garbage out." Further, many standard statistical techniques can be applied only if the population under analysis possesses certain statistical properties, and in the absence of information to the contrary it is a common practice to *assume* the existence of such properties. However, when the data are known to possess special statistical characteristics—for example, when the distribution of observations is highly skewed or the distribution is bimodal—appropriate techniques for the analysis of these special characteristics should be adopted.

The second point concerns the substantive interpretation of statistical results, particularly of differences and similarities suggested by simple comparisons. If, for example, we are told that average family income is $800 per month in one community and $900 per month in another community, how justified are we in concluding that there is a substantial difference in income between the two communities? The answer is not as simple as it may seem. If we question only one individual in each community and learn that one has an income of $800 and the other an income of $900, we can be quite certain (apart from misrepresentation) that there is a difference between the incomes of the two *individuals*. However, we will certainly *not* conclude, in the absence of other evidence, that these observations indicate overall differences between the two communities. On the other hand, if we obtain a complete census of incomes in the two communities, so that all members of each community are enumerated, and if we compute these average figures from these data, we can be quite certain that there is a $100 difference in average monthly income between the two communities.

What happens in the intermediate (but more typical) case when two different average values have been obtained from samples of individual incomes in each community? Under these circumstances, we will want to see whether the difference between the averages that have been computed for the two communities are **statistically significant.** Many different statistical tests may be used to examine this problem, and different kinds of tests are appropriate if we are dealing with means, proportions, or other comparative statistics. These tests provide an answer to the question: How likely is it that these two sample statistics could have been obtained from samples drawn from the *same* population? The tests take into account the size of the samples, the dispersion of sample observations, the size of the populations, and other population characteristics (if known). Results of the tests permit us to make such statements as the following. "It is very unlikely (say, less than five chances out of a hundred) that these sample results could have come from the same population; thus it may be concluded that average income in the two communities is truly different." Or in the contrary case: "It is quite likely (say, fifty chances out of a hundred) that these two sample results would have been obtained when the true values are the same; thus we should not take the $100 difference in sample means to indicate a difference between true mean income in the two communities."

Statements such as those above relate to the **statistical significance** of results; and only statistically significant results should be subjected to substantive interpretation. If it is quite likely that the two communities in our example have different average incomes, they may be treated as having different incomes in subsequent analyses, and vice versa. However, not all statistically significant results are of substantive importance. The $100 difference in the communities' average incomes may indeed be a true value, but it may be quite irrelevant to particular marketing problems.

If, for example, we are studying the demand for housing, we may find that $100 differences in average income within this range do not make a substantial difference in a community's housing demand, although differences between $700 to $1000 and $1000 to $1500 monthly income communities are quite substantial. Under these circumstances, the two communities may be grouped in the same category for analytical purposes, even though there is a statistically significant difference in their average income levels.

Analytical Models

An analytical model is a generalized, abstract description of a complex phenomenon, and is designed to isolate the latter's salient characteristics and key relationships. Models may be verbal or quantitative, formal or informal, simple or elaborate. Even the simplest sort of descriptive analysis requires some kind of conceptual model, implicit though it may be. If we have in mind no model whatsoever of the determinants of buyer behavior, we cannot know which of the myriad characteristics of households to begin observing in a consumer demand study. If we choose to describe family income as a potentially important factor in such a study, we will be investigating an implicit model of a relationship between income and buyer behavior; and we will have simultaneously eliminated such characteristics as hair color and state of family happiness from our model at least temporarily.

The use of formal analytical models carries this approach to a higher level. In such models explicit relationships among selected variables are formally expressed. For example, we may state that household purchases increase along with increases in household income. This statement—which constitutes a simple but formal model—may be presented in words (as above), or in mathematical symbols [$X = f(Y)$, where X stands for purchases and Y for income], or in charts or diagrams. To implement or test the model, we assemble relevant data and see whether the model provides a useful general description of the observed phenomena. We may find that the model *always* proves true. More likely, however, we will find that the model provides a reliable statement about the general relationships in many but not all cases. On the other hand, the model may not be consistent with the data, and we will have to discard it entirely and search for a different set of relationships and for additional factors that may be at work.

Chapter 7 describes in some detail the construction and implementation of an econometric model for forecasting the total annual purchases of new automobiles in the United States. This forecasting typifies both a classic kind of scientific investigation with the use of formal models and an important use of quantitative models in demand analysis. Many of the behavioral concepts of demand analysis discussed in chapter 8 can also be incorporated into formal models, and the development and use of such models is becoming increasingly characteristic of behavioral demand studies. Also, another type of quantitative model is illustrated in chapter 8 in the discussion of purchase probability studies.

Summary

Demand analysis is intended to describe, explain, and predict the behavior of potential buyers—individuals, households, firms, and other organizations—under current conditions and in response to changes over time. **Qualitative** information is essential for specifying the demand situation under analysis and for establishing the framework for investigation; and the final results of analysis must be interpreted in qualitative terms. However, the most significant studies of actual marketing behavior and opportunities rely heavily on the collection, analysis, and interpretation of **quantitative** materials.

Collections of data that deal with buyer characteristics and behavior are of two principal types, **census** (a complete enumeration) and **sample** (a partial enumeration intended to indicate the characteristics of a whole population). A **panel** is a sample in which the same individual units are observed repeatedly over time. Census and sample data can be gathered in time series or on a cross-sectional basis; panel data always have a time dimension, and frequently a cross-sectional dimension as well. Data generated or assembled for the specific purposes of a particular research study are termed the **primary** data of that study. A considerable part of the primary data of demand studies in marketing, particularly studies relating to individual firms and products, are based upon **surveys.**

The initial phase of every analytical study is an **appropriate description** of the situation under investigation. The critical problems in this phase are **relevance** and **accuracy.** That is, the description must be made in terms that are relevant to the purpose of the investigation (although they may not be relevant to some other, equally valid purpose), and it must be accurate both in the numerical sense and in the more important sense of accurately establishing concepts and categories. Serious attention to these fundamental requirements is particularly important when **secondary** data, data collected for some purpose other than the problem at hand, are being analyzed.

Statistical techniques may be used to estimate the validity of sample data and the range of accuracy of descriptive numerical results. These techniques are also useful in estimating the properties and validity of formal analytical models. However, although statistical tests can be used to determine whether a particular set of numerical results justifies substantive interpretation, the fundamental tasks of problem definition, research design, and interpretive analysis require qualitative and conceptual rather than mere quantitative and numerical skill.

References

Boyd, Harper W., and Ralph Westfall. *Marketing Research,* rev. ed. Irwin, 1964.

Burk, Margerite C. "Survey of Interpretations of Consumer Behavior by Social Scientists in the Postwar Period." *Journal of Farm Economics,* Vol. 49, No. 1, February 1967.

Ferber, Robert, and P. J. Verdoorn. *Research Methods in Economics and Business.* Macmillan, 1962.

Green, Paul E., and Donald S. Tull. *Research for Marketing Decisions.* Prentice-Hall, 1966.

Wasson, Chester R. *Research Analysis for Marketing Decision.* Appleton-Century-Crofts, 1965.

Zeisel, Hans. *Say It with Figures,* 5th rev. ed. Harper & Row, 1968.

7

Econometric Analysis and Forecasting

Econometric analysis involves the construction of a formal model of relationships among economic variables and its implementation or testing by means of empirical data. Because it is almost impossible to describe the nature and value of econometric analysis in general terms, this chapter will present an extended example of the construction and implementation of an econometric forecasting model. Forecasting is by no means the only use of econometric analysis, but it is an important use, particularly in connection with the study of demand and buyer behavior.[1]

Forecasting Models

There are three essential steps in forecasting future demand or sales with an econometric model:

1. From a general analysis of the market under consideration, and from a knowledge of other studies and possible models, an ele-

---

1. Two general texts on econometrics are Johnson (1936) and Klein (1962).

mentary formal model is developed. In constructing the model, the analyst tries to limit the number of variables, to use only variables for which data can be readily obtained, and to choose the form of the relationship so as to minimize difficulties in computation and interpretation.

2. Past data are gathered for each variable, and the parameters of the model are estimated by statistical procedures. Then the accuracy of the model as a description of these data is examined. The effect of adding or eliminating variables, and of changing the form of the relationship, may also be investigated.

3. Known or estimated values of the independent variables are inserted into the model and an estimate of the value of the dependent variable is obtained. This estimate constitutes the forecast. In general, the term **forecast** is reserved for estimates derived from formal analysis for which some expectation of future occurrence is seriously entertained. The term **projection** is often applied to the mere extrapolation of past experience, without any implication for actual expectations.

The simplest forecasting model is a time trend. If we believe that some variable of interest tends to increase regularly through time, we may forecast its future levels on the basis of this belief. We may state the forecast verbally ("I expect sales to increase at a rate of 10 percent per year") or we may express it more formally, in a mathematical statement. Two standard forms of simple forecasting statements are:

$$X_t = X_0 + b_1 t \tag{1}$$

and

$$X_t = (1 + b_2)X_{t-1} \quad \text{or} \quad X_t = X_0(1 + b_2)^t \tag{2}$$

In these expressions X_t represents the forecasted variable in period t; X_{t-1} represents the value of the variable in the immediately preceding period; and X_0 represents its value in some base period. Periods, which may be any appropriate time unit, are counted from the base period. If the base period is the year 1960, estimates for 1970 will be obtained by inserting a value of 10 for t. Equation 1 states that the variable X increases by equal *amounts* (represented by b_1) per period; equation 2 states that X increases by equal *percentages* or *rates* (represented by b_2, a decimal fraction). Figure 7–1 illustrates graphically the shapes of the two forecasting equations. The choice of either of these, or of other and more complex time-trend models, must initially be made on logical and theoretical grounds and after an inspection of the data to see the types of patterns that appear.

Figure 7–1   Two Possible Time Trends

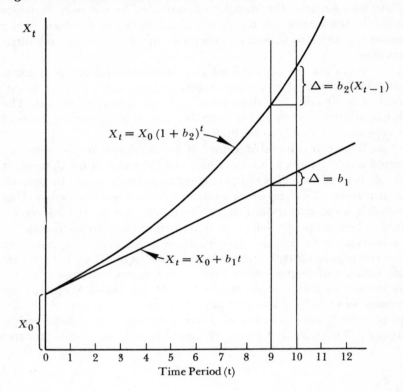

If several different models are developed and implemented, statistical tests can be used to evaluate their relative accuracy and the importance of their sources of error.

An Example: New-Automobile Purchases

The idea of formal econometric analysis is conveyed well enough in the simple time-trend example, but the importance and usefulness of the econometric approach can be indicated only by consideration of a more complex problem, such as an econometric analysis of purchases of new automobiles in the United States. The importance of auto purchases in the total economy and the availability of pertinent data have permitted many different studies of automobile demand to be made over the years, and, as a result, a contemporary investigator of automobile demand can compare his methods and results with the work of others. Thus a careful comparison of several automobile demand studies is one of the most useful ways to gain an understanding of the variety and value of econometric analysis in marketing. Our example is based upon Dyckman's study (1965), which is well worth careful reading in its entirety.[2]

The Model

From previous studies and inspection of available data and known relationships, Dyckman identified four variables as potentially important determinants of total new-car purchases: income (Y), car prices (P), the total stock of automobiles accumulated from past purchases and not yet worn out (S), and credit conditions (C). The size of the population, obviously a fifth factor of importance, was accounted for by the reduction of the first three variables to a per capita basis. Since some of the variables may be subject to similar long-term trends, the analysis was conducted in terms of year-to-year changes in each variable so that the shorter-term relationships among them could be more clearly identified. The relationship among these variables was assumed to be logarithmic, as follows:

$$X_t = aY^{b1}P^{b2}C^{b3}S^{b4}$$

where X_t is the year-to-year change in per capita new-car sales and the four independent variables are as indicated above. All variables are expressed as year-to-year changes and, where relevant, in per capita terms.

This form of relationship is selected for both theoretical and computational reasons. In principle, we would expect the variables to be multiplicative rather than additive, price effects to interact with income effects, and so forth. For computational convenience, the equation reduces to a linear form in the logarithms, as follows:

$$\log X_t = \log a + b_1 \log Y + b_2 \log P + b_3 \log C + b_4 \log S$$

The coefficients in this equation may be interpreted as **elasticity** values, which permit direct comparison between Dyckman's results

2. Dyckman's original notation has been somewhat simplified in the following summary.

and those obtained by other investigators who used different data and methods.[3]

Implementation

Each of the independent variables may be observed and measured in many different ways, and Dyckman and other investigators have examined a wide range of alternatives. Income is analyzed both in terms of disposable income (defined as personal income less income taxes) and discretionary income (for which an estimated level of subsistence expenditures is deducted from the disposable income figure). Other investigators have used less refined income concepts, such as gross national product per capita, or more refined concepts, such as changes in income distribution among households. Measurement of the price variable is complicated by changes in general price levels, in automobile quality over time, and the crucial importance of used-car prices.

To take account of the latter, Dyckman followed Chow (1960), who estimated a price index on the basis of the advertised prices of new cars in the hands of used-car dealers in December of each year. This index was then adjusted for general price-level changes, but no further adjustment was made to take account of automobile quality changes over time (see Adelman and Griliches, 1961).

Credit terms were treated as a "dummy" variable and were assigned a value of plus one when terms were substantially eased and zero in all other years. An alternative procedure, used in a study by Suits (1958), would be to combine the price and credit variables in an index of the average monthly payment, reflecting prices, length of credit period, and interest rates. Suits also emphasized the *rate* (not amount) of change in income from period to period. The stock-of-cars figure was taken directly from available data. The model was estimated for the period 1930–1962, with the years 1942–1948 omitted.

Statistical estimation of the model for these twenty-six year-to-year change values yielded the following results (all coefficients highly significant):

$$\log X_t = .004 + 1.749 \log Y - 0.748 \log P + 0.052\, C - 1.675 \log S$$

Coefficients of multiple determination (R^2) for this and other formulations that Dyckman examined are all above 0.90. This means

---

3. For an explanation of elasticity, see the appendix to this chapter.

that the four independent variables provide a statistical explanation for more than 90 percent of the variation in the dependent variable (changes in new-car purchases) over the period in question. It does not, of course, mean that changes in the former *caused* changes in the latter. However, the statistical results are consistent with such a hypothesis.

It should be emphasized that the size of the coefficients in an econometric equation is *not* a measure of the relative importance of each of the several independent variables in explaining the total variation in the dependent variable. Auto sales may be very responsive to changes in income and much less responsive to changes in prices, but if prices change very substantially and incomes change hardly at all over a particular period, price changes will be the more *important* factors for explaining the auto sales record.

It is possible to standardize regression coefficients in order to obtain indexes (called beta coefficients) of the relative importance of the variables over specific time periods. When Dyckman did this, he found that income changes had been by far the most important factor in explaining variations in auto sales over the period; price changes were about half as important as income changes; and credit and stock changes were of lesser, but about equal, importance (Dyckman, 1965, p. 262). These differences in relative importance might not be found in another period, however, even if the basic relationships of the econometric model proved to be valid over time.

Results

The coefficients of income and price variables, which may be interpreted as elasticities, are of particular interest. Read directly, they indicate that—other things being the same—an increase of, say, 10 percent in the year-to-year change in per capita income will be associated with an increase of more than 17 percent in the year-to-year change in new-car sales per capita. Similarly, the price elasticity indicates that an increase of 10 percent in the year-to-year change in new-car prices should be associated with a decline of more than 7 percent in the change in new-car sales.

Of course, these are only the most likely values within a range of possible values, but they provide an interesting basis for comparing Dyckman's results with those of earlier investigations (shown in table 7–1). The studies cover different periods and use different measurement concepts and estimating techniques; however, all of them have yielded estimates of the relative responsiveness of car sales to changes in prices

Table 7–1   Statistical Demand Studies of Price and Income
Elasticities of Automobile Demand

	Elasticity	
	Price	Income
Suits (1958)	− 0.6	+ 4.2
Suits (1961)	− 0.7	+ 1.7
Dyckman (1965)	− 0.7	+ 1.7
Dyckman (1965)—employing the "real disposable income" concept	− 0.8	+ 4.0
U.S. Senate (1958)		
Study 1	− 0.7	+ 4.1
Study 2	− 1.2	+ 3.9
Study 3	− 0.6	+ 4.4
Nerlove (1957)	− 0.9	+ 2.8
Chow (1960)	− 1.2	+ 3.6
Atkinson (1952)	− 1.4	+ 2.5

and incomes. In general, the studies suggest that price elasticity of demand for automobiles is not very different from −1.0. That is, total *expenditures* on automobiles do not vary substantially in response to price changes—purchase quantities will be higher or lower in approximately the same proportion as prices are lower or higher. On the other hand, all the studies indicate that automobile demand is highly responsive to changes in income. The elasticity estimates imply relative changes in new-car sales that range from just under twice to over four times as great as relative changes in the associated income variables. (Lower elasticity values associated with relative changes in year-to-year differences in income—as in the Dyckman study—are not inconsistent with higher values associated with relative changes in income variables themselves.)

The stock of cars (S) proved to have a substantial negative coefficient, a result also obtained earlier by Suits. This means that the greater the change in the stock of cars, the less the change in new-car demand, which suggests that the total demand for automobiles in each year of this entire period was met to a substantial extent from the supply of vehicles purchased in previous years.

This result is not surprising, but two factors would give rise to a positive coefficient under other circumstances. The first factor is the process of wearing out and obsolescence: the greater the total stock of cars, the greater the need for new cars to replace those that go out of service during each period. For this reason alone—in an economy with stable population and income—one would expect the stock variable to be positively related to total new-car demand (although not necessarily to the year-to-year change in new-car demand.) Secondly, there is the effect of past automobile purchases on tastes and life styles, so that the more cars are purchased and driven (i.e., the greater the stock), the more demand for additional cars increases. This "taste" or "demonstration effect" is undoubtedly important in explaining the rapid expansion of automobile demand in the developing countries.

A recent large-scale study of demand in major consumer expenditure categories in the United States used a stock (or "past purchase") variable in analyzing and forecasting expenditures over the period 1929–1970 (see Houthakker and Taylor, 1966, and Perry, 1967). This coefficient would be expected to be negative with respect to most durables, as was found in the case of automobiles (above), and positive with respect to expenditure categories in which habits and tastes develop as a result of past usage. Positive values, indicating habit formation, were found in fifty of the eighty-four expenditure categories, including alcoholic beverages, electricity, education, travel, toilet articles, and drugs. Further, the stock of TV sets was shown to have a negative effect on demand for newspapers and magazines and motion pictures. The stock of washing machines had a negative effect on demand for cleaning and laundering services; and so forth.

Thus it appears that the stock of durables and the past purchases of nondurables may be of substantial importance in explaining and predicting demand development over time.

Qualifications

In spite of interesting and highly plausible results, the application of econometric techniques in marketing is subject to some important qualifications. First, the results of such investigations are no better than the models and data selected for analysis. Critical relationships may be lost in an imperfectly specified model and spurious relationships may be introduced.

A special warning is necessary in the treatment of variables that follow similar, but not clearly related, time trends. When two series —such as GNP per capita and population, for example—have risen together over the long term, high statistical correlations can be obtained between them; however, such statistical results are of no substantive importance. Although econometric analysis cannot be said to prove the existence of causal connections among variables, the purpose of the analysis is to examine the consistency of substantive hypotheses, not simply to produce numerical results of doubtful import.

The second qualification is that the results of econometric analysis are always subject to margins of error, and individual period-to-period forecasts may well be wide of the mark. Dyckman's estimate of changes in new-car sales for 1962–1963, for example, amounted to only about half of the actual change. The result was an error in the total sales estimate of almost 5 percent, or about 350,000 cars in a total of 7.5 million new-car sales. Such an error in a single forecast is statistically very small, but it may be either very trivial or very important in the context of a particular marketing problem.

Third, it is important to recall that econometric analysis attempts to identify the smallest number of variables necessary to provide a statistically valid prediction of past observations. Whether they are in fact the important variables for explaining past experience, and whether these same variables will continue to be important in the future, are questions for qualitative analysis and judgment.

Finally, the application of statistically valid explanatory models for forecasting purposes is limited by the unavailability of data for future periods. In order to forecast with the Dyckman model, for example, one would have to predict the values of the necessary income, price, credit, and stock variables for subsequent periods, then insert these variables into the model in order to predict the change in new-car sales.

Summary

Econometric analysis necessitates constructing a formal model of relationships among economic variables and implementing or testing the model with empirical data.

Forecasting demand is one of the principal applications of the econometric approach. Forecasting techniques range from simple projections of past experience through statistical time-series analyses to complex econometric models that contain many variables.

The Dyckman study of new-automobile purchases illustrates the character and value of a sophisticated econometric analysis. On the basis of previous studies and his own original analysis, Dyckman identified four variables that might be closely associated with new-car purchases: income, car prices, the existing stock of cars in operation, and credit conditions. Expressing the first three variables on a per-capita basis, he set up models that related changes in the four variables to changes in new-car purchases per capita. All data were measured for the period 1930–1962, with the years 1942–1948 omitted.

Dyckman found that each of the four selected variables was statistically significant and that together they explained more than 90 percent of the variation in year-to-year changes in per capita new-car purchases over the period. His findings were consistent with those of several previous studies.

In general, these studies indicate that new-car purchases change relatively little in response to price changes (only enough to keep the total expenditure on new automobiles about the same as it would have been in the absence of the price changes), but that car purchases are highly responsive to income changes. The stock of cars was shown to have a dampening effect on new-car purchases; that is, the larger the stock, the fewer the purchases, other factors being the same.

This relationship between new-car sales and the existing stock of cars suggests the importance of interproduct demand relationships, which can also be analyzed in terms of the "cross-elasticity" concept.

Econometric analysis provides important tools for the study of market demand and buyer behavior. However, its results are always limited to the particular model, data, and time period examined, and may be subject to wide margins of error in particular forecasting applications. The usefulness of econometric demand studies depends not only upon their technical quality but also upon the skill with which they are interpreted and their results applied to specific marketing decisions.

Appendix: A Note about Elasticity

Elasticity is one of the most useful concepts in economic and econometric analysis. The elasticity index measures the *responsiveness* of one variable to changes in another when both variables are expressed in *relative* terms. The concept was originated to describe differences in the responsiveness of sales of quantities of various commodities to changes in their prices. For example, if the prices of both gasoline and motion-picture tickets rise by 10 percent, the sales volume of gasoline will remain about the same but motion-picture attendance will decline somewhat. Thus ticket sales are responsive to price changes whereas gasoline sales are not.

We may express this difference more explicitly by computing the price elasticity index (or point elasticity) for each item:

$$\text{Price elasticity} = \frac{\text{Percent change in quantity purchased (sold)}}{\text{Percent change in price}}$$

The index for gasoline will be very nearly zero; the index for motion pictures will be a significant number, probably greater than one. (In fact, Houthakker and Taylor (1966) estimated the static price elasticities as $-.09$ for gasoline and -9.8 for motion pictures on the basis of data for the years 1929–1961. Some statistical problems are posed by these figures but they indicate the appropriate orders of magnitude involved.) Note that price elasticities would ordinarily be expected to have negative signs; that is, as individual prices rise, purchases and sales would decline, if all other prices remain unchanged.

Income elasticity is computed in the same way, but with changes in income substituted for changes in price in the formula. Income elasticity values are normally expected to be positive; however, "inferior goods," such as dried beans and potatoes and low-grade cuts of meat, may be subject to negative income effects. Note that both price and income elasticities may be different at different price and income *levels,* even for the same products and purchasers.

The concept of **cross elasticity,** which measures the responsiveness of sales of one commodity to changes in the price of another (the price of the former remaining unchanged) is particularly useful in marketing analysis. The measurement of these effects permits us to identify important cases of marketing **complementarity** and **substitution.** If increases in the price of one item lead to *increases* in the sales of another, we may describe the two as *substitutes.* If *decreases* in sales occur, the second item may be *complementary* to the first. The computed cross-elasticity index,

$$\frac{\text{Percent change in sales of } A}{\text{Percent change in price of } B}$$

will be *positive* for substitutes and *negative* for complements.

Note that in a simple two-commodity example, relationships of complementarity and substitution will always be reversible: if A is a substitute for *B*, *B* is a substitute for *A*. In the real world of multiple commodities, however, the relationships may vary substantially, depending upon *which* price changes and the *direction* of change. In retail food marketing, for example, *increases* in pork prices have been found to lead to increased sales of chickens and other cheaper meats, not to increased purchases of beef. *Decreases* in pork prices, on the other hand, lead to increases in beef purchases (Zwick, 1957). Hence the relationship between the prices and the sales of pork and beef varies substantially, according to the specific type of price change involved.

Elasticity values are not only descriptively useful, they are easily computed from econometric models in certain forms by the use of standard techniques. Because they are ratios between two percentages, the elasticity values for different commodities, time periods, geographic areas, and so forth can be readily compared. The usefulness of such comparisons was illustrated in table 7–1 and in the related discussion.

References

Adelman, Irma, and Zvi Griliches. "On an Index of Quality Change." *Journal of the American Statistical Association,* Vol. 56, September 1961.

Atkinson, L. Jay. "Consumer Markets for Durable Goods." *Survey of Current Business,* Vol. 32, April 1952.

Chow, Gregory C. "Statistical Demand Function for Automobiles and Their Use for Forecasting." In *The Demand for Durable Goods,* ed. Arnold C. Harberger. University of Chicago Press, 1960.

Dyckman, Thomas R. "An Aggregate Demand Model for Automobiles." *Journal of Business,* Vol. 38, No. 3, July 1965.

Houthakker, H. S., and Lester D. Taylor. *Consumer Demand in the United States, 1929–1970.* Harvard University Press, 1966.

Johnston, John. *Econometric Methods.* McGraw-Hill, 1963.

Klein, Lawrence R. *Introduction to Econometrics.* Prentice-Hall, 1962.

Nerlove, Marc. "A Note on Long-Run Automobile Demand." *Journal of Marketing.* Vol. 22, July 1957.

Perry, George L. "Consumer Demand in the United States: A Review

Article." *American Economic Review,* Vol. 57, No. 4, September 1967.

Suits, Daniel B. "Exploring Alternative Formulations of Automobile Demand." *Review of Economics and Statistics,* Vol. 43, February 1961.

————. "The Demand for New Automobiles in the United States, 1929–1956." *Review of Economics and Statistics,* Vol. 40, August 1958.

U.S. Senate. Subcommittee on Antitrust and Monopoly of the Committee on the Judiciary, 85th Congress, 2nd Session. *Hearings on Administered Prices: Part 6, Automobiles.* U.S. Government Printing Office, 1958.

Zwick, Charles. "Demographic Variation: Its Impact on Consumer Behavior." *Review of Economics and Statistics,* Vol. 39, No. 4, November 1957.

8

Behavioral Aspects of Demand Analysis

The greatest growth in the volume and variety of market demand studies in recent years has resulted from the application of techniques and concepts from the behavioral sciences—sociology, cultural anthropology, psychology, and social psychology—to the analysis of marketing problems. The enthusiasm these new approaches has generated is, in part, a reflection of their novelty and sophistication, and in part a reflection of dissatisfaction with routine descriptive studies and formal, somewhat mechanical, statistical and econometric analysis.

More fundamentally, the expansion of behavioral demand studies has resulted from the widened role of noneconomic factors in purchasing decisions in more affluent societies, and the correspondingly increased emphasis on such factors in the marketing activities of sellers. Further, since the impact of marketing effort on the mental state and behavior processes of buyers is less readily observed than, for example, the impact of changes in prices or distribution methods, a need for behavioral studies arises in order to monitor the success of marketing activities aimed at behavioral goals.

The idea that social and behavioral factors influence buying behavior is, of course, scarcely new. The connection between personal consumption activities and psychic and social values has been noted throughout the world's literature, and as long ago as 1899 Veblen coined the term "conspicuous consumption" to describe household purchases aimed at satisfying the need for status in the eyes of others. The essence of modern psychological work in marketing was made memorable by John W. Cable, an early advertising man, in the advice "Don't sell the steak; sell the sizzle."

The new elements that have been added by recent behavioral science developments are a more fully articulated conception of the individual, with his various social and individual characteristics, and a more elaborate collection of techniques for describing, recording, and analyzing behavioral phenomena that had previously been thought to lie beyond the limits of systematic investigation.

The conceptual base of the behavioral sciences has evolved from attempts both to explain the totality of human behavior in a suggestive and almost artistic way and to examine relatively narrow and formally specified behavioral hypotheses with rigorous scientific methodology. These two sources of conceptual development interact, each receiving stimulus from the other, and the behavioral sciences have not yet yielded a standardized set of analytical categories or a commonly accepted order of presentation for related ideas. Therefore it is impossible to refer to a comprehensive and definitive inventory of behavioral science concepts; and it is also impossible to convey the richness and variety of behavioral research in marketing in a few pages.

The basic idea of a behavioral approach to marketing analysis is that the purchase and use of goods and services, particularly those for household consumption, is a part of human activity *as a whole*. Thus buying behavior is interpreted as reflecting the full range of human characteristics and motivations, not simply responses to physical needs and economic stimuli.[1] Analysis based on the behavioral approach shifts from a physical economic view of demand to a cognitive symbolic view and, correspondingly, to a group of concepts and research techniques that are appropriate for behavioral analysis. Some of the concepts and techniques that have been most prominent in marketing analysis are briefly described in this chapter. For purposes of presentation, the concepts are grouped into those relating to the mind of the individual (psychological concepts) and those relating to the individual in interpersonal and social contact (sociological concepts). It will be evident, however, that even this distinction is, at the margin, somewhat arbitrary.

---

1. Comprehensive reviews of consumer and buyer behavior are Engle, *et al.* (1968), Zaltman (1965), Howard and Sheth (1969), and Robertson (1970). Key selections from the periodical literature are collected in Kassarjian and Robertson (1968).

The Psychological Model

The psychological approach to the analysis of buyer behavior focuses on various characteristics of the individual personality and the processes by which these characteristics are formed and changed. The key personal characteristics are motivations, attitudes, images, and decision processes. Individual psychological development is analyzed in terms of perception, cognition, and learning. The psychological interpretation of behavior sees continuous interaction among (*a*) the basic characteristics of the individual, (*b*) his perception and retention of stimuli, and (*c*) his behavioral responses (see Howard, 1963, pp. 31–113; and Bayton, 1958).

The validity of this broad conception of human activity can scarcely be challenged; and the generalized stimulus-response model set forth in chapter 5—as well as a very large part of all current theoretical and applied work in marketing research—rests on this general framework of analysis. In the psychological model, the individual is described as receiving a multitude of **perceptions** or cues, both from his own internal information system (e.g., hunger) and from outside sources. On the basis of past experience and other information, these perceptions take on meaning (**cognition**), and the individual develops ways of responding to them. Satisfactory responses that can be repeated over time in various contexts become **learned**; that is, they become part of the individual's information and decision structure itself.

Once a pattern of information, attitudes, and learned responses has been developed, new perceptions are evaluated in terms of that pattern. Perceptions consistent with the established pattern may be readily received and acted upon; stimuli suggesting that an established impression or image is incorrect, or that a learned response is no longer desirable, may be rejected. (The notion of conflict between an established psychological state and the content of new perceptions has been fully developed in the concept of **cognitive dissonance**—see Festinger, 1957.)

Matching Images

The principal focus of applied psychological research in marketing has been the analysis of brand preferences, advertising themes and techniques, and buyer attitudes and images with respect to narrowly defined products and product groups. The early motivation researchers, deriving their inspiration from European schools of psychology, began by asking the question: What *is* a product? They then attempted to develop answers that would include all relevant aspects of the purchase and use of a product as they might appear in the mind of the consumer. The goal of the analysis was to relate the "product image" or "brand image" (i.e., the characteristics of the product as perceived by the individual) to the individual's "self-image" (i.e., his perception of his own charteristics) so that the underlying continuity between his psychological state and his observed behavior would be revealed. The relationship might be a direct matching of similar images, a choice of products that would compensate for perceived inadequacies in the self-image, or a more complex pattern. In any case, the notion of symbolic matching as a principal aspect of buyer behavior was emphasized (see Meyers, 1968).

Applied research reveals that the discrepancy between objective evidence and subjective images can be very great. A study of diet-food users found that the classifications "overweight," "normal," and "underweight," as determined by medical standards, did not provide useful descriptions of the principal buyer groups (Newman, 1957). On the contrary, a great many technically overweight people thought of themselves as normal in size and therefore felt no need for diet foods, whereas many medically normal people were regular diet-food users. Evidently, quite different approaches to product development and advertising would be appropriate for these two different potential customer groups.

The same kind of differences between objective evidence and images occur with respect to product images. For example, "low price" and "expensive" are psychological as well as economic characteristics, and buyers' impressions that a product of "high" or "low" quality may depend to a great extent on the place and manner in which it is sold, its price, the character of its advertising, and so forth, rather than on its objective characteristics. Similarly, many "status" aspects of consumer goods require neither social recognition nor correspondence with observed behavior. If a person associates certain status attributes with a product, he may acquire that status in his own eyes by using or owning the product, even though no one else knows or cares that he is doing so, and even if other persons in the relevant status group do not, in fact, use it. In such circumstances, the "status" aspect of buyer behavior may be quite different from Veblen's concept of conspicuous consumption.

Buying Intentions and Purchase Probabilities

An aspect of individual buying behavior that is receiving increasing attention in marketing research is the *likelihood* that certain types of purchases will take place during certain periods. If we wish to predict new-automobile sales for next year or a branded consumer product's sales next week, we may frame our research question in terms of the likelihood that particular groups of individuals (or all individuals) will make these purchases. If, during the next period, the average potential buyer is as likely to buy as not, we may say that the average purchase probability is 0.50, and we may forecast the next period's sales as equal to half the number of potential buyers.

Two approaches are currently being applied to the analysis of the likelihood of specific household purchasing activities. One of these employs direct-questioning techniques to ascertain the buying intentions and attitudes of a representative sample of households. The other approach records actual purchase behavior and from this record computes "implied" purchase probabilities, based on naive or complex formal models. Both approaches, of course, may be combined in any specific study, although they have developed from diverse origins. And each approach merits brief consideration.

Economic Psychology and Intentions Surveys

The modern study of "economic psychology" originated with George Katona and his associates at the Survey Research Center of the University of Michigan. Its central idea is that economic variables—income, prices, and so forth—do not directly affect household behavior but filter through perceptions, attitudes, and expectations. Hence these psychological factors, along with economic factors, jointly determine spending, saving, and other major household economic decisions.[2]

Over many years of research, Katona and his associates have accumulated masses of empirical data that reflect individual attitudes and expectations about economic conditions, have developed predictions based on these data, and have compared them with actual buying

2. For a general discussion of this approach, see Katona (1960). A more detailed treatment of intention surveys is to be found in Juster (1966).

decisions. Most of this research activity has been based upon direct questioning and observation. For example, a statistically selected sample of respondents is asked such direct questions as "Do you think your income will increase or decrease over the next period?" "Do you think this is a good time to buy (product)?" "Do you intend to buy (product) within the next period?" The point, of course, is not that this sample of households is more prescient or that its purchase decisions are in any sense more important than the average but that the sample responses will reveal typical tendencies throughout the entire household population in the economy.

Many persons who report intentions to buy during a specified period will not in fact do so; many others will buy who previously stated that they would not. In the aggregate, the two groups may balance out, but most intentions surveys now take account of differences in the certainty of purchase commitments by providing a probability scale for responses. If, for example, two individuals are asked "Do you intend to purchase a car next month?," and their responses are scored on "yes-no" and "likelihood" scales, the results might be as shown in table 8–1 (the probability values are given in parentheses).

Table 8–1   Purchase Probability Responses

Respondents	Yes (1.0)	No (0)	Certain (1.0)	Likely (0.75)	Don't Know (0.50)	Un- likely (0.25)	Defi- nitely Not (0)
Individual 1	x				x		
Individual 2		x					x

The average purchase probabilities for the sample (in this case a sample of two) can be computed from either group of responses, and the example was chosen so that both results are the same: a purchase probability of 0.50. The advantage of using a likelihood scale is that gradations of purchase intentions can be identified, taken into account in making overall estimates, and made the subject of special analysis if this is desired.

The principal application of this approach to buying-intentions analysis has been in macroeconomic forecasting, and the collection of this type of information is now financed and reported by the Federal Reserve Board as part of its general economic information program. The results of a buying-intentions survey, which illustrate the relationship between economic variables and expectations in determining purchase probabilities, are shown in table 8–2. Note that past *increases*

Table 8–2   Purchase Probabilities Computed from a Buying-Intentions Survey (*Consumer Buying Prospects,* Summer 1969)

Question (asked in April 1969): Do you intend to buy an automobile, new or used, within the next 12 months?

Respondents	*Purchase Probabilities (Chances in 100)*
All families	18.3
Families with income of $3000–$4999	11.5
Families with income of $10,000 and over	28.8
Families with "much higher" income over the past year	35.9
Families with the "same" income over the past year	11.3
Families expecting substantial increases in income	31.1–36.2 [a]
Families definitely not expecting increases in income	12.9

a) Depending on the estimated probability of income increase.

in income and positive income *expectations* result in the highest purchase probabilities in the table, while relatively high *levels* of income ($10,000 and over) have a lesser impact. The substantive significance of the "$10,000 and over" category is somewhat ambiguous, however. Median family income in the United States in 1968 was $8630, but the modal income class, containing 25 percent of all families, was "$10,000 to $14,999." An additional 15 percent of all families had incomes of $15,000 and above.

Intentions surveys have been less widely used in connection with the analysis of purchase probabilities for low-price products and specific brands. One reason for this is that the size of the samples required for obtaining accurate predictions by this method is rather large and, as the average purchase probability decreases, the required sample size increases (in order to obtain a minimum number of likely purchasers). A second limitation on the use of intentions surveys for smaller-scale marketing problems is the fact that their primary predictive value is in indicating the *direction* of change in buying activity and not the *amount* of change, whereas some estimate of the amount of change is generally required for decision making at the firm level.

Implied Probabilities and Probability Models

An alternative approach to the analysis of purchase probabilities is to compute actual purchase frequencies for sample households and then to use these frequencies to estimate the underlying probabilities. An advantage of this approach is that it permits the application of formal models of probabilistic processes to the analysis of marketing behavior.[3]

The buying records that are used to estimate purchase probabilities for these purposes are generally obtained from household consumer panel studies. In a panel study (as explained in chapter 6) the same individuals and households are observed periodically over time, so that a sequential record of their purchases is obtained. If we analyze this record with respect to a particular consumer product, we may find that some families purchase only a single brand of the product throughout the period while others purchase several different brands. We may describe the first group of families as "brand loyal"—or, more formally, we may say that their purchase probability for the brand they bought within the product group is almost 1.0 and that the probability of their purchasing other brands is almost zero. (In a rigorous probability analysis, the extreme values of zero and one are never used because all outcomes are assumed to be possible.)

If, in contrast, a family buys several different brands over the period, and if no obvious time pattern appears among these choices, we may say that this family chooses brands at random and that its relative frequencies of purchase reflect the probabilities of each random choice. Thus if a family purchases Brand A 60 percent of the time and Brand B 40 percent of the time, and purchases no other brands within the product group, we may say there is a 0.60 probability of

3. For an important early example, see Frank (1962).

its purchasing A and a 0.40 probability of its purchasing B during any particular shopping trip or time period.

An initial question to be raised with reference to this type of data is whether there are substantial differences in purchase probabilities among households in the sample. If the differences are not substantial, we may wish to use the typical results as estimates of purchase probability for the entire relevant population and compute expected future purchase amounts and market shares accordingly. However, if there are substantial differences among the computed probabilities for different families, the focus of the analysis shifts to identifying the economic and behavioral factors that account for these differences. In this task two somewhat different approaches are used. One approach is to group the households and individuals that are already known to possess common characteristics, such as family size, income level, or location, and ask (1) whether the units within these groups have similar purchase probabilities and (2) whether the differences, if any, in purchase probabilities between such groups account for the principal differences in purchase probabilities among all the households. The alternative approach is to group households that have similar purchase probabilities and then seek the common characteristics that account for this similarity.

The latter is the more imaginative and also the more scientific approach. However, the former approach is still widely used, principally because results obtained in terms of standard economic and demographic categories can be readily compared with the results of other studies and extended to provide market-wide forecasts. By contrast, the search for underlying similarities among buying units with similar purchase probabilities, if successful, is more likely to lead to the identification of important new variables and relationships for future observation and analysis.

Formal probability models. Purchase probabilities can be used to forecast buyer behavior from one period to the next by simple extrapolation. However, a more comprehensive analysis of probabilistic processes can be accomplished by means of formal model construction and implementation. Many of the probability models used in analyzing buying behavior are concerned with the effects of the passage of time, and two elementary propositions are often involved in such models:

1. The probability of repetition (or the memory) of a satisfactory experience tends to decline with the passage of time.
2. The probability of repetition (or the memory) tends to increase with the regularity or frequency of repetition (or exposure).

These two propositions are illustrated in figure 8–1. In both diagrams of the figure (a and b) it is assumed that the initial purchase probability is 0.5 (i.e., the purchase and the nonpurchase of Brand A are equally likely). If no purchase is made during period 1, and no subsequent purchase or other stimulus maintains the probability of buying, a typical pattern of future purchase probabilities may be estimated from a "decay" function, as in figure 8–1(a). On the other

Figure 8–1   Purchase Probabilities (a) with Decay Process
           (b) with Reinforcement

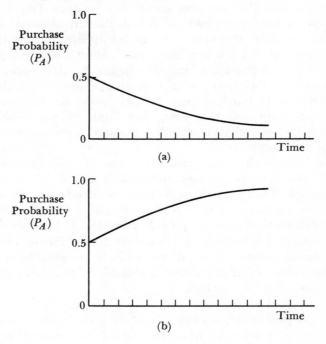

(a)

(b)

hand, if a purchase is made in the initial period, and if this is followed by satisfactory experience with the product, repeat purchases, or other forms of "reinforcement" over time, then purchase probabilities may increase through time, so that at some later period the likelihood of purchase is nearly one.

Such time paths have been estimated on the basis of questionnaires and entries from purchase diaries kept by members of organized consumer panels. Kuehn and Day (1964) have integrated both decay and reinforcement patterns over time into a hypothetical purchase probability record for Brand A, subject to competition from Brands B and C. Their schematic diagram (reproduced as figure 8–2) shows

Figure 8–2   Changes in P_A over Time with Purchases and Exposures to Advertising (Kuehn and Day, 1964)

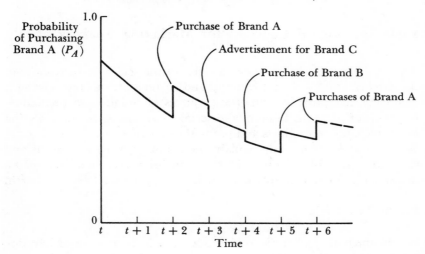

how purchase probabilities for Brand A might be subject to natural decay through time, reinforced through periodic purchases of A, and reduced by exposure to advertising for C and by the purchase of B. This same pattern of relationships can be analyzed in terms of a "probability tree" or other diagrammatic or mathematical constructions.

Because the application of probability models to problems of market demand analysis is only in its infancy, many of the studies reported thus far will probably prove to be false starts in the light of later developments. Even now there is considerable dispute as to whether observed purchase data can be given a valid probabilistic interpretation in terms of brand choices and detailed socioeconomic and behavioral characteristics. On the other hand, much purchase activity appears to be intrinsically probabilistic in character, and probability models have provided important insights—and even useful research results—in some instances. A probabilistic approach is a valuable supplement to the maximum-likelihood estimates provided by econometric techniques, as well as a means for obtaining rough orders of magnitude and estimates of interaction among less easily quantified behavioral variables. A particularly important aspect of purchase probabilities developed from buying-intentions surveys is their indication of the direction of change in aggregate household or industrial purchases. Such surveys results may therefore be useful for aggregate economic forecasting and marketing conditions analysis, even when they are less reliable as indicators of specific product or brand sales.

Some Sociological Concepts for Marketing Analysis

The analysis of buyer behavior in terms of the social characteristics of the buying unit, both individually and in relation to other elements in society, has provided important sources of insight and prediction. Concepts of life style, fashion, and social status are useful in analyzing buyer response to products and promotion activities. Concepts of social contact and influence help explain the adoption of new products and the elimination of old ones. This section briefly reviews some of the major sociological concepts that are used in buyer behavior research.

Family Life Cycle

A fundamental characteristic of the household is its state of development as a social unit, which may be described in terms of the stages of a family life cycle:

young, single individual, on his own
young married, no children
married, young children
married, older children
mature married, no children at home (the "empty nest")
older single (including widow and widower)

There are many reasons why household buying behavior would be closely associated with life cycle stages, since the life cycle concept is a composite indicator of age, marital status, domestic needs, income, assets, and so forth. Typically, major purchases (housing, automobiles, furniture, and appliances) and major service expenditures (entertainment, health, and education) are closely associated with life cycle stages. Some investigators contend that life cycle data, although difficult to obtain, provide more valid predictive and interpretive insights than the more familiar demographic and economic information.

Social Class and Status

A consumption unit or a household may be characterized not only by its distinctive social attributes but also by its relationships to other members of society, and a gross indicator of these relationships is its membership in a broad social class or status group that is made up of many similar units. Although the terms "social class" and "status" tend to be used interchangeably, it is customary to describe large societal groups as **classes** and individuals or smaller groups as possessing **status,** relative to either their own class or society as a whole.

Social class is a composite concept that involves individual characteristics and the perception and evaluation of these characteristics by other members of society. Although income, age, vocation, education level, and other more objective characteristics are frequently correlated with social class, it is itself a broader concept. Detailed social-class structures and characteristics differ widely among regions and communities, but the major divisions shown in table 8–3 are generally recognized throughout the United States.

The major social-class groups are important for market analysis because, at any point in time, each group is likely to have adopted one or more characteristic styles of living and behavior that lead to the purchase or use of certain types of consumer goods. As a result, it is possible to draw characteristic profiles of typical buying units within each main group and to anticipate their buying behavior and preferences.

The fact that the major social classes have distinct consumption and marketing profiles leads to the curious result that one way of shifting one's class position is to adopt the life style of some other group. Thus the purchase patterns of households not only change as a *sign* of their moving from one social class to another, they also change as a *means* of attaining a different class position.

Socialization and Reference Groups

Within the major social classes, and within smaller local and family groups as well, continuous processes of socialization, acculturation, and learning take place. Newcomers join a group by birth and marriage, and by physical movement and communications contact; and established members of one group come into contact with members of another group. As a result, the members of a society observe similari-

Table 8–3 Principal Social Classes in the United States

Upper Class	Persons with inherited wealth or large personal fortunes, holding high executive positions and exerting social and civic leadership
Middle Class	
Upper-Middle	Second-level executives, heads of smaller companies, distinguished professional people
Middle-Middle	Small businessmen, professional men, upper-level white-collar workers
Lower-Middle	Clerks and white-collar workers, minor public officials, blue-collar workers with seniority who are members of strong unions
Lower Class	Blue-collar workers
Lower-Lower Class	Not a single group, but a collection of special groups, each with its own special characteristics; composed of racial minorities and groups disadvantaged with respect to location, skills, and/or education

ties and differences in the social behavior of others and adapt and respond to these observations through their own behavior.

The members of society or a group to which an individual refers in the development of his own attitudes and behavior patterns are termed his **reference group.** Reference-group contacts may be personal or impersonal, formal or informal, conscious or unconscious. These groups may consist of specifically identified individuals, such as friends and family members, or a general class of individuals, such as young executives or students. **Socialization** is the process of an individual's adaptation to his reference group, or, as it is sometimes described, the learning of tastes and behaviors. Note that an individual may refer to many different reference groups for guidance with respect to different aspects of his behavior—to one group for his professional standards, another for entertainment, another for home and personal-life conduct, and so forth. Also, reference-group membership may vary from one individual to the next. If I pay close attention to the kind of car you drive but you are indifferent to the kind of car I drive, you are in my reference group but I am not in yours. Further, the individual may recognize a **negative** reference group, one whose life style or behavior pattern is to be avoided.

However, many important reference-group relationships involve mutual contact, or at least mutual awareness, among the group members. Within such contact networks, specific influence processes have been analyzed in terms of **leadership-followership** patterns. The transmission of influence from leaders to followers may not be overt or intentional; that is, no questions may be asked or instructions given—leaders may, in a sense, be passive and unaware of their leadership qualities. On the other hand, they may consciously seek and exercise their leader or teacher role. And leadership, like other phases and aspects of reference-group membership, may be either relatively permanent or subject to rapid change.[4]

It is sometimes useful to distinguish between developments that tend to increase or to decrease the stability or uniformity of behavior, or cohesiveness of attitude, among members of a social group. Child rearing and the explicit teaching of tastes and behavior patterns to novices are examples of uniformity-increasing socialization processes. Leadership, however, may have either type of effect. Thus leaders may hold to established norms and behavior patterns or, in contrast, may take an active role in introducing changes into society. In some instances, initiative in introducing change may be a leadership qualification in itself.

Some examples. The concepts of social learning, reference groups, and leadership have been most extensively applied in marketing analysis in studies of household consumption expenditures. Some of the empirical questions raised in such studies are: How are reference-group memberships and leadership positions determined? By what process are changes in buying behavior transmitted among networks of social contact? What determines the speed of adaptive behavior within and between reference groups?

A classic investigation of these questions is the early study by Coleman, Katz, and Menzel (1957) of the adoption of a new drug by physicians. In their search for leader-identifying characteristics, these

4. A comprehensive analysis of these relationships is presented in Katz and Lazarsfeld (1955).

researchers examined (*a*) the extent to which a physician was profession-oriented, as opposed to patient-oriented, and (*b*) the extent to which each doctor was "integrated" into his professional group, as reflected in the comments of other doctors. In general, they found that if a doctor was profession-oriented he was also highly integrated, and that such doctors (who occupied high-status positions within their groups) were early users of the new drug. Also, because of their status and contacts, these doctors seemed to influence their colleagues in the use of the new drug; although, relatively isolated physicians, who were not subject to this influence, apparently became acquainted with new drugs only through advertisements and the work of field salesmen.

Although this study indicated that doctors who adopted the new drug at an early date carried out a traceable leadership role with respect to their colleagues, many documented instances of early adoption do not seem to have involved specific leadership-followership relationships. Indeed, there may be important consumption categories in which established leaders resist new product introduction. For example, a number of studies have indicated that families who move to new localities, particularly in connection with promotions or other favorable job changes, are early adopters of new consumer products. Young families, and particularly young housewives, are also found to be especially receptive to new purchase alternatives.

These findings may not be surprising inasmuch as families that change their residence and work environment may readily accept other changes at the same time, and young housewives may be looking for ways to solve household problems that older housewives have learned to cope with or ignore. However, both of these findings conflict with previously held conceptions of behavior and influence patterns. If the primary motivation of newcomers to a reference group (a community or work group) were to duplicate the consumption patterns of the group, they would *not* be innovators; on the contrary, they would pattern themselves as closely as possible on the established members of their new group. Similarly, traditional family-influence patterns involve the old teaching the young, not vice versa.

The strength of the forces that tend to change, rather than perpetuate, life styles is characteristic of modern, as opposed to traditional, societies around the world, and this tendency is especially strong in socially fluid countries, such as the United States. Under these circumstances, the early adoption of consumption innovations may be interpreted as primarily *barometric* rather than *leading*. Early adopters *foreshadow* changes but do not necessarily bring them about in a direct causal way.

Behavioral Research Techniques

The use of behavioral science concepts in marketing analysis has been paralleled by the increasing application, and even the innovative development, of behavioral research techniques. Direct observation of behavior, either in the field or in laboratory settings, and the collection of data from interviews, individually administered tests, and projective techniques have been of paramount importance. Many observational studies deal with the mechanics of perception and reaction. Photographing eye movements, measuring physiological responses, and monitoring in-store shopping behavior are typical examples. These studies are designed to identify the kinds of stimuli that cause people to stop and take notice, and to measure the speed with which attention shifts from one external stimulus to another.

Other observational and interview studies deal with the process of decision making in a more formal way. The time spent in reaching a household or organizational purchasing decision and the specific considerations bearing upon it can be recorded by participants or observers. Intensive interview studies may be made of families that have made certain types of purchases so as to determine the length of time spent in decision making, the sources of information consulted, and the specific decision criteria applied.

In these latter investigations it is somewhat difficult to separate "rationalizations" (the reasons and procedures one considers acceptable for open discussion and reporting to outside parties) from perhaps more powerful but less easily stated motives and practices. Many studies of households in the United States have indicated that a large percentage of purchases, including purchases of durable goods, are not the results of long periods of conscious deliberation but are made on the basis of a sudden "need," or simply a sudden change in purchasing ability or marketing contact. However, it would be a mistake to conclude from such studies that the bulk of household purchases are impulsive or unplanned. On the contrary, the development of purchasing criteria and the accumulation of information about consumer goods may be such a constant and pervasive process in our society that most households have latent plans for purchases of many items whenever funds become available, market contacts occur, or specific "needs" arise.

Other types of interview studies and more sophisticated testing procedures attempt to seek information on attitudes, motives, and impressions that need not be associated with a particular past purchase or other observable incident. The questions that are framed for this purpose may be direct and/or indirect. The distinction lies in whether the question directly identifies the information sought or whether the respondent is guided toward responses from which an answer may eventually emerge. Examples of direct questions are "What kind of car do you like?" "Why do you enjoy (a particular type of entertainment)?" "What do you like or dislike about (a food or beverage)?" Indirect questions, by contrast, attempt to elicit information in a less restrictive way. For example, a respondent may be asked very general questions—What new products or brands have you recently purchased or noticed?—and then led to express various tastes and attitudes in conversation.

If a respondent is known to have been exposed to some new product, a particular piece of advertising, or other external stimulus, a response dimension of special interest is the length of time that elapses before he voluntarily mentions the specific stimulus and the number and nature of his unsolicited comments. As another example, the importance of an automobile or particular automobile characteristics may be clearly indicated by how long a conversation about a car trip goes on before the car itself, or any of its features—good or bad—are mentioned.

Additional insight into buying behavior may be obtained by the use of **projective techniques,** that is, exercises in which the respondent is allowed to project himself into a hypothetical or unspecified situation. The simplest projective question is, What would you do if . . . ? More subtle ways of asking this question involve the use of pictures, cartoons, shopping lists, or interrupted narratives, and asking respondents to describe the suggested circumstances or to complete the story. Studies of these types have revealed that instant coffee and baking mixes are associated with lazy and careless housewives, that insurance advertising that emphasizes low premium costs is not readily believed, and so forth. Investigations of this type involve role playing, in the imagination if not in overt actions. Similar results may be obtained from sentence completion, word association, and other spontaneous response tests in which the role-playing element is not so prominent. The ultimate limit in these open-ended investigations is reached with the psychiatric (or "depth") interview, in which respondents are invited to speak freely about a wide range of experiences and ideas.

Behavioral research techniques have revolutionized marketing analysis because they have made it possible to conduct serious investigation of many important but previously neglected aspects of buying behavior. At the same time, their validity, in marketing and elsewhere, has been subjected to serious question and criticism. Many of these questions arise from the very novelty of the techniques and the fact that summary results of their use in many similar circumstances have not been available. As a result, it is difficult to appraise the validity of any particular test or application.

Other criticisms are made on the ground that the concepts of the behavioral sciences, upon which these research techniques are based, describe fundamental, pervasive, and continuing human characteristics, whereas household buying decisions can usually be described as relatively superficial, scattered, and transient. There may be substantial and strong links between an individual's social relationships and psychological makeup and his choice of products and brands in some instances; in others, the suggestion of such a linkage seems ludicrous.

It would seem, therefore, that the value of psychological studies in marketing depends as much on the intuition and imagination that underlie their design, and on the creative insight that is brought to bear on their interpretation, as on their substantive content and accuracy. However, the substantive results of these studies serve as important reminders that buying behavior cannot be fully understood without considering the ideas, decision process, and personality characteristics of individuals. Fortunately, all of the questions and criticisms are subject to evaluation and correction through continued study and experience. Some data-gathering procedures will be validated over time; others will be improved or rejected. Some types of purchases will be shown to be particularly responsive to changes in behavioral variables; others will appear unresponsive. The value of these research tools will be determined by their usefulness in application, not by argument.

Marketing Research: A Final Comment

In these chapters we have described some of the main ideas and approaches to the analysis of market demand, but only in a very selective and summary way. It may be unnecessary to add that most of the concepts, models, and techniques used for this purpose may also be applied to many other analytical tasks, including aspects of marketing that are only remotely related to final purchase activities. For example, statistical and econometric techniques may be applied to the choice of geographical locations, the analysis of costs, and many other aspects of business operations. Behavioral research techniques are particularly useful in analyzing personnel problems (including, very importantly, the behavior of sales personnel) and in studying high-level management organization. Our description of the various research methods has ignored these applications only for the sake of brevity.

In conducting and appraising applied research work in any of these areas, it is important to distinguish between exploratory studies and formal methodological studies designed to provide specific information or to test substantive hypotheses. Exploratory studies, by definition, are concerned with problems about which little is known; therefore their value depends on the extent to which they include many dimensions of a problem and examine significant alternative explanations. Because an exploratory study can rarely be fully designed in advance, its most valuable conclusions will be stated in terms of the areas it has identified as probably fruitful and unfruitful for further analysis. By contrast, a formal research study can be undertaken only if the basic problem is sufficiently understood to permit specific research methods and hypotheses to be selected in advance. Success or failure in formal, substantive research depends primarily on careful **methodological design,** in which a research question is so framed, and the research techniques so selected, that *the implications of all possible results are known in advance.*

A familiar example of a methodological design is the test for the quality of a solution in elementary chemistry. We are taught to ask the question "Is this solution acid or basic?" and we answer this question by dipping a piece of litmus paper in the solution. We know in advance that if the paper turns red, the solution is acid; if it turns blue it is basic; and if there is no change it is neutral. No other color changes are likely, and therefore we know in advance precisely *how* our research question will be answered in response to our technique, although we do not know *what* the specific answer will be until we have immersed the paper. (Note that we have not asked or answered the more difficult question, "What is *in* this solution?") Although marketing research can rarely achieve this degree of exactness and simplicity, careful attention to methodological design in each phase of an investigation, and particularly in the framing of research questions and the structuring of possible answers in advance, will increase both the validity and the value of research results.

This reference to the *value* of research results suggests a final comment concerning the costs and benefits associated with such studies. Costs set limits to the scope of marketing investigations, and we can never afford to gather every piece of data or conduct every analysis that might conceivably be useful. Although difficult to apply, the criterion for determining research expenditures, like any other economic decision, is the relation of value received to cost incurred.

Summary

The fundamental idea underlying a behavioral approach to demand analysis is that the purchase and use of goods and services is an integral part of human activity, and therefore it requires analysis in terms of the complete range of the psychological, social, and cultural factors that affect human life. To accomplish this analysis, various concepts and research techniques have been taken from several basic behavioral science disciplines and applied to marketing.

The **psychological approach** to buyer behavior emphasizes the continuous interaction between an individual's psychological characteristics (attitudes, motivations, and decision processes) and his perception of new stimuli. This interaction leads both to changes within the characteristics themselves (**learning**) and to behavioral responses. An important theme within the psychological approach is that buying behavior is to be understood as a **matching** process in which the product or brand image of the purchased item is matched against the self-image of the buyer.

Another important feature of behavioral analysis is the idea that purchase decisions are based upon **probabilistic,** rather than deterministic, processes. Purchase probabilities have been investigated both by means of direct questioning about attitudes and buying intentions and in terms of formal probability models implemented with empirical data. The former approach has been of greater usefulness in short-run forecasting, but the latter holds greater promise of providing a comprehensive explanation of buying behavior.

Sociological concepts that are now widely used in marketing studies include the family life cycle, social class and status, reference group, and socialization-acculturation (the learning of tastes and behaviors). These concepts are particularly useful in identifying the typical purchase patterns of important segments of society and in tracing the process of new-product adoption and behavioral change within social groups and over time.

These behavioral-science concepts have been investigated through the use of a wide range of research techniques, many of which are still in the experimental or developmental stage. Some of these techniques involve direct observation and questioning, others the application of mathematical relationships to empirical data, and still others the projection of substantive conclusions on the basis of indirect evidence.

The early state of development of many of these concepts and techniques, and the great variety of the concepts being investigated and the techniques being applied, have led to some apparent inconsistencies in results and to professional controversy. In spite of these problems, it is apparent that behavioral science approaches have opened new dimensions for the study of buyer behavior and other aspects of marketing as well. An even more fruitful development of these concepts and techniques in marketing analysis will follow from their continued adaptation and application in methodologically designed research studies.

References

Bayton, J. A. "Motivation, Cognition, Learning: Basic Factors in Consumer Behavior." *Journal of Marketing,* Vol. 22, No. 1, January 1958.

Coleman, James, Elihu Katz, and Herbert Menzel. "The Diffusion of an Innovation among Physicians." *Sociometry,* Vol. 20, December 1957. Reprinted in *Marketing Models,* ed. Ralph L. Day. Intext, 1964.

Engle, James F., David T. Kollat, and Roger D. Blackwell. *Consumer Behavior.* Holt, Rinehart and Winston, 1968.

Festinger, Leon. *A Theory of Cognitive Dissonance.* Stanford University Press, 1957.

Frank, R. E. "Brand Choice as a Probability Process." *Journal of Business,* Vol. 35, January 1962.

Howard, John A. *Marketing Management,* rev. ed. Irwin, 1963.

————, and Jagdish N. Sheth. *A Theory of Buyer Behavior.* Wiley, 1969.

Juster, Thomas F. *Consumer Buyer Intentions and Purchase Probability,* Occasional Paper No. 99. National Bureau of Economic Research, 1966.

Kassarjian, Harold H., and Thomas S. Robertson, eds. *Perspectives in Consumer Behavior.* Scott, Foresman, 1968.

Katona, George. *The Mass Consumption Society.* McGraw-Hill, 1964.

————. *The Powerful Consumer.* McGraw-Hill, 1960.

Katz, Elihu, and Paul F. Lazarsfeld. *Personal Influence.* The Free Press, 1955.

Kuehn, Alfred A., and Ralph L. Day. "Probabilistic Models of Consumer Buying Behavior." *Journal of Marketing,* Vol. 28, October 1964.

Myers, John G. *Consumer Image and Attitude.* University of California Institute of Business and Economic Research, 1968.

Newman, Joseph W. *Motivation Research and Marketing Management.* Harvard University, Graduate School of Business Administration, 1957.

Robertson, Thomas S. *Consumer Behavior.* Scott, Foresman, 1970.

Zaltman, Gerald. *Marketing: Contributions from the Behavioral Sciences.* Harcourt, Brace & World, 1965.

Part III

The Tasks
of Marketing Management

9

Goals, Strategies, and Decision Models

Managerial activity in marketing involves two principal tasks: (1) formulating marketing policy, based upon appropriate combinations of marketing strategy variables, and (2) implementing policy and strategy through planning, administration, review, and revision. By far the larger share of expense and effort goes into implementation, and effective implementation is an essential aspect of any marketing program. However, the critical decisions for policy and strategy must be made before implementation can take place. These decisions, therefore, establish the framework for the entire marketing effort of the firm.

The four chapters of Part III focus exclusively on the decision-making aspects of marketing management. In this chapter, the principal strategy variables are identified and some important goals and models for managerial decision making are introduced. The remaining chapters deal selectively with three principal strategy variables: product, promotion, and price. The fourth principal variable, the place of the firm within the larger context of marketing organization, was dealt with in Part I. These four key marketing strategy variables, **product, promotion, price,** and **place,** are generally referred to as the elements of the **marketing mix.** This terminology is meant to suggest that each firm can mix various combinations of the four variables in order to develop its own marketing program. The geographic dimension of marketing is generally considered, along with the selection and use of marketing channels, as part of the *place* variable. However, geographic aspects of marketing, including the choice of market locations and the impact of transportation modes and costs on marketing activity, are not discussed in any detail in this book.[1]

Goals and Decision Criteria

The essence of management is making decisions and taking actions to implement them. The five essential steps are (1) setting goals, (2) establishing decision criteria related to the goals, (3) gathering the information required in order to apply the criteria, (4) making decisions, and (5) taking action. In some simple circumstances the actions to be taken (or *not* to be taken) may be obvious from the decisions themselves. As a rule, however, a range of possible actions might be taken as a result of any specific decision, and the choice of actions requires a subsidiary goal-decision structure.

The role of goals and decision criteria is so important that it may merit further discussion in a simple example. Suppose that you are leaving the house and wondering whether or not to take your umbrella. Your goal is to stay dry, if possible; and your decision criterion is therefore the likelihood of rain. The information required may be obtained from weather reports, direct observation, and the comments of others. From this information you decide whether the circumstances of the day meet your criterion for carrying the umbrella.

It all seems very simple, but notice how your action depends on your decision criterion: the likelihood of rain. You may be a cautious soul, who carries an umbrella if there is only a remote chance of a shower; on the other hand, you may carry it only if rain is actually falling or is almost certain according to your weather report. In addition, you may wish to consider other goals, such as convenience (if carrying an umbrella is considered a form of inconvenience) or fash-

---

1. Three important general texts in the marketing-management area are Howard, *Marketing Management: Analysis and Planning* (1963); Kotler, *Marketing Management: Analysis, Planning, and Control* (1967); Sturdivant *et al., Managerial Analysis in Marketing* (1970); and Davis, *Marketing Management* (1966).

ion, and include these goals within your decision system. Finally, note that if the decision process becomes too complicated and time consuming, or if it comes to depend upon a volume or quality of information that is unavailable or unduly expensive (your own weather station!), you may never get out of the house at all. It may then be necessary to adopt a routine form of behavior (always carrying an umbrella or never carrying an umbrella), or a simplified decision system that makes "wrong" decisions part of the time, with the cost of these errors being less than the cost of a decision system that would eliminate them.

Most of the decision models for marketing management that are available in the professional literature and textbooks are cast in terms of a single goal: profit making for the firm. Therefore the decision criterion that is built into the analysis is typically one of the following: (a) minimizing costs for a given (or unknown) revenue, (b) maximizing revenue for a given (or unknown) cost, or (c) balancing additions to costs against resulting additions to revenue until the two are equal. The last is the familiar marginal criterion of economic theory: Profits are at a maximum when the rising marginal cost equals the falling marginal revenue.

Limitations

Plausible as these decision criteria may appear, their application in actual decision making is rarely easy, for many reasons. The reason that is stressed in most general discussions of the problems of decision making is the lack of requisite information. Not only are critical pieces of data difficult to obtain; available data often are not in the appropriate form for efficient use. Cost data, for example, generally report some history or projection of actual expenditures for principal expenditure categories, whereas the costs relevant for decision making are the *necessary* expenses associated with particular activities or results, which may be quite another thing. On the revenue side, the principal informational problems are lack of sales data by relevant customer classifications and uncertainty about the range and stability of revenue possibilities.

Informational problems such as these severely limit the ease with which simple and precise decision criteria can be applied on a routine basis. However, the more significant limitations on the use of simple profit-maximization decision rules in marketing are of a different character. These limitations may be summarized under three principal headings.

Multiple goals. The goals of modern business management—what they are and what they should be—are the subject of a large literature (see White, 1960). Even if long-run profit maximization is acknowledged as the most general goal of managerial activity in the private sector of the economy, this single goal becomes fragmented and qualified in the context of specific managerial decisions. Thus marketing management decisions frequently aim at a complex of goals, including (a) profits at least as great, in amount or rate of return, as some minimum level; (b) market-share level or rate of growth; (c) physical volume of sales or activity; (d) stability or specific time pattern of costs and revenues; (e) organizational goals, such as maintaining a qualified staff and a regular pattern of staff development; and (f) social, industry, and community goals of various sorts. This multiplicity of goals makes any decision that is based upon a single-goal criterion subject to limitation or revision because of conflicts and inconsistencies among the goals themselves.

Interaction among decision variables. In marketing, perhaps more than in other aspects of business management, the results of apparently quite distinct decisions are inherently interrelated. For example, it seems sensible to search for the profit-maximizing price for a particular product under particular distribution and promotion conditions. And it also seems sensible to try to develop the best promotion strategy, or the best distribution methods, for a particular product with a particular price. But the optimal marketing mix—the one that the marketing manager really hopes to develop—involves the best combination of product, price, promotion, and distribution method. Holding some of these marketing strategy variables constant, while examining the effects of changes in others, is the usual means of developing marketing policy; and it is the only feasible approach in many circumstances. At any point in time, any on-going organization will have operating policies in force and established products and prices; as a result, some elements in the marketing mix may be fixed, or severely restricted, while others are more readily variable. Subsequently, the initially fixed elements may be brought into balance with those that have been altered. However, piecemeal adaptation of individual strategy variables over time may never result in their optimal combination since the effect of undesirable marketing mix combinations in the past may be to foreclose the possibility of highly desirable combinations in the future.

Large and small changes in strategy variables. The marginal approach to decision making applies specifically to decision variables that are subject to change in relatively small increments—to prices reduced from \$10 to \$9 to \$8, to advertising budgets increased from \$100,000 to \$110,000, and so forth. Thus where small and continuous variations are possible, decision systems and criteria based upon marginal calculations have their greatest value. However, many key decisions in marketing involve qualitative variables, so that incremental changes and comparisons are not feasible or relevant. For example, the critical feature of a product may be whether or not it is highly advertised, not how much it is advertised within the "high" or "low" advertising range. Similar distinctions may be drawn among price levels, product quality features, distribution methods, and forms of marketing organization. For decisions among choices of this type, a decision system appropriate for the analysis of small adaptive changes may be of little value.

Some Marketing Mix Models

The formal integration of marketing mix variables into the simple profit-maximization model of the firm is a relatively easy task; however, implementation of such a model for purposes of analysis and marketing planning is quite difficult. For this reason, the most advanced analytical models for marketing planning now in use are based on complex computer programs that permit sequential examination of strategy alternatives and provide options for decision making in a YES-NO-CONTINUE format. In this section we briefly indicate the place of the marketing mix variables in a simple profit-maximization model, and then we present two examples of large-scale computer models for marketing planning.

Profit Maximization

The simple mathematical model of the firm includes (1) a cost function, $C = f_1(q) + C^*$, and (2) a demand function, $q = f_2(p)$, where q is quantity, p is price, C is total cost, and C^* is the total fixed cost.

Total revenue (R) is defined as $R = qp$. Total profit (Π) is $\Pi = R - C$. The criterion for profit maximization is that marginal cost be equal to marginal revenue:

$$\frac{dR}{dq} = \frac{dC}{dq}$$

To integrate the marketing mix variables into this model, we simply expand the demand function as follows:

$$q = f_3(p, V, A, M)$$

where V represents product quality features (variety), A advertising, and M distribution channels and methods. All of these added marketing variables result in additions to cost, so that the cost function now becomes:

$$C = f_4(q, V, A, M) + C^*$$

If we consider that separate and identifiable cost and revenue effects are associated with each of the marketing variables, the marginal profit-maximization criterion becomes:

$$\frac{dR}{dq} = \frac{\delta C(V)}{\delta q} = \frac{\delta C(A)}{\delta q} = \frac{\delta C(M)}{\delta q} = \frac{\delta C(q)}{\delta q}$$

where the parentheses identify the particular cost factors and $C(q)$ is the marginal production cost.

This notation is formally correct, but it makes very little sense since it appears that the variations in quantity are producing the changes in marketing costs, rather than vice versa. Therefore a more suggestive expression for any given value of δq is the following:

$$\frac{\delta R}{\delta C(V)} = \frac{\delta R}{\delta C(A)} = \frac{\delta R}{\delta C(M)} = 1$$

This says that profits are maximized when the marginal costs of each marketing variable necessary for generating a given addition to total volume are equal to the marginal revenues obtained from selling that volume, with price adjusted to the appropriate level in each instance.[2]

It may be helpful to visualize these relationships in terms of the familiar demand-curve concept, as in figures 9–1 (a), (b), (c), which suggest hypothetical relationships between quantity sold and each of

---

2. For a recent elaboration of the economic approach to marketing-management analysis see Palda (1969).

Figure 9–1   Demand Curves for Marketing Mix Variables

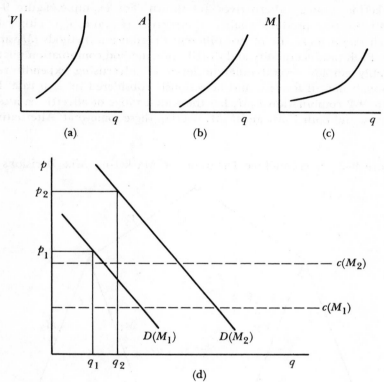

(a)   (b)   (c)

(d)

three marketing variables, with all other variables held constant. Figure 9–1(d) illustrates the price-quantity demand curves resulting from two different distribution methods: a high-cost method (M_2) and a low-cost method (M_1). In each instance, both price and quantity are adjusted to profit-maximizing values (the marginal revenue curves are not shown). The profit-maximizing distribution method would, of course, be the one that yields the greatest excess of total revenue over total cost, which in this case appears to be method 2. Similar partial maximization results could be illustrated for various product quality levels (V) and advertising expenditures (A). The global maximum— the greatest possible profit available with all factors variable—would, of course, include the interaction of all marketing mix variables, but this cannot be illustrated in a two-dimensional diagram.

Another useful way of looking at the profit-maximization model is in terms of a tree diagram in which only significant and distinct marketing strategy alternatives are shown. For example, figure 9–2 illustrates two product quality alternatives (V_1 and V_2), either of which might make use of two different distribution methods (M_1 and M_2). Each product-quality and distribution-method combination might suitably employ several different levels of advertising expenditures, although not all levels would be seriously considered in each case. In figure 9–2 combination V_1M_1 has the widest range of advertising alternatives, and both V_1M_2 and V_2M_1 overlap these somewhat. Alternative

Figure 9–2   Decision-Tree Diagram for Marketing Mix Decisions

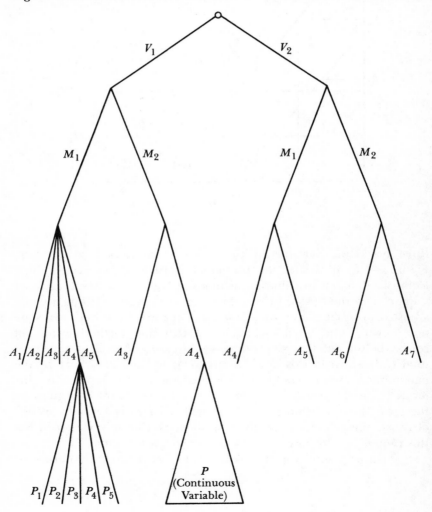

V_2M_2 would involve a choice among other advertising policies (A_6 and A_7). At the end of each branch of the tree, price might be considered either in terms of a few significant price-level choices (say, the $25 range, the $10 range, and so forth) or as a continuous variable. In either case, the significant choices that require close attention might be reduced to a manageable number, and the profit-maximization criterion could be used to select among the several important, but widely scattered, alternatives, as well as to determine the final values of continuous variables by means of marginal adjustments.

Computer Models

The large computerized models that now are coming into use in marketing planning require the arraying of alternatives and criteria, and the tracing through of decisions and effects, in something like the pattern of the tree diagram in figure 9–2. These models are distinguished not only by their use of computer technology but also by their great complexity and their integration of large amounts of operating-cost and revenue data and a variety of managerial decision criteria into a single analytical system. Two of the most important recent models have been developed primarily as means of evaluating new-product decisions. However, their scope is so broad that they may well be considered general models of the planning process for all marketing strategy variables.[3]

The *Demon* Model

The DEMON (*DE*cision *M*apping via *O*ptimum *N*etworks) model for new-product appraisal was developed for an advertising agency, Batten, Barton, Durstine, and Osborn (see Charnes, 1966, and Learner, 1965). The idea incorporated into the model is that a new product should be subjected to a series of increasingly specific marketing tests, after each of which one of the following three decisions is possible:

GO The product should be introduced as soon as possible because it appears certain to meet the sales, profit, and other criteria initially set forth by the responsible managers.

ON The product should be subjected to further tests because the evidence is not yet clear.

NO The product does not meet requirements and should be rejected.

A schematic diagram of the model is shown in figure 9–3.

3. This discussion is based on Kotler (1968).

Figure 9–3 A DEMON Information Network (Kotler, 1968)

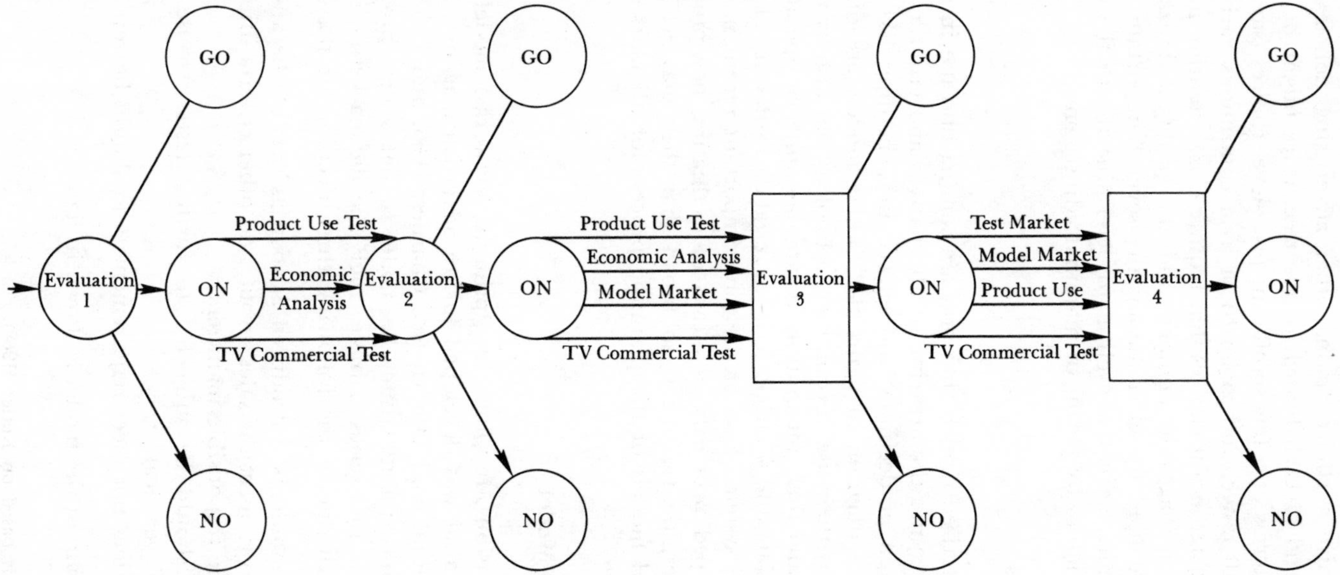

Application of this model requires a full statement of managerial decision criteria: minimum profit and sales levels, length of the planning period, minimum levels of prediction confidence required for decision making, and so forth. In addition, the demand structure is a critical feature of the DEMON model. Since the entire analysis was developed from the viewpoint of new-product introduction, explicit attention is given to the effect of advertising expenditures, sales promotion, and distribution techniques on the number of individuals who learn about the new product and the extent to which these individuals try it and become regular users.

The model also allows for the explicit introduction of competitive effects, through the loss of lead time, if the firm chooses to continue testing the new-product rather than take advantage of its ability to enter the market earlier.

The *Sprinter* Model

THE SPRINTER (Specification of *PR*ofits with *IN*teractions under *T*rial and *E*rror *R*esponse) model was developed by Glen Urban (1968) for analyzing the impact of new products on the total product assortment and profit outlook of a firm in a dynamic context. In addition, variations in competitive conditions throughout the life history of the new product are explicitly considered. The two key measures of the new product's impact are **discounted differential profit** (the present value of annual profit differences on the whole product line due to the new product) and **differential uncertainty** (differences in the variability of profits with and without the new product). The model incorporates a GO ON NO framework similar to DEMON. A flow diagram of its principal steps is shown in figure 9–4.

Urban was able to test his model on data supplied by a large chemical company for a new product it had recently introduced on a nationwide scale, and the model produced a NO decision on the basis of the data. However, Urban later learned that the company had deliberately understated the size of the expected market to see whether the model would reject the new product for this reason.

Careful scrutiny of both the DEMON and the SPRINTER models underscores two points that were made earlier in the discussion.

1. The integration of marketing strategy variables into a comprehensive marketing program is a task of great complexity. Thus it is little wonder that rules of thumb come to be widely followed and that significant problems of suboptimization arise and persist over time. Even in these large and complex computer models, important aspects of market response are necessarily omitted and key behavioral factors are drastically simplified.

2. All the models, and all marketing planning decisions, rest on the initial goals and decision criteria adopted by enterprise owners and managers. Formal models provide methods of working out the implications of various circumstances and decisions in order to see which ones will prove most satisfactory in terms of the initial management goals. However, the goals themselves must come from outside the models.

Figure 9–4   Flow Diagram of the SPRINTER Model (Kotler, 1968)

A
↓

Informed executives supply estimates and data on:
1. A reference marketing program matrix (P_i, A_i, D_i) over the planning period for the new product and for any interacting products.
2. Estimate of probable time of competitive entry and marketing program of competitors. (Also high and low estimates.)
3. Estimates of market share of competitors in new-product market over planning period and effect of industry marketing effort on demand. (Also high and low estimates.)
4. Planned plant capacity for each year in the planning period.
5. Estimate of the reference life cycle demand for the new and interacting products on the basis of the marketing programs. (Also high and low estimates.)
6. Executive estimates of the demand response of the new and old products to systematic variations in (P_i, A_i, D_i), including cross-product response functions. Also needed is an estimate of the shift in the reference life cycle in response variations to the marketing program. (Also high and low estimates.)
7. New-product development costs and production for new and existing products.
8. Management constraints on advertising budget, plant output capacity, technical service, and price.
9. Management requirements regarding the minimum profit necessary for a GO decision (Z_G), the minimum profit for an ON decision (Z_O), the minimum probability necessary for a GO decision (Pr_G), and the minimum probability necessary for an ON decision (Pr_O).
10. A reference marketing program matrix for the old line (on the assumption that the new product is not introduced).

|
B
↓

Calculate the total discounted profits for the new line and the old line under the new reference marketing program and the old reference marketing program. (All constraints must be satisfied.) Subtract old line discounted profit from new line discounted profit to find total discounted differential profit.

|
C
↓

Specify alternative values for price, advertising, and distribution and for each combination find total discounted differential profit. Select the marketing program that yields the maximum total discounted differential profit.

|
D
↓

Calculate the differential uncertainty.

|
E
↓

Plot the estimated maximum discounted differential profit and differential uncertainty on the GO, ON, NO decision grid. Does the estimate fall in the GO region?

| |
Yes   F   G   No
↓   ↓

Introduce the new prod-   Does the estimate fall
uct with the prescribed   in the NO region?
marketing program.

                                | |
                                H   I
                                ↓   ↓

                        Drop the   Determine the best mar-
                        product.   keting study according to
                                            expected value of infor-
                                            mation/cost of informa-
                                            tion criterion. After the
                                            information is gathered,
                                            return to A.

Summary

Managerial activity in marketing involves policy formulation and implementation with respect to the four key marketing mix variables: **product, price, promotion,** and **place** (distribution channels and location). Although implementation is the more costly and time-consuming activity, policy formation and decision making is logically the prior activity, and it sets the limits within which implementation takes place. Therefore the principal focus of our discussion is on the decision-making phase of marketing management.

Systematic decision making requires the establishment of **goals** and **decision criteria** and then relating information and experience to the criteria in order to select a course of action. The practice of decision making is complex and difficult because most organizations have multiple goals and because the decision variables interact in complex ways. Further, a decision-making approach that is appropriate with respect to relatively small changes—particularly marketing mix variables—may not be appropriate with respect to larger changes or other variables, and vice versa.

A simple economic model of profit maximization including marketing mix variables states that additional expenditures should be made on each marketing mix variable (e.g., for product improvement, increased promotion, or price reduction) until the additional cost is just offset by the additional revenue. This is the simple and appropriate **marginal decision rule.** The large number of alternative specific marketing expenditure decisions, and the complex interrelationships among them, may make the application of such a rule very difficult. It is possible, nevertheless, to apply a marginal decision rule or criterion to individual segments or discrete alternatives within the marketing mix.

The availability of computer technology has led to the development of **complex decision models** (such as DEMON and SPRINTER) in which large collections of marketing data are interrelated and manipulated in order to test the impact of a variety of possible market conditions and decision choices. Although this approach to managerial decision making is still in its infancy, and although it requires very considerable expenditures and a high degree of technical skill, it will probably become the principal means of achieving integrated managerial analysis and planning of marketing activity in the future.

References

Charnes, Abraham. "DEMON: Decision Mapping via Optimum GO-NO Networks—A Model for Marketing New Products." *Management Science,* Vol. 12, No. 11, July 1966.

Davis, K. R. *Marketing Management,* 2nd ed. Ronald, 1966.

Howard, John A. *Marketing Management: Analysis and Planning,* rev. ed. Irwin, 1963.

Kotler, Philip. "Computer Simulation in the Analysis of New-Product Decisions." In *Applications of the Sciences in Marketing Management,* ed. Frank M. Bass, *et al.* Wiley, 1968.

————. *Marketing Management: Analysis, Planning, and Control.* Prentice-Hall, 1967.

Learner, David B. "DEMON New-Product Planning: A Case History." In *New Directions in Marketing,* ed. Frederick E. Webster. American Marketing Association, 1965.

Palda, Kristian S. *Economic Analysis for Marketing Decisions.* Prentice-Hall, 1969.

Sturdivant, Frederick D., and others. *Managerial Analysis in Marketing.* Scott, Foresman, 1970.

Urban, Glen. "A New-Product Analysis and Decision Model." *Management Science,* Vol. 14, 1968.

White, C. Michael. "Multiple Goals in the Theory of the Firm." In *Linear Programming and the Theory of the Firm,* ed. Kenneth E. Boulding and W. Allen Spivey. Macmillan, 1960.

10

Some Concepts for Product Planning

Products and Services

Business enterprises and other economic organizations employ and consume economic resources and produce tangible and intangible output results: merchandise, services, noise, trash, environmental effects (beautification/pollution), and so forth. The production of some of these results is the primary purpose of the enterprise; others are secondary or simply inevitable consequences of the principal activity. The distinction between principal and secondary products and services, as well as between products and wastes (or services and *dis*-services), depends primarily upon demand conditions. Output results that others will purchase are economic goods or, less formally, "products." Output results that are discharged free into the environment, or that others must be paid to accept, are wastes or nuisances. For many decades a major aspect of product development and planning in most manufacturing industries has been the transformation of wastes into products and of low-value into high-value products. This task has been accomplished primarily through scientific and technological research. However, market research and market communication also play an important role in discovering uses that might be made of new technological possibilities and in acquainting potential users with them.

The outputs of an enterprise that have value to other units in the economy are usually described as physical products (tangible outputs) and services (intangible outputs). Some types of economic activity, such as manufacturing, result primarily in physical products; others, such as banking and retailing, result primarily in services. However, most product-producing enterprises also generate a stream of associated services (sales calls, repairs, financing, etc.), and most service-producing enterprises jointly provide some physical products along with their service output. In retailing, for example, the connection between physical products and the services of display, storage, selling, and financing is obvious and essential. A general analysis of product planning and strategy necessarily involves product and/or service policies. It is not, therefore, necessary to restate the importance of product-service combinations and purely service outputs at every stage of our discussion.

Product Classifications

Physical products of economic activity take many different forms, are subject to a wide variety of cost and demand conditions, and are marketed through an incredible diversity of marketing arrangements. A crude classification of major types of products is useful, therefore, as a basis for analyzing the physical, locational, cost, and demand factors that condition specific product planning activities. Any such classification is subject to the usual qualifications of arbitrariness and incompleteness, and there is inevitably some overlapping among the descriptive categories. However, the following terms are frequently used to describe the principal physical product categories and to suggest their important differences in marketing problems.

Primary products and raw materials. Almost without exception, these products are marketed in large-volume transactions, and their value per unit of bulk or weight is very low compared to that of other product types. (For example, typical values for raw materials are well under $100 per ton or freight carload, but automobiles are valued at about $5,000 per ton or $40,000 per carload.) Hence a critical determinant of marketing practices that involves these products is the need to reduce transportation, storage, and transaction costs by substituting distant communication, long-term contracting and centralized

trading for direct inspection and negotiation in scattered, small transactions.

The two principal subcategories within this major product classification are **agricultural products** and **metals and minerals**. The
former are typically characterized by seasonality in production, re-
producibility over time, and perishability in storage (natural fibers
being a nonperishable exception). Metals and minerals, on the other
hand, do not share these characteristics to any significant extent.
Mitigating the effects of production periodicity has therefore been a
more important consideration in the development of marketing
arrangements for the former group of products than for the latter.
Examples of this are futures markets and auction marketing.

Industrial or "producer" goods. These terms are usually applied to products that are purchased primarily by industrial and
construction organizations for use in producing additional products
and services. The three principal subcategories are:

1. **Materials and semifinished products:** the physical resources to be
   transformed into final goods. (Note that industrial raw materials
   reappear here.)
2. **Equipment:** the durable machinery, processing facilities, transportation vehicles, and so forth through which the materials pass
   in the transformation process
3. **Supplies:** the auxiliary items that are used up during the production process but do not become part of the final product [1]

The industrial goods category thus includes a full range of
products, from large, complex, and permanent pieces of industrial
equipment to inexpensive, expendable supplies such as cleaning materials. Marketing practices and strategies for industrial goods vary correspondingly. However, since industrial users typically purchase even
low-value products in relatively large volume, the use of marketing
methods that involve high costs per transaction, and particularly large
amounts of personal selling effort, is not unusual throughout this
class of products. A key consideration in determining product and
price policies with respect to industrial goods is the relationship between the unit prices of these inputs and the unit values of the resulting outputs; low-value final products must be made from low-value

---

1. It will be obvious that the two principal industrial cost items not listed here
are (1) labor and (2) use of finance capital, both of which are service (not product)
inputs into the production process.

materials, and so forth. A further consideration is the impact that one input decision has on the requirements and costs of other inputs. New pieces of equipment and new types of materials that reduce the amount of waste, cut labor requirements, or result in subsequent outputs of higher value compete very successfully with equipment and materials that are simply cheaper in direct-purchase cost.

Consumer goods.   Goods of types and forms that are suitable for household consumption are generally described as consumer goods, regardless of the stage of the marketing process at which they may be found. Note that wholesaling agencies deal in both industrial and consumer goods while retailing agencies deal only in consumer goods. The principal subcategories of consumer goods are usually identified as follows:

1. **Durables:** appliances, automobiles, furniture
2. **Semidurables:** clothing, footwear, housewares
3. **Nondurables:** primarily foods

Unit prices and the amount of direct-selling activity that accompany individual transactions tend to decrease from one of these categories to the next whereas the frequency of purchase by final buyers tends to increase. These differences in the combination of price, service, and purchase frequency are the essential features of the distinction between "convenience" and "shopping" goods, which are stressed in much of the marketing literature (see Bucklin, 1963). Convenience goods are characterized by frequent purchase and small expenditure per purchase; and the combination of these two characteristics could result in a high ratio of purchasing effort to purchase value for the buyer. Frequent purchase also results in a high state of product knowledge on the part of the buyer, so that he could make purchases quickly and without great effort *if*—and here is the point—*if* the purchase were made convenient for him. Therefore convenience of purchase, which reduces the purchase effort associated with these frequent, routine, and low-value purchases, becomes an important factor in the purchases decision. Hence the term **convenience goods:** merchandise for which convenience of purchase is, in itself, a highly significant determinant of buyer behavior.

By contrast, shopping goods are less frequently purchased items of relatively high unit values. Buyers are, therefore, less familiar with product features, and are thus more likely to make errors in purchasing them (in the light of their own purchasing criteria); and these errors may be costly in terms of both money and satisfaction.

Therefore the commitment of considerable effort and time to comparing product alternatives and making careful decisions is justified. Hence the term **shopping goods:** merchandise for which the process of shopping and comparing alternatives is, in itself, a critical determinant of buyer behavior.

It will be evident that specific merchandise items will be convenience goods for some groups of buyers and shopping goods for others, and that various buyer groups will shift whole groups of products from one classification to another over time. For example, books and records are ordinarily thought of as shopping goods; however, rising levels of income and the expansion of mail order sales and book and record club promotions have probably shifted a major portion of the sales of these products into the convenience-goods category.

Product Space: Differentiation and Segmentation

Any major type of product can be described as possessing certain significant attributes, and any item within the product type can then be identified in terms of its possession of particular values of these attributes. If, for example, the significant attributes of an item of clothing were weight and insulating capacity (commonly referred to as "warmth"), all possible combinations of light to heavy weight and small to great insulating capacity (i.e., "cool to warm") could be shown by points on a two-dimensional grid, as in figure 10–1.

A grid of this type, conceived in terms of all of the attributes that are significant for planning and analysis of a particular product has been termed "product space" by Alderson (1957, pp. 260–61; see also Brems, 1951). In such a space, two kinds of points may be plotted. One set of points, represented by x, identifies the collection of products currently available in the market—that is, the combinations of attributes among which buyers can currently choose. The other set of points, represented by o, shows combinations of the attributes desired by potential buyers. Note that the product attributes are treated as if they were entirely objective, whereas both the attributes of actual products and the combinations of desired attributes are defined by the subjective interpretations of potential buyers (your notion of "heavy" may be different from mine). We assume, for purposes of discussion, that the objective measure sufficiently correspond to generally held subjective evaluations to be descriptively useful.

Figure 10–1   A Two-Dimensional Product Space

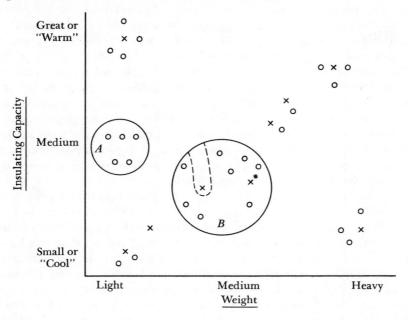

Any observed pattern of purchases within a product space can be explained as the matching of available and desired product attributes. Thus potential buyers, upon finding products that have appropriate attribute combinations, select those products. Potential buyers who desire combinations that are far removed from any available product alternative either stay out of the market or purchase the best available alternative but remain substantially dissatisfied. It may well be that substantial areas of product space—i.e., whole ranges of combinations of product features—are unattainable with existing technology. However, if a large number of buyer preference points occur in such areas, they may indicate high-priority problems for technological research.

The simple notion of product space is not only suggestive as a way of thinking about the available range of products and the existing state of buyer preferences; it permits an examination of two closely related and widely misunderstood marketing strategy concepts: product differentiation and market segmentation. The classic definition of differentiation is "securing a measure of control over the demand for a product by advertising or promoting differences between a product and the products of competing sellers." Segmentation, on the other hand, "consists of viewing a heterogeneous market . . . as a number of smaller homogeneous markets in response to differing product preferences among important market segments" (Smith, 1956, p. 6). The essential distinction between differentiation and segmentation is simply whether one, or more than one, marketing program is contemplated for a single marketing firm. If only one program is contemplated, the strategy is described as **differentiation**—distinguishing the products of this seller from those of others. If multiple marketing programs are contemplated, and each is designed to differentiate some subgroup of products of the firm from its own similar products, the strategy is described as **segmentation.**

Both strategies are illustrated in the product-space diagram (figure 10–1). The circled group of buyer preference points marked A reveals an opportunity for market segmentation for any one of the established producers. If a sufficient number of potential buyers have these preferences—whether or not they are now "making do" by purchasing one or another of the available products—it may be possible to develop a product that is specifically adapted to their requirements and thus reach a segment of the market that is being poorly served. Differentiation, on the other hand, may best be described as an attempt to establish a circle of attribute preference points for only one available product point; for example, to associate the preference points in circle B with only one of the product points (x*), leaving the other excluded (as shown by the dotted line). This might be accomplished by changing the product attributes (i.e., by moving x* to another place in the diagram), or by persuading potential buyers to alter their preferences (i.e., by moving the buyer preference points closer to x*), or—most imaginatively—by adding significant dimensions to the product space. Thus the seller whose products are represented by x* might change his product somewhat, establish a promotion program aimed at distinguishing it clearly from the other product in circles B, and simultaneously try to persuade the buyers within the circle that they would prefer his product's combination of attributes to the combination they previously favored. An important part of such a differentiation strategy might be the discovery (or invention!) of an additional product attribute (for example, style), so that the dimensions of product space would be altered and, in the new dimensions, the buyer preference points would cluster closely about the specific attribute combination of the seller's product.

Differentiation and segmentation, of course, are desirable marketing strategies for an enterprise only if they succeed in matching product attributes with the preferences of a substantial number of potential buyers. Differentiation in terms of irrelevant or undesired product attributes (pens that write under water!) and segmentation aimed at minute potential buyer groups are not generally the strategies most likely to result in additionnal sales and profits. Hence the importance of fundamental research on the identity and behavior of potential buyers as a basis for product planning and marketing strategy development.[2]

Product Life Cycle

Rapid changes in technology, income, and life style in the developed countries since the end of World War II have been accompanied by rapid shifts in buyer preferences among products and brands, the decline of many standard products and brands, and the emergence of new ones. As a result, product planning in many industries has come to be based on a product life-cycle concept. The essence of the life-cycle approach is that product histories are described as following a regular pattern of birth, growth, maturity, and eventual decay. The pattern may be stated in terms of total sales, gross margin or contribution, market share, or some other measure of market activity for particular item or product groups. The usual scheme of analysis is shown in figure 10–2. In a sample study of 258 prescription drug products during the period 1955–59, Cox (1967) found that 28 percent of all products substantially followed this type of life-cycle pattern, and an additional 39 percent followed a two-hill pattern, suggesting that a product's life span could be renewed at least once by appropriate modification, packaging, and advertising.[3]

The life-cycle concept suggests several important implications for product planning. If similar and short life-cycle patterns can be anticipated for products of a particular type, firms that market such products should structure their product planning processes in order to obtain a regular flow of new-product ideas over time and should introduce each new idea at an appropriate stage in the life of the preceding product. Under these circumstances, new-product planning and

2. Two important recent works on segmentation are Claycamp and Massy (1968) and Frank (1968).
3. Additional analytical and empirical results are reported in Bass (1969), Pessemier (1966), and Polli and Cook (1969).

Figure 10–2   The Product Life Cycle

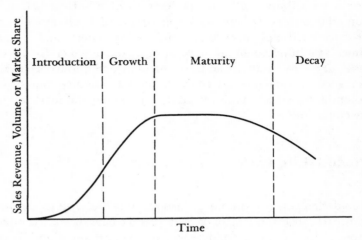

introduction becomes an essential and continuous part of normal business operations, not a once-and-for-all event that is associated with the establishment of a firm or a major reorientation in marketing activity. In order to stabilize sales volume through time, a firm that markets products with a strong life-cycle pattern must aim for a systematic mixture of new and old products, somewhat as illustrated in figure 10–3. The evidence that many firms now think in these terms includes not only the widespread discussion of life-cycle concepts in the trade literature but, more importantly, the establishment of new-product development departments and sections within the marketing organizations of many large manufacturing firms, particularly in consumer goods lines.

Establishing a normal life-cycle pattern as a reference point may also be a critical aspect of product sales forecasting. As a rule, final commitment to large-scale production and marketing of new products will be delayed, if possible, until after an extensive test marketing or initial-introduction experience has been completed. The problem traditionally associated with such postponed decisions is how to analyze the test or initial-period results. If first-season sales obtain 5 percent of the relevant market, what is the outlook for subsequent seasons? Evidently, many different pieces of information go into making a product sales forecast in a particular instance, but a standardized life-cycle model for the appropriate industry or product group can serve as an important guide to typical market development pat-

Figure 10–3   Product Sequences in the Life Cycle

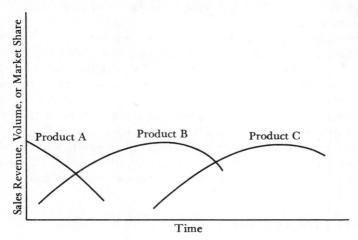

terns. Thus substantial departures from the normal pattern in the early stages can be used to predict and prepare for abnormal (favorable or unfavorable) developments later.

A third application of the life-cycle concept is made in connection with planning other marketing mix decisions (see Levitt, 1965). For example, promotion policy or price policy may vary substantially with various products within the same firm and product group, according to each product's life-cycle stage. Introduction and growth stages may be associated with heavy emphasis on promotion, and particularly on attention-getting or explanatory promotional activities; initial price policies may be designed to indicate the product's quality features. During the maturity stage, promotional activities may be substantially reduced, and may aim primarily at reminding potential buyers of the established reputation of the product, while price policies may focus primarily on the prices of competitors and on retaining customers who might be lured away by newer innovations.

Other critical relationships can be highlighted in terms of specific properties of the life-cycle pattern for an individual product. Examples of relevant questions are the following.

What length of calendar time is involved in the typical life cycle—weeks, months, seasons, or years? (Fashion products, toys, and popular books may complete their life cycles within a few months; drugs, appliances, and furniture may require several years to complete a single life-cycle pattern.)

How does the height of the life-cycle curve at various points of time compare with the break-even point in terms of production and marketing costs?

How long does the maturity phase last and what patterns of cost behavior can be anticipated during that phase? In particular, can substantial cost reductions, due to learning and the routinization of production and marketing activities, be anticipated during the maturity phase?

What is the appropriate point for discontinuing a "decaying" product, whether or not it can be replaced by a new one?

These and other important managerial questions can be clearly formulated in terms of the life-cycle model and appropriate decision rules and information systems can be developed on this basis.

Product Line and Mix

The standard analysis of product planning decisions is framed primarily in terms of cost, demand, and marketing conditions for individual products, whether considered alone or following each other in a time sequence as in the multi-product life-cycle model (figure 10–3). However, the single-product firm represents an analytical abstraction rather than a typical case. Virtually all production and marketing agencies in a developed economy deal in multiple products and therefore are concerned with the special problems that arise in multi-product management. Physical products are subject to a considerable range of variation in performance features, style, durability, and so forth, and even physically identical products may be subject to varying amounts of supplementary service and marketing effort. In particular, differences among potential customer groups may give rise to differences in production and marketing methods and costs that create sharp distinctions among units of the same basic product type.

Some marketing writers draw a sharp distinction between the "product line" of closely related items, such as variants of the same basic physical product, and the "product mix," consisting of items physically quite different, and usually having very different unit costs as well (see Stanton, 1967). This terminology may have merit for some purposes; however, it may also obscure the essential point: all product collections in the marketing system are based upon some underlying interproduct relationship, either with respect to costs or with respect to demand. The relationship on either side may be obvious and direct: two or more physically different products may inevitably result from the same production process (in which case they are termed "joint" products); two or more products may generally be demanded together (as food and beverages in restaurants). Further, particularly with respect to "shopping goods," the desire to make interproduct comparisons may be a significant feature of market demand, even though only one purchase is made from the multiproduct collection.

It may therefore be well to recall Alderson's description of the marketing process as the conversion of conglomerate resources into assortments—that is, of "natural" or cost-related collections of items into collections that are related to demand characteristics. Multiproduct activities may arise in both production and marketing at every stage of this process. In this connection, it is important to note that a multiproduct *producing* firm may or may not engage in multiproduct *marketing*. A firm will engage in multiproduct marketing only if its multiple products can be effectively marketed to the same customer groups, or if different customer groups can be most economically reached through a single marketing program embracing diverse products.

The choice of product assortments is a particularly critical decision for an enterprise engaged exclusively in marketing, for example, retailers, wholesalers, and other marketing intermediaries. The basic resources of such enterprises are financial capital, managerial skill, and location or range of potential market contact; and these resources may be applied to marketing a wide variety of products in many different ways. If we can imagine a potential marketing firm that is not yet committed to any particular types of products or services, we might describe its evolution into an active marketing unit in terms of three interrelated decisions: (1) the decision to serve a particular customer group, (2) the decision to sell the output of a particular source or sources of supply, and (3) the decision to deal in a particular line of merchandise.

Any one of these decisions might be made first, so that the others would be correspondingly limited by it. Thus a potential retailer might decide to use his capital and skill to open a store in a particular shopping area, and only subsequently look for sources of supply and apppropriate merchandise lines. Or he might choose to sell the products of a particular manufacturer, and then select his location and product assortment from those items appropriate and available within this limitation (e.g., a franchise sales-and-service operation). Or he might decide to establish, say, a men's wear store, and then seek out potentially profitable locations and supply sources. In any event, the

three characteristics—customers, suppliers, and product assortment—
define the character of the individual marketing agency.

Within the basic product decision that determines the character
of an enterprise there is room for wide variation in product assortment and associated services. In this connection it is customary to
distinguish merchandise **depth**—the range of similar products that
are differentiated by quality, style, special features, and so forth—
from merchandise **breadth**—the range of distinctly different products.
Using this distinction, we may identify specialty marketing agencies
with deep but narrow merchandise lines (e.g., large shoe stores), other
agencies that may offer broad product assortments with few variants
within each major product category (e.g., convenience food stores), and
large general-line agencies that offer both depth and breadth of product assortment within a major merchandise grouping, such as groceries, drugs, clothing, and the like.

Add or Drop Policies

Within an ongoing marketing enterprise, the assortment problem generally takes the form of discrete decisions to add or drop specific products or product groups. Large food retailers may stock up to 10,000
different items within a single store, and many lines of wholesale and
retail trade deal with several thousand items on a regular basis.
Obviously, the aggregate of choices that might be made within this
range of product alternatives defies systematic analysis. Therefore it is
customary to develop highly simplified rules of thumb to assist management in identifying items for discontinuation or for addition to
the assortment. The basic idea incorporated in such rules of thumb is
that the principal scarce productive factor within the enterprise should
yield an acceptable minimum level of revenues or profits in every possible use. For example, floor space or shelf space is frequently the
principal scarce factor in a retail store; therefore a typical rule of thumb
for retail assortment decisions is a minimum total revenue or gross
margin per space unit (per square foot or linear foot of shelf facings).
Items that yield less than this minimum will be candidates for discontinuation or reduction in space assignment. Items that yield more
than the minimum may be candidates for expansion or special display.
Potential new items will be compared with existing stock choices on
the basis of their potential contributions per unit of space.[4]

4. For an application of this rule of thumb, see Cairns (1962).

This kind of add-or-drop policy is a typical example of a product decision rule based on marginal analysis. Such a policy is a wholly acceptable and efficient way of making a large number of small decisions, each of which is substantially independent of the others. However, this type of decision rule fails, at least in its simple forms, when it is applied to large product groups in the aggregate or to individual items that have a special role in determining the character of the marketing agency. Thus a department store with a large furniture department is a substantially different kind of marketing agency than another store of similar size that carries little or no furniture. The former will attract a different group of customers—not only to its furniture but to other departments as well—than the latter. Thus marginal product decisions made with respect to one department may have an impact on the sales of other departments, and may eventually affect the total character of an enterprise. Further, some products essential to the identification of a particular type of marketing agency may violate all the rules of thumb, and yet be exempt from discontinuation. Food staples (flour, salt, sugar), for example, rarely yield a significant wholesale or retail profit but nevertheless are essential product elements of the product mix of any enterprise engaged in general-line grocery marketing.

Product Identification and Branding

In a developed economy, few products other than raw materials and fresh foods are marketed without a specific designation of their source. And most manufactured products are branded, if only for identification. The managerial decisions that arise with respect to branding are not, therefore, generally made in terms of whether or not an identifying brand should be placed on the products of the enterprise. Instead, these decisions are made on the basis of such questions as (1) what the specific brand should be and how it should be displayed, (2) what firm or organization should have control over the brand, and (3) whether brand identification, as such, can be—or should be—made an important feature of the product in the eyes of the potential buyers.

Apart from its legal aspects, the problem of brand naming is largely an aspect of advertising and promotion. One seeks a name that is recognizable, appropriate, and not already in use by others. Major consumer-goods marketing firms in the United States have adopted diverse policies with respect to the mixture of brand and company names on their products. Some firms—Procter and Gamble, American

Home Products, and General Motors (to name only a few)—have historically followed a practice of product branding. Individual and unrelated names are applied to each of their products, and little or no attempt is made to associate the products with each other or with the parent company. In sharp contrast are the company-name merchandisers—Borden, General Electric, and others—who place a single brand name on all their products and omit or minimize subsidiary product designations.

The legal status of brand naming is a special aspect of the right to ownership of ideas. Brand-name rights are specifically protected in the United States under the Lanham Act of 1946, which permits the registration of names and other identifying devices with the U.S. Patent Office. However, the responsibility for defending brand-name rights against infringers rests with the brand owner, and legal rights to a brand name may be lost if infringement is tolerated. The International Patent, Trademark and Copyright Agreement provides similar protection for brand designations in international trade.

Managerial decisions concerning control over brand names are related to problems of overall control within marketing organization and the marketing channel. Some brand names are controlled by trade associations or cooperatives, which include large numbers of firms that operate at the same level of the production-marketing process. Other brands are controlled by manufacturers, and still others by distributors who obtain merchandise from one or many supply sources and place their own brand on it. Brand-name control is generally both a sign and a means of control over other marketing variables, particularly price and promotion policy.

The significance of actual brand-name choice and of the locus of brand-name control within the marketing system depends upon whether brand identification is an important product feature from the viewpoint of buyers and final users. Brand identification may be a guarantee of performance quality over the long run, an evidence of appropriate style or taste, an indicator of fair prices or good values, or a sign of compatibility in style or function among similarly branded products. On the other hand, brands—as such—may be essentially trivial for buyers' decision making; and even extensive promotional efforts may not be sufficient to cause buyers to react differently to branded versus unbranded, or differently branded, products. There may, however, be a sharp distinction between buyer attitudes toward *all* products with well-known brand names as a group, as compared to other items of the same product type, even when individual brand names, as such, make little impact. The development of buyer response to specific brand names depends heavily on promotional activity and on the continuity of products, brands, and marketing practices over time.

Summary

The output results of economic activity are **products, services, wastes, and nuisances.** The distinction among these outputs depends entirely upon demand. Both technological and marketing research are used .to discover ways to convert wastes and low-value outputs into saleable and higher-value products. Most business enterprises engaged in marketing provide physical products *and* services in varied combinations. Therefore a general discussion of product policies includes services and product-service combinations as well.

Marketing costs, organizational arrangements, and product policy alternatives vary substantially among product categories that differ in physical characteristics, value, and uses. In general, the greater the value involved in marketing transactions, the greater the cost of their associated marketing activities. Similarly, the less frequent the transactions and the lower the level of product knowledge of potential buyers, the most costly (generally speaking) the required marketing activities. On the other hand, purchase convenience and minimum marketing costs may constitute extremely important product features for products of low value, frequent purchase, and high familiarity.

The product strategies of a firm are frequently described in terms of **differentiation** and **segmentation.** The former term means distinguishing the output of a particular enterprise from that of others; the latter term means distinguishing among potential buyer groups and varying product characteristics and other marketing-mix variables in order to adapt to the characteristics of each group. Of course, under particular circumstances, neither differentiation nor segmentation may be a more profitable marketing strategy than simply offering a standardized product to the mass market.

A product's **life-cycle** depicts its typical sales history in terms of a regular sequence of introduction, growth, maturity, and decay. Estimation of typical life-cycles in particular product groups, as well as experimentation with techniques for prolonging the maturity stage and planning for regular product replacement, provide important insight into product policy problems and their solutions.

All marketing enterprises of any importance are engaged in multiproduct operations to some degree, and the choice of appropriate merchandise and service combinations is a significant dimension of product policy. The fundamental product-mix decision determines the character of an enterprise, but within any enterprise category there is considerable room for differences in the amount and character of product variety. Systematic **add-or-drop** rules are frequently employed as a guide to routine product-mix decisions; and these rules are usually based upon simple marginal decision criteria.

The choice of source or brand-identification policies and specific names is an aspect of product policy that is closely related to promotion planning and strategy.

References

Alderson, Wroe. *Marketing Behavior and Executive Action.* Irwin, 1957.

Bass, Frank M. "A New-Product Growth Model for Consumer Durables." *Management Science,* Vol. 15, No. 5, January 1969.

Brems, Hans. *Product Equilibrium under Monopolistic Competition.* Harvard Universty Press, 1951.

Bucklin, Louis P. "Retail Strategy and the Classification of Consumer Goods." *Journal of Marketing,* Vol. 27, No. 1, January 1963.

Cairns, James P. "Suppliers, Retailers, and Shelf Space." *Journal of Marketing,* Vol. 26, No. 3, July 1962.

Claycamp, Henry J., and William F. Massy. "A Theory of Market Segmentation." *Journal of Marketing Research,* Vol. 5, No. 4, November 1968.

Cox, William E. "Product Life Cycles as Marketing Models." *Journal of Business,* Vol. 40, No. 4, October 1967.

Frank, Ronald E. "Market Segmentation Research: Findings and Implications." In *Applications of the Sciences in Marketing Management,* eds. Frank M. Bass *et al.,* Wiley, 1968.

Levitt, Theodore. "Exploit the Product Life Cycle." *Harvard Business Review,* Vol. 43, November–December 1965.

Pessemier, Edgar A. *New-Product Decisions: An Analytical Approach.* McGraw-Hill, 1966.

Polli, Rolando, and Victor Cook. "Validity of the Product Life Cycle." *Journal of Business,* Vol. 42 (October 1969), 385–400.

Smith, Wendell R. "Product Differentiation and Market Segmentation as Alternative Marketing Strategies." *Journal of Marketing,* Vol. 21, No. 1, July 1956.

Stanton, William J. *Fundamentals of Marketing,* 2nd ed. McGraw-Hill, 1967.

11

Marketing Communication and Promotion

Buyers, sellers, and marketing intermediaries engage in marketing communication to acquaint each other with purchase and selling alternatives, to persuade each other to trade, and to negotiate the terms of individual transactions. The major portion of marketing communication in an enterprise economy is conducted by potential sellers who attempt to promote their particular products and services for purchase by potential buyers; hence the term **promotion** is frequently used to encompass all phases of marketing communication.[1] However, a substantial and important part of marketing communication is also accounted for by buyers, particularly industrial and public agency buyers, who publicize purchase specifications and advertise for proposals and bids, and communication of a purely informational character may be undertaken by government units, trade associations, and other nonprofit agencies within the economy. Thus the overall scope of marketing communication is much broader than the promotional activities of sellers alone, and the content of this chapter, which is presented primarily in terms of sellers' promotional activity, could be

1. A survey of this entire field is presented in Brink and Kelley (1963).

rephrased to emphasize marketing communication by buyers or auxiliary agencies.

The Communication Paradigm

Communication is the transmission of a *message* from a *sender* to a
receiver. The message may be simple or complex; its content may be
factual or analytical, or it may be primarily attitudinal, persuasive, or
artistic. (This sentence is itself a message from the writer to the
reader; it illustrates, by example, the nature of a simple message.) Messages cannot ordinarily be transmitted from one mind to another
without the use of some communication medium: speech, other audi-
ble sounds (e.g., music), gestures, writing, pictures, films, and so forth.
Therefore the simple paradigm of the communications process shows
the message contained in some communications medium during transmission from sender to receiver, as follows:

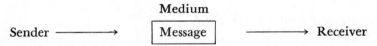

Medium

Sender ⟶ Message ⟶ Receiver

Reference to this simple paradigm is an easy way to keep the
essential features of marketing communication, or any other communications activity, in mind. One obvious point is that the message
receiver is an integral part of àny communication process: mere message sending is *not* communication. A second point is the necessity for
compatibility between the medium and the message, a point that has
become familiar in the popular cliché "the medium *is* the message."
Everyday communications activities illustrate the essential link between message content and means of transmission. You cannot *tell*
someone how to drive a car, you have to *show* him; but you cannot
show someone why you hold certain political views, you have to *tell*
him.

Because most messages have to be transmitted by means of sounds
and symbols (words, pictures, and the like), many writers on communications theory stress the importance of the **message-encoding**
activity by the sender and the **decoding** activity by the receiver. This
phase of the communication process, however, does not concern us
here in any detail, although the encoding-decoding problem is a
critical aspect of creative work in marketing communications.

The marketing communications messages that most senders desire to convey are both general and complicated: the product is very good (general) and it has many physical attributes and performance features (complicated). In order to make this type of message both transmissible and understandable, extensive simplification and encoding are required. If one tried to acquaint potential buyers with product quality and performance features by compiling a comprehensive, descriptive list, with all the appropriate illustrations and explanations, one might well find that the message was too lengthy and bulky to be readily transmitted and that potential message receivers were simply unable to understand and utilize this abundance of detail. Therefore the message sender may distill his message into a few highly generalized statements, examples, and illustrations so that they can be both easily transmitted through the available media and readily received and comprehended by the intended recipients. The test of successful communication is whether or not the message receiver actually receives the same thought or impression that the message sender intended to convey.

Planning a Promotion Policy

The four essential steps for developing a promotion policy for an enterprise or agency concerned with marketing a particular collection of products and services are:

1. Identifying the appropriate groups of message recipients (i.e., the potential buyers or users of the products and services)
2. Developing relevant and effective messages for conveyance to these groups
3. Selecting appropriate means of transmitting these messages to the intended receivers
4. Determining the necessary costs associated with promotional activities, and the corresponding revenues, so that a comprehensive promotion policy can be selected and promotional activity can be integrated into the total production and marketing effort of the enterprise.

It is worth noting that these tasks are not uniquely associated with profit-making firms; public agencies engaged in promoting the products, services, business locations, or other features of their respective jurisdictions face the same set of decision problems.

The problem of market identification is a fundamental aspect of marketing planning and management, and thus is not a special or unique aspect of promotional activity. However, if potential buyers and users are not homogeneous, or if basically similar customer groups cannot be reached by the same communication media, then the explicit identification of groups of intended message receivers (i.e., market segmentation) for promotional purposes may be necessary.

Given the product-service offering and the intended message recipients, the development of appropriate messages is a combination of analysis and art. Economic and demographic data, as well as studies of buyer behavior, attitudes, and ways of thinking, provide necessary background for the development of creative promotional ideas. However, the actual content of promotional themes—words and phrases, illustrations, and sales approaches—depends heavily on the insight and artistic skill of individual marketing personnel and promotion specialists. The final selection of promotional messages can be importantly aided by sample interviews, test-market results, and follow-up studies, but there is no substitute for the imaginative and creative element in designing and executing promotional messages and programs.

Several different types of promotional activity can be used to convey marketing messages, and advertising alone offers an almost incredible range of media choices. The principal promotional activities are described briefly in the following section, and the problems of selecting advertising media are discussed in the section "Media Selection Criteria." The problem of overall promotion budgeting and the integration of promotional activity with the total marketing program of an enterprise is considered in the final section of this chapter, as well as in the analysis of marketing-mix decisions in chapter 9.

Promotional Activities

A critical feature of promotion policy planning is the selection of appropriate types and combinations of promotional activities in order to accomplish specific marketing goals. Promotional activities use personal and impersonal media to transmit the promotion message to intended receivers, and thus they play a central functional role in the communications process. In addition, these activities comprise the principal cost categories in the promotion budget. Expenditures for market research and creative work—that is, for market identification and message development—are typically very small in comparison with expenditures for transmitting the appropriate messages to the selected potential buyers.

Four principal types of promotional activity are generally recognized in marketing planning.

1. Advertising: the use of commercial communications media to transmit a single marketing message to multiple receivers. (The remaining sections of this chapter place primary emphasis on advertising planning and budgeting.)
2. Personal selling: the use of direct personal contact to convey marketing messages.
3. Other sales promotion activities: displays, distribution of free samples, trade shows, and so forth. These activities generally are not aimed at making direct or immediate sales but rather at providing a background of information and experience upon which future sales contacts can be based.
4. Public relations of a more general sort: activities that are not aimed at marketing objectives as such but rather at the public image of an enterprise or organization, its contribution to community life, and similar goals. Many public relations activities cannot be described as promotional in a narrow sense. That is, they are not intended to promote specific things, but they may use the same promotional techniques and personnel and may overlap with more specifically promotional activities in many instances.

Personal Selling and Advertising

The two largest elements in total promotional expenditures in the economy are personal selling and advertising. These two types of promotional activity are alternatives that may be used in various combinations in particular promotional programs, and there are sharp differences in their relative importance in the promotional efforts of different firms and industries. In consumer goods industries, promotional expenditures are typically weighted toward mass media advertising. The principal reasons for this are that (1) it is ordinarily appropriate for consumer goods marketers to send the same promotional messages to large numbers of potential message receivers, and (2) the average value of consumer goods transactions is relatively low, so that only small expenditures on promotion *per transaction* are economically justified.

Personal selling contrasts with mass media advertising in three important ways: (1) Each sales contact is unique; and it is possible, therefore, to adapt the basic marketing message to the particular interests and requirements of each message receiver. (2) Personal sales calls can be an important source of market information for the message *sender,* so that communication becomes a two-way rather than a one-way process. (3) Personal sales calls *may* be joined with order taking and even with completing transactions, and thus physical distribution and promotion are combined.

Because of these three special features, personal selling is more important than advertising in industries that have the following characteristics: (*a*) highly complex products and marketing messages, so that appropriate information cannot be conveyed by mass media; (*b*) great diversity among customers, so that sending a single promotion message to many receivers is not appropriate; and (*c*) high average values per transaction, so that high promotional expenditures per transaction are justified. Industrial equipment marketing depends almost entirely on personal selling effort, as does the marketing of real estate and insurance. Examples of the categories of relatively large personal selling expenditures in consumer goods marketing are automobiles, furniture, and (in order to influence marketing intermediaries: doctors and pharmacists) prescription drugs.

Most promotional programs involve mixtures of personal and impersonal communications media that are aimed at different message receivers within the marketing system and at the same receivers in a particular time sequence. Consumer goods marketing agencies depend heavily on personal sales contacts to stimulate product availability throughout the distribution channel, and industrial goods marketers make extensive use of industrial advertising, mailing pieces, and catalogs to prepare potential customers for personal sales calls and to provide sales reminders and ways of placing orders in the interim between personal contacts. As with many other aspects of marketing planning, the development of promotional programs is not a choice between extremes but rather a choice among many possible combinations of complementary and supportive activities. In addition, it should be noted that the use of an unusual promotional technique may be an important and effective form of marketing innovation. Thus the choice of promotional activities that are quite different from those that would ordinarily be expected on the basis of conventional analysis *may* result in a substantial increase in market impact and sales.

Advertising Planning

Many aspects of promotional activity, and particularly personal selling and sales force administration, are closely interwoven with the physical distribution and marketing-channel policies of an enterprise.

Mass media advertising, however—although necessarily integrated with all other elements of the marketing mix—gives rise to such a large portion of total marketing expenditures and such a specialized group of decision problems that a detailed consideration of advertising planning is required. The principal topics discussed are a firm's goals in advertising, advertising media characteristics and selection criteria, and the problem of planning total advertising expenditures and appraising their effectiveness.[2]

Advertising Goals

A decision to advertise, followed by the choice of a particular level of advertising expenditures and a combination and sequence of advertising media, implies the existence of certain goals or purposes toward which the advertising is directed (see Colley, 1964). Similarly, an *ex post* appraisal that a particular advertising activity has been successful (or unsuccessful) means that there must be some criteria by which its effects can be evaluated. How can the principal goals of advertising activity be described and the success or failure of individual advertising programs be appraised? [3]

It is easy to say that private business firms advertise in order to make sales; however, this is not very informative. Most firms could make some sales even if they did not advertise, and many firms do precisely that. Development of an advertising plan requires a judgment that sales will be greater, more regular, more certain, more profitable, or in some other way more desirable if advertising is provided than if it is not.

Many advertising activities are developed and evaluated in terms of cognitive and attitudinal goals. For example, an advertising program may be designed to make a certain group of potential buyers aware of the existence of a product, or to cause them to remember the product over time, or to create favorable attitudes and associations. These are all valid aims of advertising planning. Yet the ultimate purpose to be served must inevitably be stated in terms of sales, and cognitive and attitudinal goals are simply intermediate steps toward an eventual sales objective. After all, recognition, memory, and even

2. Two recent surveys of the problems and managerial practices in advertising are Robinson and Luck (1964) and Dalbey, Gross, and Wind (1968).

3. This discussion focuses exclusively on marketing goals related to sales. Advertising activities aimed at public relations and other nonsales goals are not considered here, although they may be very important in particular advertising programs.

highly favorable attitudes are of little economic value, and hence would not justify substantial expenditures—unless the persons who hold these attitudes are potential buyers of goods and services. It is its essential connection with sales that distinguishes advertising in marketing from other mass communication entertainment, information, and propagandistic activities.

It is useful to summarize the principal goals of advertising in the business firm in terms of the familiar demand-schedule concept of elementary economics. We do not imply that advertising planning is normally—or should be—cast in these terms. They simply provide a convenient way of identifying and distinguishing some important goals that seem to be reflected in actual advertising plans.

Advertising to create a specific demand (through differentiation). The demand schedule for an individual firm or product in undifferentiated competition is generally shown as a horizontal line at the market price, as in figure 11–1(a). Four circumstances are summarized in such a diagram: (1) the firm is one of many small units in the market; (2) its products are very similar to those of its competitors; hence (3) it cannot offer a sufficient quantity for sale to bring the market price down, and (4) it cannot attract any customers at a price above the market level. A principal objective of advertising by individual firms is to free themselves from this market situation, to insulate themselves against the risks of the market and to create a basis for managerial discretion with respect to price and other marketing policy variables. Product and marketing channel decisions are also, of course, important elements in a differentiation strategy. However, the identification of products and the advertising of product names and features is an indispensable strategy ingredient.

Advertising to shift demand. Advertising to shift demand is intended to permit larger quantities to be sold at each possible price level [see figure 11–1(b)]. This goal—increasing sales possibilities at all prices—is probably the most commonly held idea of the purpose of advertising. And, indeed, many advertising campaigns are initiated with this goal in mind, and specific sales increases are often cited as evidence of advertising effectiveness. However, it is important to note that advertising with the intent of shifting demand for an individual firm is a feasible goal only for products for which a differentiated demand is already established. Thus some significant questions with respect to a demand-shifting advertising program are: Where are additional sales expected to come from? Is it anticipated that

Figure 11–1   Demand Diagrams Illustrating Principal Goals of Advertising: (a) Form Demand Through Differentiation; (b) Shift Demand; (c) Increase; (1) or Decrease (2) Demand Elasticity; (d) Stabilize Demand

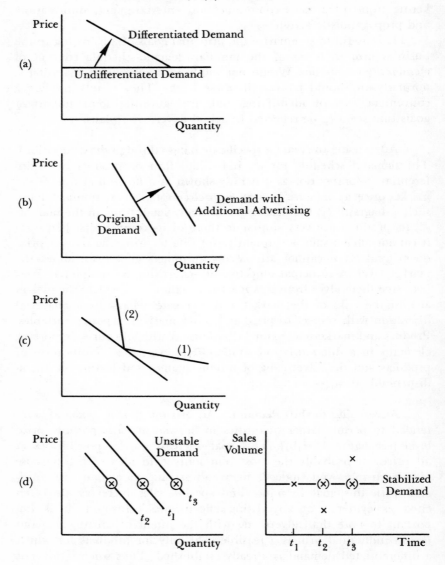

total market demand will expand and the firm will retain its proportional share? (If so, what is to prevent new or established competitors from taking most of the increase?) Or is it anticipated that sales will be taken away from competitors? (If so, what are the competitors likely to do in response?) In either event, is it anticipated that additional sales will be made to established groups of customers or that new buyer groups will be attracted as a result of the advertising?

The difficulty in answering these questions—and the impossibility that all firms, including banks and savings institutions, can simultaneously expand their activities through advertising—suggests that shifting demand at all prices is perhaps not the most common purpose of advertising activity in the economy. (Or if this *is* the purpose, marketing managers must be content with a very low level of accomplishment.)

Advertising to change demand elasticity.   A special kind of demand shift that might be made the goal of advertising planning is a change in elasticity, a term that refers to the responsiveness of total sales to changes in marketing variables, particularly prices (see appendix to chapter 7). As part of an overall marketing strategy, it might be desirable for a firm to try to change the responsiveness of its customers to price changes in either direction. For example, a *decrease* in elasticity might be desirable if a price increase were contemplated, or if it were anticipated that the prices of competitive products were going to be reduced. On the other hand, an *increase* in price elasticity might be desirable if one's own price were to be reduced, or if small and temporary price reductions were being offered for promotional purposes. The use of special price promotions in grocery product lines is a familiar example of the latter practice. An unadvertised price change of less than 10 cents per unit is apt to pass unnoticed by the majority of shoppers; hence the special newspaper announcement, the window and end-of-counter display, and the large bright label saying "6¢ off." Devices such as these are aimed at making demand more elastic than it would otherwise be in order to expand sales substantially on the basis of small price reductions.

Advertising to stabilize demand.   The marketing of most types of products, and particularly of individual brands of consumer goods, is conducted in an environment that is full of potentially destabilizing forces. Purchase quantities vary widely within short calendar periods and climatic or fashion seasons; tastes change with changes in popular interests and life styles; new products appear and competitive activities by other marketers upset established marketing patterns. As part of its total effort to reduce risks and to gain any benefits that may arise from regularity and continuity of operations, firms may desire to stabilize demand conditions. Such stabilizing activities may aim either at reducing some observed pattern of periodic instability or simply at increasing the probability that favorable demand conditions will prevail in the face of destabilizing but as yet unknown future events. (The contrast between stable and unstable demand situations is illustrated in figure 11–1(d).) Advertising that is focused on such attitudinal goals as "brand loyalty" and such specific sales goals as "increasing repeat purchases" is essentially aimed at stabilizing demand. The prominence of such goals in the current literature and in advertising planning discussions suggests that stabilizing demand and insulating the market position of an individual firm and product against unfavorable developments is, in fact, one of the most important purposes of promotional activity at the present time.

No one of these four goals of advertising policy is necessarily desirable for a particular enterprise, nor are the goals themselves mutually exclusive. The identification of goals in this general way, however, provides some basis for planning and appraising particular advertising campaign strategies, media combinations, and expenditures.

Principal Advertising Media

Total reported expenditures for advertising in the United States were in excess of $17 billion in 1968, more than 2 percent of the total gross national product, and advertising expenditures have increased as much or more in proportion to increases in total economic activity almost every year since the relevant data were first collected. Several firms spend more than $200 million per year on advertising, although these large expenditures vary from less than 2 percent (General Motors) to more than 10 percent (Procter & Gamble) of their total sales values. All these expenditures are made primarily to place advertising messages in commercial advertising media, of which eight principal categories are usually identified.

Newspapers. Still the largest class of media expenditures, accounting for about 30 percent of the U.S. total, newspapers are characterized by their broad and diverse audiences within their individual geographic circulation areas. Newspapers are also distinguished from many other media in that their advertising content is a positive feature for many audience members, who seek **out and** read advertisements for informational purposes.

Magazines. Household and farm magazines have accounted for about 8 percent of total advertising media expenditures in recent years, a figure that has declined over the long term partially as a result of the rise of television expenditures. Magazines are extremely diverse, ranging from general consumer and news magazines with very broad nationwide audiences to specialized publications aimed at residents of particular localities and at narrow interest groups. The products featured in magazine advertising generally acquire the qualitative images associated with the magazines in which the advertisements are carried. Magazine advertising, like newspaper advertising, may be of intrinsic interest and value to particular groups of readers.

Business and trade publications. These media are distinguished from general newspapers and magazines because of their special audience and, hence, their suitability for industrial goods and services advertising. They account for about 5 percent of total advertising media expenditures. An important factor in the steady expansion of expenditures in these media has been the rapidly rising cost of the alternative promotional activity for industrial goods—personal sales calls.

Direct mail. Direct mail offers the highest degree of selectivity with respect to the recipient of advertising messages since each mailing piece can be directed to a specific individual or firm, or to a particular location in a geographic area by means of "occupant" mailings. It is also the most flexible form of advertising with respect to both timing and level of expenditures. Mailing pieces can be as simple or elaborate as the advertiser wishes and any number of pieces can be mailed at any time. Expenditures for direct mail advertising have risen steadily in recent years to about 15 percent of total media expenditures, but there are two significant limitations on their continued growth. One of these is the rising cost of postal service; the other is the competition of the increasing number of mailing pieces for the attention of each direct mail receiver.

Television. Over the past twenty years television has brought dramatic changes in advertising and all other forms of mass communication throughout the world. Television advertising now accounts for about 16 percent of total media expenditures, and this figure has continued to rise gradually over time. However, recent expenditure increases are more largely due to rising costs and rates than to increases in the total amount of TV advertising or programming.

The early growth pattern of TV advertising followed the nationwide network format previously established for radio. The minimum size of network advertising purchases was extremely large by comparison with minimum expenditures in other media, and the very large and diverse potential audience was considered inappropriate for many products and firms. TV broadcasters have adapted to this situation by making "spot" advertising available on individual network stations so that an advertiser can reach selected geographic areas within the network programming format. The result has been an increase in the flexibility of TV advertising, with respect to both cost and time-and-place combinations, and a corresponding shift in TV advertising expenditures toward spot rather than network advertising. In addition, TV programming has become substantially separated from TV advertising, so that programming decisions now rest primarily with the networks and stations, and advertisers simply place their materials within the available time periods.

Radio.   After the introduction of TV in the early 1950s it appeared that radio might die out as a major advertising medium. However, during the 1960s radio proved to be a lively and innovative communications medium, and now it accounts for about 5 percent of total advertising expenditures. The secret of this success has been the establishment of large numbers of local radio stations, each aimed at special audience groups. Nationwide radio programming and advertising is now associated almost exclusively with international and national news and sports coverage, and the great bulk of radio advertising is now accounted for by marketing messages aimed at specific local audiences. The relatively low cost of radio station operations, the universal availability of radio sets (counting car radios, there is more than one radio set per capita in the United States), and the ease with which radio listening can be combined with other activities have served to maintain radio as a significant advertising medium.

Outdoor advertising.   Highway billboard and other outdoor advertising has tended to decline somewhat, and now accounts for less than 2 percent of total advertising expenditures, partially because of government restrictions on the construction of advertising boards along certain types of highways. Outdoor advertising continues to be an important medium within densely populated metropolitan areas, although there is some likelihood that public policy developments will restrict its expansion here as well.

Miscellaneous media.   Some 20 percent of total advertising expenditures is accounted for by transit facility advertising, point-of-purchase and display materials, local and regional periodicals of various types not covered by nationwide reporting services, skywriting and other "happenings," handbills (the earliest form of print advertising), and other promotional techniques. Some of these probably should not be considered mass media in a strict sense, and total expenditures in these categories are only rough estimates at best. However, it is important to remember that the full range of advertising media choices includes this wide array of activities, which are subject to very different cost conditions and capable of achieving extremely diverse effects on their potential audiences.

Media Selection Criteria

Marketing agencies engaged in mass media advertising are confronted not only by choices among the principal media categories but also by a wide range of specific media alternatives within each category, and by a limitless variety of media combinations and sequences. The casual observer is most impressed by the qualitative differences among media—a television program is so unlike a newspaper!—but for purposes of advertising planning it is necessary to establish some bases for comparison among media so that appropriate selections and combinations can be determined.[4] There are three principal bases for such comparisons.

Audience size and characteristics.   Advertising media differ very substantially with respect to (a) the total number and the characteristics of the individuals and households that may be reached through each medium and (b) the accuracy with which the number and characteristics of these units may be identified in advance. Some forms of advertising (direct mail) can be sent to selected message receivers in any number desired by the advertiser; other media simply aim at broadly classified groups of potential message receivers, whether few or numerous, and many of whom may not come into contact with a particular

---

4. For a review of computer-based techniques for comparing and evaluating media, see Gensch (1968).

advertising message. The potential audiences of magazines and newspapers, for example, may be identified from subscriber lists, although there is no certainty that each subscriber will observe each advertisement, nor even consult each issue of the publication. On the other hand, potential audiences for broadcast media can be identified only in a very general way—all persons with a radio or a television set who live within the reception range of a given station—and the size of the audience that actually receives a particular advertising message varies widely even within short time periods.

With respect to audience characteristics, media differ in their ability to reach particular audience groups (housewives, executives, teen-agers, etc.) and in the extent to which their audiencies are homogeneous or heterogeneous. Audiences may be homogeneous with respect to very general characteristics—upper-income families, for example—or they may be identified by some highly specialized criterion, such as the pursuit of a particular hobby or recreation activity.

Of course, the desirability of various audience sizes and characteristics depends upon the particular products and services being advertised. Large audiences—and particularly large *potential* but elusive audiences—are not necessarily more desirable than smaller ones. Carefully selected and identified audiences, similarly, are not necessarily more desirable than more diverse and anonymous ones. It is interesting to note that some very specialized audiences may be reached most effectively through broad-audience media, because the audience members lack distinguishing characteristics by which they can be identified in advance. An example is suggested by the television advertising of Xerox Corporation, a leading manufacturer of copying machines. No doubt, only a small percentage of Xerox's television program audience consists of potential copying machine buyers; however, it may well be that a large percentage of all potential copying machine buyers and users are reached by this form of advertising. If people who might purchase or use a product have nothing *else* in common, they will probably have to be reached by broad-audience media.

Advertising costs.   Advertising media may be compared both with respect to the total cost of each use of the medium to a message sender, which we may describe as the cost per message *sent,* and with respect to the average cost of each message *received.* The latter, of course, is the cost per message sent divided by the number of receivers. Both of these cost factors are influenced by technological considerations and audience size. The actual production cost associated with a page of magazine advertising is likely to be greater than the production cost associated with a similar page of newspaper advertising. In addition, media that have large audiences tend to charge higher rates per unit of media time or space (i.e., higher rates per message *sent*) than media with small audiences. Hence the cost of a one-time full-page advertisement in a national magazine will usually be greater than the cost of a similar advertisement in a newspaper because of differences in production costs and the larger audience reached by the magazine, which makes its space more valuable. On the other hand, the cost per message *received* (i.e., the total cost divided by the number of audience units) may be lower in the medium with the greater total cost. Within each principal media category, the quoted advertising rates are generally higher per time or space unit, and lower per audience units, in large-audience media than in small-audience media. Large metropolitan daily newspapers, for example, quote higher rates per page and lower rates per thousand circulation than small local papers. National consumer magazines differ in the same way from regional and special-interest magazines.

Media also differ substantially with respect to their flexibility of use by individual advertisers. In some media (newspapers and direct mail) the frequency of advertising and the amount of expenditures may easily be varied by each advertiser over a very wide range. In other instances it is necessary to choose among large and discontinuous expenditure commitments and to adapt the periodicity of an advertising program to regular publication and broadcasting schedules.

Impact. The qualitative differences among media are taken into account in considering their communications impact on the audience (Lucas and Britt, 1963). Can the desired message be transmitted and received over different media? Does it require illustration, demonstration, or extensive explanation? What differences are there among media in the clarity of presenting the message? In believability? In memorability? Is the message receiver able to refer to the message again, or to retain a reminder of it for future use? Is the audience able to scan the medium for material of special interest or must it either receive or avoid all messages? The answers to these and similar questions are indicators of media impact; and impact differences are especially important in determining the combinations and sequences of media to be incorporated into total advertising programs. For example, media with a strong attention-getting quality may be used to introduce a new product line or advertising theme; then media of greater explanatory capacity and high believability may be employed to provide details and persuasive evidence; finally, reminder media may be used to keep the name and principal characteristics of the product alive in the minds of potential buyers.

Promotion Budgeting: Expenditures and Effectiveness

No aspect of marketing management is subject to greater controversy than the budgeting of promotion expenditures, particularly expenditures for mass media advertising. The marginal decision rule, of course, is very simple: Continue to spend for promotion, and for each promotional activity, until the cost increments equal the revenue increments. This rule may be usefully applied in such decisions as determining the appropriate amount of expenditures for individual promotional activities or individual advertising media, the allocation of a specific total budget among media, and the allocation of expenditures among potential customer groups or market areas. However, the multiplicity of goals, the variety of promotional activities that might be undertaken, the complexity of their effects, and the diversity of themes, methods, and creative content that might be selected present insuperable difficulties for a comprehensive analysis. As a result, most promotional budgeting decisions tend to rely on conceptually less satisfying, but operationally simpler, approaches. Among these, two stereotypes may be noted. One is the production (sometimes called the task) approach to promotional budgeting; the other is based upon rules of thumb with respect to the ratio of advertising expenditures to sales revenues.

The production or task approach requires the definition of a specific task or goal that the promotional program is intended to accomplish. Thus one might aim for recognition of the product name or its qualitative features by some percentage of the total potential buying population; or one might aim for a specific number of new customers, or a specific share of total market sales, within a specific time period. An analysis of media, audiences, impact, and cost is then made to determine one or more detailed plans for accomplishing this task. In this approach, promotional activities are treated as factors of production, and the defined task or goal is the output that results from their use.

An almost opposite approach is represented by the use of routine percentage-of-sales rules as guides for promotional budgeting. The ratio of advertising expenditures to sales varies widely among industries, from well below 1 percent in industrial goods and raw materials to 20 or 30 percent in cosmetics and toiletries. Even within broad industry categories, ratios for individual firms vary widely. (One reason for this is that the number of products and brands also varies among firms, and firms that have many product lines tend to have higher advertising budgets than firms with fewer products but the same sales volume.) The logic involved in using these historical records as a guide to planning is that an industry's average advertising level, and a firm's past advertising activity in relation to this average, establish a "normal" level of advertising expenditures for planning purposes (see Weinberg, 1960). If a firm continues its normal policy, and other firms do likewise, advertising should contribute to the stability of the firm's market position over time. If, on the other hand, an increased market share is desired, the historic data provide a reference point for a planned increase in advertising activity.

In actual budgeting decisions, task and percentage-of-sales approaches are combined to establish expenditure levels. The former serves as a guide to the expenditure levels necessary for accomplishing specific results. Whether these results are worth the cost must be determined in the final budgeting process. Historic patterns, on the other hand, indicate the minimum expenditure levels necessary for maintaining relative market positions, if unusually aggressive activity by competitors is not anticipated. Of course, promotion budgeting, and all other aspects of marketing planning, require effective integration of the major marketing mix variables, on one hand, with the detailed articulation of the promotion program—activities, media, themes, and creative content—on the other.

Summary

Communication, an essential element in the operation of markets, is a highly developed activity in modern marketing. The essence of communication is the transmission of a message from a sender to a receiver. Apart from telepathy and other extrasensory processes, communication requires the encoding of messages in sounds, signs, and symbols that are transmitted to the receiver and decoded by him. The critical aspects of communication are the choice of messages and codes and the choice of media by which the encoded messages are to be conveyed. In personal communication, the process of encoding and transmission occurs almost simultaneously; in nonpersonal communications, however, each step constitutes a discrete, although highly interrelated, problem.

Promotional communication in marketing involves identifying the potential message receivers, developing messages, selecting appropriate media combinations and sequences, and determining total expenditures. The two major promotional activities are advertising and personal selling, which may be used separately or in combinations. The choice of promotional activities depends primarily on the number of message receivers to be reached and their similarities and differences. Large numbers of very similar message receivers can appropriately be sent the same message through mass media advertising; smaller numbers of receivers, characterized by considerable diversity, may be more appropriately reached by personal contact.

The goals of mass media advertising include differentiating the products of an individual enterprise from those of others in the market, increasing the demand for specific products, changing demand elasticity, and stabilizing demand against competitive developments and other changes over time.

A great variety of advertising media are available, and the media in each principal category possess various distinct performance and cost characteristics. In addition, each medium reaches a somewhat different audience group, at a different cost per message sent and received and with different impact. These differences are taken into account in the media selection process.

In establishing overall advertising budget levels, the two principal approaches are (1) building up media combinations and expenditure requirements in order to accomplish particular marketing goals and (2) following rules of thumb that are based on percentages of normal or estimated sales.

References

Brink, Edward L., and William T. Kelley. *The Management of Promotion: Consumer Behavior and Demand Stimulation.* Prentice-Hall, 1963.

Colley, Russell H. *Defining Advertising Goals for Measured Advertising Results.* Association of National Advertisers, 1964.

Dalbey, Homer, Irwin Gross, and Yoram Wind. *Advertising Measurement and Decision Making.* Allyn & Bacon, 1968.

Gensch, Dennis H. "Computer Models in Advertising Media Selection." *Journal of Marketing Research,* Vol. 5, No. 4, November 1968.

Lucas, Darrell, and Steuart H. Britt. *Measuring Advertising Effectiveness.* McGraw-Hill, 1963.

Robinson, Patrick J., and David J. Luck. *Promotional Decision Making: Practice and Theory.* McGraw-Hill, 1964.

Weinberg, Robert S. *An Analytical Approach to Advertising Expenditure Strategy.* Association of National Advertisers, 1960.

12

Pricing Policies and Practices

Prices are the terms of exchange among goods and services, or between goods and services and an accepted medium of exchange: money. In developed and relatively stable economies, prices are ordinarily stated and analyzed in terms of standard monetary units—for example, dollars and cents, pounds and shillings. In primitive societies, prices are often quoted in barter terms—so much wheat for so many cattle—or in terms of materials prized for their own sake: gold, precious stones, religious objects. Implicit barter relationships exist, of course, among goods and services in monetary economies. And the comparison of effective barter prices for important purchase alternatives may suggest new dimensions for price decisions. For example, among consumer goods it is relevant to examine the amounts of food or clothing, automobiles or housing, and so forth that can be purchased with equal dollar expenditures. Similarly, in industrial goods the barter alternatives among materials at various stages of processing, and between materials and equipment, often suggest new pricing possibilities to buyers and sellers alike. Barter prices also become prominent in highly developed countries during periods of rapid change in the general price level, particularly during hyperinflation, when the standard monetary unit is no longer considered reliable.

208

In this chapter we consider three aspects of pricing in some detail and relate the discussion throughout to the relationship between price and other marketing mix variables. The analysis focuses primarily on the viewpoint of the seller, who is most often the price setter in our economy. However, the equally important viewpoint of the buyer, who may take the pricing initiative under some circumstances, is implicit throughout and is explicitly considered where it is particularly relevant. The first topic, of central importance to both seller and buyer, is the fundamental relationship between prices and costs, both in an individual firm and among groups of firms, industries, and markets. Next, several important dimensions of price policy decisions are identified and the bases for policy choices within each dimension are examined. A brief discussion of price administration, including both traditional rules and behavioral procedures, follows. The final section of the chapter highlights the essential relationship between price and other elements of the marketing mix and thus serves as a short integrating summary of this part of the book.[1]

Prices and Costs

Do costs determine prices? Or do prices determine costs? Or is the connection between costs and prices only indirect and conditioned by important intervening variables? The paradoxical answer to all these questions is *yes*. Both within the individual firm and among competitive firms, costs exert an important and sometimes determining effect upon prices. However, buyers will not pay a particular price simply because a particular seller has incurred costs in some particular amount. Thus a potential seller's decision to incur costs rests upon the belief that potential buyers will be willing to pay prices that are at least sufficient to cover these costs some time in the future. And if buyers are willing to pay substantially more for higher-cost products than for lower-cost ones, sellers may find it desirable to increase costs in order to obtain more than equally increased prices, and thus greater profits. In this sense, then, prices determine costs, rather than vice versa.

Finally, in spite of both of these close links between prices and

1. A recent review of many aspects of pricing is contained in Phillips and Williamson (1967), epecially chaps. 12–16. The standard theoretical text is Stigler (1966).

costs, empirical data reveal a great variability in price-cost relationships among industries and products, which suggests that many other factors may be at work. For example, the average margin (sales values minus direct costs) in manufacturing industries in the United States in 1963 was approximately 25 percent of sales values. Among individual industries, however, margins ranged from less than 10 percent on such products as leather gloves, cheese, and soybean oil to more than 50 percent on such products as cutlery and toiletries.[2] Some of these differences are explained by differences in the ratio of capital costs to direct costs among industries; that is, margins will tend to be higher in more capital-intensive industries. However, a substantial portion of the differences seems to be accounted for by (a) whether industries are primarily engaged in producing and marketing consumer or producer goods and (b) whether total industry activity is relatively concentrated among a few firms or widely dispersed among many firms of more nearly equal size. In general, and with important exceptions, price-cost margins are higher in consumer goods industries and in more highly concentrated industries, even when differences in capital intensity and some additional factors are taken into account (Collins and Preston, 1969).

The relationship between costs and prices also varies substantially among the different products of a multiproduct firm. Indeed, a significant dimension of marketing strategy in such firms is the development of an assortment of products with varying life cycles, sales volumes, and profit margins in order to maintain a stable level of business activity over time and to balance opportunities for growth against protection from sales decline. In manufacturing industries it is not unusual to find that the largest volume of *sales* is accounted for by products with the lowest profit margins—the basic products of the firm, which are probably very similar to competitive offerings of other firms—whereas the largest share of total *profits* will be gained from smaller-volume, but higher-margin, specialty items. In retailing, similarly, staple products in each line of business (sugar and cigarettes in the supermarket, sheets and underwear in the department store) tend to carry lower margins than other items. For example, one study of supermarket pricing found that average margins were about 20 percent of the purchase price, but margins varied from less than 10 percent (on the two staples listed above) to 50 percent and more on some small-volume specialty items (*Progressive Grocer*, 1958). These pricing

---

2. Computed from Bureau of the Census (1966).

patterns will be referred to below in the discussion of market basket pricing.

In summary, prices and costs are interrelated in a variety of ways, and the connection between them in every instance will be significantly affected by many other market conditions, including the intensity of demand, the strength of competitive forces, and the assortment of products being purchased and sold simultaneously. However, two fundamental connections between prices and costs exert a pervasive effect on marketing activity, although their impact may not be detectable in a single transaction or at one moment of time. One of these is the necessity, for the individual firm, that total revenues obtained from sales cover all costs, including direct, overhead, and investment costs, and return a sufficient profit to justify continued operation of the enterprise over time. This does not mean, of course, that the price obtained in any single transaction must cover more than its own direct costs; indeed, it may even be desirable to sell below direct cost under some circumstances. However, prices obtained on *some* transactions must be in excess of the associated direct costs, and the aggregate of all the resulting price cost margins must be sufficient to meet all the cost and profit requirements necessary to the continuity of the firm. Thus, the relationships between selling prices and the firm's own costs determine its ability to remain in operation through time.

Under competitive conditions, however, the selling prices obtained by a firm are not determined by the individual firm's *own* costs, but rather by the costs incurred and prices charged by its competitors. The reason is that these other firms will offer to sell at prices favorable to themselves, and any individual competitive firm will have to adapt to these prices or find itself unable to dispose of its own output. Developing competitive prices does not require specific matching of prices and products among firms. It does, however, require adapting prices and products so that only "competitive" differences remain among them. For example, under competitive conditions, a slightly better quality of product may command a slightly higher price, but the price difference will be closely related to the cost required to obtain the product improvement. In this way the costs of competitors—and even of somewhat distant or potential competitors— determine the prices that can be obtained by any individual firm. It also follows that a firm that has only a few remote competitors may well have a wide range of choice in price-cost relationships and thus may be able to establish prices that maximize its profits, without much regard for the activities of others. Under such near-monopoly conditions, costs become only a point of reference in the pricing process, and price-cost relationships depend primarily on demand considerations.

Much of the traditional analysis of price decisions in marketing appears to be cast in terms of monopoly. Indeed, a certain departure from perfectly competitive conditions must be assumed if the individul firm can be said to make a price decision at all. However, it is clearly an error to analyze individual-firm pricing behavior as if most firms were isolated monopolies in their particular markets. On the contrary, it is essential that price decisions arrived at on the basis of a single firm's costs and demand circumstances be reexamined in the light of potential competitive alternatives and responses. If executives who are engaged in pricing do not scrutinize their initial decisions in the light of possible competitive developments, they are likely to discover the effects of competitive response through costly market experience.

One final connection between costs and prices is worth noting: the *timing* of changes in the two variables, particularly with respect to increases. Whether the costs and prices of firms and industries are relatively close together or quite far apart, it is a common practice to announce price changes in response to industry-wide changes in costs. It is also common to find that suppliers of goods and services, and particularly organized labor, attempt to change their prices (i.e., to raise costs) whenever a change in final-goods prices occurs. These timing patterns would be expected in perfectly competitive markets, where prices and costs are very closely linked. Cost increases would necessitate price increases if competitive firms are not to leave the market. Similarly price increases would raise the value of the productive factors employed, thereby creating a basis for cost increases. However, these timing patterns also prevail in industries with very wide price-cost margins, where the linking of price changes to cost changes may be simply an effective means of price coordination among firms that seek to avoid price competition.

Price Policies and Strategies

Managerial decision making, with respect to prices, is often discussed as if the principal problem were establishing specific dollar-and-cents prices on individual products and items. In fact, however, establishing and revising prices is a routine activity and usually is governed by standard operating rules and procedures (some of these will be discussed below in connection with price administration). In contrast with these routine operations, the task of selecting and developing basic price policies is a fundamental and difficult aspect of marketing planning. These key policy decisions identify the considerations that will be taken into account in routine price administration and the operations and information that will be necessary for setting and revising prices on a continuing basis.

The discussion of price policies and strategies in this chapter is necessarily highly selective. It is organized about four major topics: (1) single-price versus multiple-price policies, (2) multiproduct pricing, (3) the time dimension of pricing, and (4) price policies involving resellers.

Single-Price versus Multiple-Price Policies

The simple economic model of the firm depicts a single-product firm selling all units of its output at a single price. However, as we have noted in previous chapters, the typical firm in a developed economy is engaged in multiproduct activities; hence the analysis of decisions that involve multiple products and prices is a central topic in marketing. Not only do most firms produce and market merchandise items that are physically different in some respect, they are also able—if they choose—to charge different prices for essentially the same, or very similar, products and services when these are sold to different customers, or in different quantities, or at different times. An initial price policy decision for the firm, therefore, is whether to develop and take advantage of its ability to make different transactions on different terms or to ignore the differences among its potential customers and treat them all alike for price-setting purposes.

Price discrimination. The theory of price discrimination is a special topic in the study of monopoly pricing.[3] Its essential idea may be illustrated by a simple example. Suppose that you inherit from a deceased relative a plot of ground in his home community on which a free-flowing spring of mineral water is located. The residents of the community have a taste for mineral water and no other source is available, although they have ample access to plain water for regular use. There is no financial constraint on their water purchase: all of the residents are sufficiently well off that they are *able* to pay much more

---

3. For a classic review of the many forms of price discrimination, see Machlup (1955).

than they would be *willing* to pay in order to consume the mineral water. However, some of them have a stronger taste for it than others and are willing, therefore, to pay more in order to obtain it. The quality of the water is such that people who drink it ordinarily consume one glass per day—neither more nor less—and they bring their own glasses to the spring. No costs whatsoever are involved for the spring's owner. Your problem is to develop a price policy that will obtain the maximum income from your unique inheritance.

The typical student response to this problem is to draw a demand schedule, as in figure 12–1(a), showing the amount of money that each individual in the community would be willing to pay for his one glass of water per day. The student then estimates the single price that will produce the largest total revenue (P^*) and, since no costs are involved, concludes that this price should be posted for all glasses of water sold at the mineral spring, that Q^* glasses of water will be sold at this price, that all potential buyers who are willing to pay less than P^* per glass will get no water, and that all unsold water will flow away into a creek.

It is true that P^* and Q^* are the profit-maximizing single price and quantity choices in figure 12–1(a). However, the above analysis is *not* the best answer to the problem. On the contrary, a much greater total revenue and profit may be obtained if you devise a way to sell *each glass of water* to *each resident* at his own maximum price—that is, at the price he would pay rather than do without the water, as indicated by the demand schedule. Thus residents with a strong taste for the water would pay prices above P^* and residents who are less eager to have a daily glass would pay lower prices. If you are able to devise such a pricing scheme, your total revenue (and profit, since you have no costs) will be represented by the entire area beneath the demand schedule. All residents who are *willing* to pay any price greater than zero for the water will be served, and the total volume of water consumed (Q') will be substantially greater than it would be under a single-price policy.

The profit-maximizing policy for the mineral spring owner is, therefore, a policy of **price discrimination**. Price discrimination may be briefly defined as selling units of the *same* product to different purchasers at different prices; the higher-price purchasers are discriminated *against* while the lower-price purchasers are *favored*. Possibilities for discrimination arise whenever there are differences in the intensity of demand, accompanied by ability to pay, among potential buyers. When such differences exist on the demand side, when costs are not affected by the practice of discrimination, and when

Figure 12–1   Monopoly Price and Price Discrimination

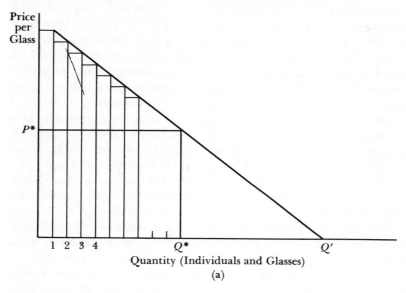

(a)

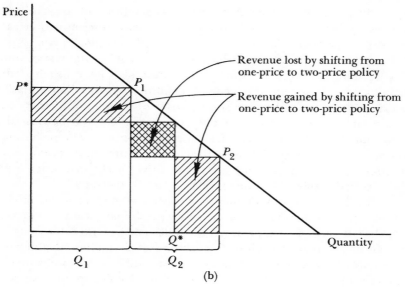

(b)

the lower-price buyers are not able to resell to the higher-price buyers, a policy of price discrimination will *always* lead to greater total profits and larger total sales volume than a single-price policy. This is true whether it is possible to charge *each* customer his maximum buying price or whether only two, or a few, customer groups are identified for pricing purposes. In figure 12–1(b), for example, the demand schedule of figure 12–1(a) is reproduced to illustrate a two-price policy, the next most profitable alternative after the P^*Q^* combination. It should be evident from inspection of the figure that these two monopoly prices $(P_1$ and $P_2)$—which divide the total possible demand into thirds, the lowest-price third being excluded from the market—result in substantially greater total revenues and profits than a single price.

The definition of price discrimination merits brief additional comment. What is meant by "the *same* product" in this context? Some physical similarity among the units sold is certainly implied; however, physical similarity is a matter of degree and depends, in part, on the knowledge and perspective of buyers. The essential similarity among product units sold at discriminatory prices is on the cost side; that is, product units are "the same" when they have the same costs or come from a single production process in which the specific costs of individual units cannot be identified. This emphasis on cost similarity widens, rather than narrows, the scope of price discrimination as a marketing practice. For if the sale of product units having equal costs at different prices is described as discrimination, the sale of units having different costs at equal prices must also be considered discriminatory. Thus, in the general definition, price discrimination occurs whenever a seller sells similar units of output to different customers at different cost-price ratios or margins. On the basis of this definition, it is obvious that price discrimination is a widespread marketing practice. It is also very likely that many more instances of discrimination occur because the same price is charged when costs differ than because prices differ when costs are the same.

It is important to note that the description of a particular pricing pattern as discriminatory in some respect is by no means a criticism, nor does it carry any implication of undesirable or illegal activity. It simply means that the selling agency or firm is taking advantage of differences in cost and/or demand to obtain different amounts or percentages of profit on different transactions. Note also that when a single buyer purchases a variety of items with different price-cost ratios or margins from a single seller, the situation can no longer be appropriately described as involving price discrimination. Under these circumstances, the buyer's decision to purchase items of different prices indicates that he sees distinct differences (not similarities) among them.[4]

Discrimination and segmentation. It was noted in chapter 10 that varying product quality, distribution methods, and promotional activities are important means of segmenting heterogeneous markets into more homogeneous subgroups of potential buyers. Many of these segmentation techniques involve specific costs that are traceable to the various market segments, and thus they create a basis for differences in prices and price-cost relationships among segments. In addition, price differences themselves may be an important segmentation technique in some instances. If the sales price of a particular type of product conveys a significant image of its quality, it may well be possible to market identical product units to different customer groups at different prices, with the price itself serving as the primary differentiating feature. As a rule, however, different distribution outlets and somewhat different packaging and branding practices are also involved. Indeed, in the more usual situation the segmentation policy is pursued *because* it, in turn, permits the establishment of differences in prices and profit margins among various customer groups.

As an example of a segmentation strategy problem, let us again consider the mineral spring. Once we know that the demand conditions that justify a price discrimination policy are present, our problem is to segment the market so that different customers can be charged different prices. Segmentation by distribution channels might be attempted. For example, we might establish an auction, with each successive glass of water sold to the highest bidder. However, the obvious fact that the mineral water is freely flowing—and thus that additional glasses will be available—would probably restrain the bidding, and a daily auction would be extremely inconvenient for the water drinkers. As an alternative, we might establish a delivery service, thereby incurring a slight additional cost but setting the price per glass of delivered water at some arbitrary level. Presumably, many of the residents who are willing to pay at least this much for water at the spring, as indicated by the demand schedule, would be willing to purchase delivered water at this price, while those with a less intense desire for the water, or those unwilling to pay the premium for delivery, might continue to

4. Holdren (1960) has described the retailing practice of charging different margins on different products as "product discrimination." He argues that the original seller, not the final buyer, of high margin merchandise is being discriminated against because his products are being priced for resale on relatively unfavorable terms.

buy it at the spring at an appropriately lower price. Segmentation possibilities through product variation (bottling, providing special glasses,
and so forth) and through promotion (branding and associating different—but hopefully not false!—advertising appeals with each brand)
also come to mind. Of course, these various segmentation strategies
might be pursued simply to reach different buyer groups and without
any price discrimination impact.

Discriminatory price differences would probably be even more
prevalent in the economy than they are at present if substantial costs
were not involved in administering multiple-price marketing programs
and in preventing resales from low-price to high-price customers. On
the other hand, discrimination arising from price uniformity, where
costs differ, continues—even where disadvantaged buyers are well
aware of it—because the cost of eliminating it would be too great.
For example, bottled soft drinks sell at the same prices in almost
every outlet throughout the United States, yet it is impossible that the
costs of production are the same in every bottling plant, and that
transportation and service costs are equal for each outlet served by
each plant—or that the two sets of cost differences invariably balance
out. Therefore it must be true that buyers from low-cost plants and
outlets are discriminated against while buyers who pay the same
prices for soft drinks from high-cost plants and outlets are favored.
Nevertheless, it is probably more satisfactory for buyers and sellers
alike to adhere to the uniform price rather than compute the cost differences and vary prices in small amounts from place to place.

Legal aspects of price discrimination.   Price discrimination that
tends to lessen competition in the economy was made illegal in the
United States by the Robinson-Patman Act (1936), an amendment to
section 2 of the Clayton Antitrust Act (1914). This legislation was
aimed primarily at the marketing practices of manufacturers and distributors who deal simultaneously with very large and relatively small
reseller-buyers. It was alleged that large reseller-buyers used their
bargaining power to obtain prices from suppliers that were lower than
the prices obtained by smaller reseller-buyers. As a result, the large
reseller-buyers were able to offer prices in final markets below those
that would yield a profit to smaller resellers. Since the smaller firms
could not match these low prices, final buyers would purchase all
their requirements from the larger firms, and the competition of
smaller firms with larger firms and among themselves would be eliminated. The Robinson-Patman Act extended the prohibition of price
discrimination to quantity discounts, advertising allowances, broker-

age allowances, and other marketing arrangements that might produce the same net effects. Price differences are allowed among customers, however, when they can be justified on the basis of cost differences (although the specific pattern of cost-price differences that might be legal was left to be determined on a case-by-case basis) and when they arise from meeting the competitive prices of other firms "in good faith."

As a result of this legislation, discriminatory price structures in intermediate markets may be called into question at any time on the basis of their potential anticompetitive impact on any group of re-seller-buyers or on subsequent customer groups within the marketing channel. However, price discrimination as such—in the absence of anticompetitive effects—is by no means illegal. On the contrary, almost any price structure that is subjected to detailed examination can be shown to have significant discriminatory aspects.

Multiproduct Pricing

Pricing multiple products, both complements and substitutes, each of which represents a distinct purchase possibility for the potential buyers, is essentially an extension of a market segmentation strategy. Of course, there are multiproduct firms that face such a wide array of competitive products from other sources that they simply price each product on its own merits, and with regard to the total competitive environment, without taking into account the specific interproduct relationships among them. However, in the more typical case, the marketing planner wishes to take specific account of both demand and cost relationships among products within his own market offerings. It will be recalled from chapter 10 that variety in the product line may be an important means of attracting customers to the merchandise of a particular firm; added variety also creates the possibility of making additional sales to all attracted customers. The goal of the marketing planner is to develop an assortment of products and prices that is varied enough to attract appropriate customer groups and optimal with respect to both (1) additional sales revenues that may be obtained through sales complementarity and (2) unnecessary or avoidable costs of overlapping and substitute products.

The establishment of multiple prices for related products is an essential element in the development and selection of product assortments. In some industries, readily substitutable variations within a single basic product type are routinely developed to coincide with an established multiproduct price structure. This practice is known as

price-lining. Price-lining occurs, for example, in the women's apparel industry, where items are routinely designed and produced in conformity with established final resale price lines: $9.95, $14.95, $19.95, and so forth. When changes occur in consumer tastes or production costs, the quality of products in, say, the $14.95 price line may be changed and the items in that line shifted to a different price within the established price structure. Rarely, however, will this type of merchandise be priced at $13.35, $16.21, or other prices that are not among the traditional price lines.

Market basket pricing. A different kind of multiple-product pricing problem arises when the products involved are complementary in purchase—that is, the sale of one product directly stimulates the sale of another. In these circumstances, which may be termed **multipurchase marketing** (because each buyer may make multiple purchases from a single seller), the pricing problem is to develop a combination of prices for the various products that will lead to the optional sale of product combinations. Since this situation is particularly characteristic of retail marketing, and particularly of supermarkets, the term **market basket pricing** has been coined to describe this pricing strategy (see Preston, 1963).

In market basket pricing, the price setter seeks to take advantage of both individual product demand conditions and inter-product demand relationships in order to obtain maximum profits. In practice, this means that he tries to select individual items whose prices are well known, or items to which customers are known to be particularly price-sensitive, and to feature them at strikingly low prices both in advertising and within the store. Thus, by attracting customers to a store to purchase the "specials," the retailer is also in a position to sell them their regular purchase requirements at regular prices. And thus, by selling a combination of "specials" and regular-price items to each customer, he hopes to attain greater sales and profits than if he offered all items at their regular prices. The items that are featured at unusually low prices for this purpose have traditionally been termed "loss leaders"; however, Holton (1957) has noted that they might more accurately be termed "profit leaders," since the purpose of their selection and use is to bring about an increase in profits.

The basic strategy of market basket pricing extends far beyond the field of retailing. All tie-in sales arrangements are essentially market basket pricing problems. For example, when production equipment is sold along with expendable supplies, or when merchandise and related services (say, equipment and maintenance contracts) are sold together, the optimal price policy is the one that leads to the most profitable total of combined sales. Indeed, whenever two outputs are sold and priced separately, but nevertheless related in demand and use, the price combination problem arises. For example, if users of a piece of industrial equipment could be compelled to purchase the supplies or services associated with the equipment solely from the original equipment supplier, and at very profitable (for the supplier) prices, it may pay the supplier to provide the equipment itself free of charge. The possibility that tie-in arrangements and requirements contracts might be used to protect or extend monopoly positions in the economy has led to their specific prohibition, when they tend to have anticompetitive effects, in the Robinson-Patman Act.

Pricing Strategies over Time

All of the previous discussion has dealt with price decisions for a single market period or with once-and-for-all decisions taken on the basis of anticipated typical cost and demand conditions over time. In fact, however, many pricing policies include explicit consideration of the relationship between prices and marketing activity through time. In these instances an attempt is made to establish a time pattern of prices so that sales and profits will be maximized over the life history of individual products or in perpetuity for the firm. Two clearly distinct types of time-related pricing policies are of particular importance: (1) policies related to stages in the product life cycle and (2) policies that involve periodic price variation as a merchandising technique.

Pricing in the life cycle. The initial price decision for a new product is part of the overall marketing plan for its development and introduction. The initial price helps identify the product in the eyes of the potential buyers, who will compare the price and product, both with similar products at various prices (if there are any), and with other purchasing alternatives in the same price range.

The principal alternative introductory pricing policies are sometimes described as **skimming** and **penetration**. A skimming policy prescribes the choice of a relatively high initial price, within the range of possible prices that might be selected, and the selection of other marketing mix variables so as to concentrate sales among potential buyers who are willing to pay this price. The purpose is to "skim" the profits available from a relatively small volume of initial high-margin sales before its lower, long-run price level becomes established. The contrary policy of penetration requires setting the introductory price at, or even below, the expected long-run price level and choosing other marketing mix variables so as to expand sales volume rapidly. The objective is to reach the sales level associated with the maturity stage of the product's life cycle as quickly as possible.

Either skimming or penetration may be a profitable and success-ful policy under appropriate conditions. A skimming policy may be indicated when a new product is substantially different from any other product on the market and when it is known to appeal strongly to some group of potential buyers who possess ample purchase ability. Under these circumstances, skimming—which amounts to discriminat-ing in price between initial and later purchasers—may yield greater profits than would be obtained from a single-price policy over time. On the other hand, a penetration policy is indicated if substantial dif-ferences among potential buyers do not exist, or if the profits available from buyer differences are more than offset by profits arising from economies of scale and continuity of operations for the introducing firm. In addition, penetration pricing may be particularly attractive for products subject to rapid taste and habit formation, so that the initial source and brand becomes established in the leading position within an entire product group.

An introductory skimming price, by definition, is expected to decline over the course of the product life cycle, as skimming condi-tions give way to conditions of normal market acceptance and matu-rity. Penetration prices also may change over time, as a result of demand and cost changes and competitive developments. When penetration prices are established *below* the anticipated normal long-run price for a product, they are ordinarily identified as "special in-troductory offers" or similar designations. The intention behind this type of merchandising is to use the "regular" price as an indicator of the quality status of the product, as well as to prepare the buyer to pay a higher price if he chooses to purchase the product on a con-tinuing basis. Many times, of course, the rate of product acceptance at the introductory price level is not sufficient to permit a price increase, and thus the price remains at the "introductory" level over time or the product has to be withdrawn. Regrettably, a "special introductory offer" may also be used as a form of deceptive advertising when no new product introduction or anticipated regular price level is in-volved.

Variable-price merchandising. The second major type of time-related pricing strategy is the use of perpetual or periodic price vari-ations for individual products within a multiproduct assortment in order to draw attention to a firm or outlet and to differentiate it from its competitors. This strategy has been termed "variable-price mer-chandising," because it involves the use of price variability, not sim-ply specific prices or price levels, as a key dimension of marketing policy (see Nelson and Preston, 1966).

Variable-price merchandising, which is most familiar in food retailing, is closely related to the strategy of market basket pricing discussed above. However, the optimal mix of market basket prices need not be variable over time. On the contrary, the best combination of prices for products with related demands may remain unchanged from one period to the next. Further, effective use of a variable-price merchandising strategy is not limited to situations in which the indi-vidual customer purchases multiproduct assortments. Thus the peri-odic use of "sale" promotions, featuring different product groups at different times, and of unadvertised "special" prices within a store or catalog—both of which are forms of variable price merchandising—attracts to the firm or outlet the attention of various potential buyers, including those who purchase only the special-price merchandise and those who purchase none of it.

It is curious that variable price merchandising has come to be so strongly associated with food retailing, where the great standardization of products and outlets might be expected, *a priori,* to lead to price uniformity among firms and price stability over time. The explanation seems to be that product lines can be so nearly the same among out-lets, and other store features can be so closely imitated, that the only low-cost means of sharp differentiation among them is the selection of different products for special pricing and advertising. Also, as a critical condition for continuing this type of price behavior, enter-prises *must not* simply and simultaneously duplicate each other's price and product choices since, if they did so, they would no longer be dif-ferentiated in this respect. Empirical studies of retail food pricing indicate that competing firms do *not* tend to advertise the same items or the same prices at the same time, and also that the prices of heavily advertised products do not tend to stabilize at a single level for all firms over time. Thus this particular pricing strategy, although clearly competitive, does not lead to the equilibrium results that would be anticipated on the basis of a simple single-product single-period com-petitive pricing model.

Reseller Price Policies

All of the above pricing policies and strategies may be employed by marketing intermediaries who purchase merchandise for resale, as well as by original producers, fabricators, and branders. Some of these policies, such as market basket pricing and variable-price merchandising, are particularly—but by no means exclusively—associated with pricing by resellers. In addition to these resale price policies, independently developed and practiced by resellers, it is also common for original merchandise producers and branders to develop pricing policies that explicitly include reseller price levels and practices. In these instances, the original seller of the merchandise seeks to suggest or prescribe the minimum, maximum, or specific prices that resellers may charge in dealing with subsequent customers. When this control over prices is formally established by means of contracts and price notification procedures, it is referred to as "resale price maintenance" (RPM) or, more euphemistically, "fair trade" or "quality stabilization" pricing. Similar results may be obtained, with less resort to contracts and legal proceedings, by means of price suggestions and the inclusion of price information on packages and labels.

Resale price maintenance. There are a few historic instances in which resale price maintenance has been used by original producers and branders to hold down the prices of their products in final markets. However, the more typical purpose of RPM is to maintain final prices at or above certain minimum levels, that is, to prevent price cutting by resellers. A question immediately arises: Why would any original producer or brander wish to do this? A priori, one would suppose that any producer would be happy to have resellers charge the lowest possible resale prices (provided his own prices to resellers remained unaffected) in order to achieve the greatest possible sales volume in final markets. There are, however, a number of reasons why manufacturers and branders might choose to follow an RPM policy, and some of the most important ones may be briefly summarized. (See also Telser, 1960, and Gould and Preston, 1965.)

Price-quality relationships. The role of price as an indicator of merchandise quality for final buyers has been mentioned previously. Where these price-quality "image" effects are extremely important, a price reduction by resellers may reduce total demand and sales by suggesting a lower quality level, or a tendency toward deterioration, for the product.

Reseller services. If the marketing program of the manufacturer requires the maintenance of specific types of reseller facilities and the performance by resellers of relatively costly special services, some means must be found to motivate resellers to operate in the desired manner and to compensate them for the costs involved. Various means may be found for accomplishing these objectives, including special allowances and direct payments for services rendered. However, when the desired activities are continuous and very general in nature—such as providing displays and demonstrations, maintenance and repair services, and intensive selling efforts—the establishment of relatively wide unit profit margins may be a highly efficient means of accomplishing the desired goals. If this means is chosen, an RPM arrangement may be required to ensure that some resellers do not use the wide margins as a basis for price reductions, thereby undermining the competitive status of the resellers who follow the desired operating practices.

Number of outlets. Aggregate sales of particular items and brands of merchandise may be importantly affected by the number of resale outlets in which they are available to potential purchasers. This is true not only because each outlet provides additional sales opportunities but also because routine shelf displays and catalog listings establish and maintain high levels of product awareness and recognition among potential buyers. Thus it may be in the original producer's interest that his product be made available through the largest possible number of appropriate outlets. For any particular aggregate product sales volume, however, the larger the number of outlets, the smaller must be the average number of product units sold per outlet. Reseller outlets generally require some minimum level of total revenue and total gross profit margin for each item or brand of product handled in order to justify providing their facilities and services for it. Evidently, if the original producer can assure resellers of higher prices and unit profit margins—and also assure them that other resellers will not undercut these levels—these minimum revenue and profit requirements can be met from the sale of smaller numbers of product units than would otherwise be required. Hence RPM may enable an original producer to expose his products to a larger number of outlets, each of which sells relatively fewer units of his product, but with the intended result being a greater aggregate of total sales than he would obtain if prices and margins were lower and the outlets handling the product correspondingly fewer. (In much of the practical literature, this matter is discussed in terms of the danger of *losing* outlets and exposure if prices and margins are allowed to vary freely among resellers.)

Reseller cartel. Many students of RPM have concluded that one of its principal functions is to establish a cartel-like arrangement among resellers so that all of them are restrained from engaging in price competition with each other. The political support among reseller business groups for legislation permitting or strengthening

RPM arrangements lends credibility to this allegation. However, it is not likely that large firms that manufacture and market highly advertised and well-established branded goods would cooperate in RPM practices unless it were in their own interest to do so.

Legal aspects. The control by one person or firm of the prices and marketing practices of others not under the same ownership is at variance with the common conception of property rights and is generally held (in the United States) to be an illegal restraint upon trade. Yet the practice of RPM involves precisely such control. Therefore, to legalize RPM arrangements it has been necessary to secure legislation that explicitly permits this practice as an exception to the usual standards applied to agreements among independent buyers and sellers. In the United States, federal legislation has permitted the separate states to enact resale price maintenance laws and to enforce them in interstate commerce among the enacting states. Some states have never enacted such laws, and the specific provisions and legal status of the laws adopted by the various states are diverse and continually changing.

The greatest difficulty arises because of the need to force uncompliant resellers to adhere to the pricing instructions of suppliers. Yet keeping these resellers "in line" is at the heart of an RPM program, since resellers who desire to maintain the designated prices can do so in response to suggestions, without resort to a formal RPM arrangement. The policing of RPM agreements is entirely up to the supplier, and the cost and complexity of price inspections, merchandise retrieval, and prosecution of resellers who depart from the designated prices have served to reduce the use of RPM in the United States in recent years. It remains, however, an important feature of marketing policies in some industries (drugs and toiletries and some lines of apparel) and some states (particularly California).

One alternative to RPM is the announcement of suggested resale prices by manufacturers and branders, without contractual arrangements or legal recourse against resellers who fail to follow the suggestions. This technique may establish the required cooperative behavior in some instances, although it serves as an invitation to reseller price cutting in others. A second approach is an agency relationship whereby resellers do not take title to merchandise but simply represent the principal (i.e., the original producer or brander) and follow his pricing and merchandising instructions. A few important types of consumer goods (notably light bulbs) are marketed in this way through regular retail channels. A third alternative is a franchise arrangement whereby resellers (franchisees) enter into extensive agreements with franchisors concerning product assortments, services, supply sources, business locations, and other aspects of routine operations, as well as prices. The basic price structures of franchise outlets are ordinarily controlled by the franchisors, although a certain amount of individual variation may be permitted.

Impact of RPM. One important result of RPM practices in instances where they are widespread and effective is improved marketing opportunities for lower-priced items and brands within the RPM product groups. In effect, RPM prices establish an umbrella under which cheaper products may obtain large and profitable market shares. The development of reseller brands, which usually sell at lower final prices than highly advertised and price-maintained manufacturer brands, has been particularly important in recent years. In many cases both reseller brands and manufacturer brands are produced in the same, or very similar, facilities; and the reseller's ability to purchase unbranded items for his own merchandising often results in substantially lower procurement costs, which yields him larger unit profit margins, even on items with lower final prices. The resulting expansion of reseller-brand merchandising activity and market shares has contributed importantly to the decline of RPM in some industries, where RPM products were losing their markets to lower-price non-RPM items within their product groups.

Price Administration

Basic price policies and strategies are implemented, and individual prices computed and revised, through price administration. Some pricing policies (such as detailed and lengthy haggling over each transaction) require very little administration, although they may result in very high marketing costs. On the other hand, implementation of a marketing plan that involves multiple products to be sold in various combinations to a variety of types of potential users will necessarily involve extensive administrative activity. The guiding principle of price administration is to state and revise prices so as to follow the intended price policy, as nearly as possible, without making the price quoting and price changing procedure itself either unduly expensive or an impediment to the overall marketing program. Empirical studies indicate that price administration is in most cases based on a combination of traditional markup rules and routine pricing and price-review procedures, and both of these aspects of pricing activity require brief consideration.

Markup Pricing Rules

If one asks a sample of independent businessmen and corporate executives how they set prices, the most common response is that they add a traditional or normal percentage markup to some computed or estimated unit cost and thereby arrive at a price. A little probing will reveal that the recommended markups vary among products and that prices computed from a markup rule may be revised upward or downward as a result of specific considerations or general sales experience. However, the notion of a traditional or normal markup occupies a central place in nearly all discussions of pricing practices.

What does adherence to a traditional markup rule imply? Obviously, the difference between any pair of price and unit cost figures can be computed and the result, expressed as a percentage of cost, can be termed a "markup." [5] However, if the markup is not simply an *ad hoc* statistic computed after the fact, adherence to a markup rule must guide price makers to the desirable range of actual price quotations—at least more often than not. There are several reasons why this might be so.

Costs and competition.   Pricing by means of a markup rule assures, at a minimum, that an initial attempt will be made to recover unit costs on each transaction. Many problems are involved in establishing a unit cost figure for pricing purposes—that is, in actually knowing what unit costs *are* within large and complex organizations and in making appropriate allowances for indirect costs associated with individual product groups and customers. However, once some standard cost-estimating procedure has been established, markup rules require the price maker to take these costs into account. Further, if costs—or even cost *estimates*—tend to be about the same among several competitive firms, and their marketing behavior over time has led to their acceptance of a certain cost-price relationship as "normal" for their products and markets, the revision of prices over time, as well as the development of new prices for product variations, on the basis

5. The value of the difference in money, or as a percentage of the price, is commonly termed a "margin." For example, unit costs of $8 and a price of $10 yield a difference of $2, which may be described either as a 25-percent markup or as a 20-percent margin.

of this "normal" markup pattern will reduce the likelihood that price administrators will unintentionally disrupt regular price and product relationships throughout the market. Thus a markup rule may provide a means for incorporating the outcomes of previous price competition in the setting of present prices. It is also a means of avoiding the introduction of new types of price competition where these are not desired.

Markup and rate of return.   Investment decisions for acquiring new facilities and for developing and marketing new products are generally made on the basis of anticipated rates of return over time. The pricing rules of large firms are frequently stated in terms of an overall target rate-of-return goal. The relationship between such goals and markup-pricing rules may be easily illustrated.

Let P stand for unit price, C for unit cost, Q for the number of units produced and sold, M for the percentage markup over cost, and I for the required amount of investment. (For simplicity, all variables are stated with respect to one market period only.) Then the percentage markup may be written

$$M = \frac{P - C}{C} \tag{1}$$

and the markup price as

$$P = C(1 + M)$$

The demand function is written [6]

$$Q = f(P) \quad \text{or} \quad Q = f(C, M) \tag{2}$$

Total profits are

$$Q(P - C) \tag{3}$$

And the rate of return is

$$r = \frac{Q(P - C)}{I} \tag{4}$$

6. Read "Quantity demanded is a function of price, or . . . a function of cost and margin."

By combining (1) and (4), we obtain an expression that relates the markup to the rate of return:

$$\frac{(Q)(M)(C)}{I} = r \tag{5}$$

From this expression it is clear that, for any given investment and unit cost, the demand function—that is, the relationship between Q and P (or between Q and C and M) determines the markup necessary to obtain a desired rate of return. Or, conversely, the demand function determines the rate of return that will result from any particular markup rule that might be followed. Since the relationship between markup and rate of return has been shown to depend upon the demand function, it may seem that nothing has been clarified by this piece of analysis. However, the significant point is that, for given demand conditions, costs, and amounts of investment, there is a unique relationship between markup and rate of return. And, since neither the markup nor the amount of investment directly determines the demand conditions, it is appropriate to take these conditions as given in the short run for purposes of price administration. Therefore the two most common pricing rules—markup and target rate of return— are shown to be different ways of expressing the same basic relationship.

A further implication of this analysis is that when a new investment opportunity is appraised in terms of rate-of-return criteria—and thereafter undertaken—the markup percentage that is incorporated in the initial investment decision becomes a useful guide to price administration. If costs and demand were accurately estimated during the planning stage, and if the markup originally contemplated is actually applied, the rate of return that is obtained should be approximately on target. Thus the use of such markup rules is a way of setting prices and attaining sales results that will meet the criteria applied in the initial investment decision.

Markup and elasticity. In spite of the evidence that markup rules typically play an important role in price administration, many analysts of price behavior have been troubled by the implication that the addition of a standard markup percentage to various unit cost totals should invariably yield prices that would be even feasible, let alone optimal, in actual markets. Since demand conditions are independent of cost conditions, costs may vary among products and over time without generating a related variation in demand. Therefore it would seem that application of a standard markup to these various costs might result in prices so high that *no* quantity might be sold, or so low as to result in revenues and profits far below the best attainable levels.

These possibilities can be readily illustrated under a variety of highly simplified analytical conditions, and perhaps under some actual conditions as well. However, there is one particular set of conditions under which the application of the same percentage markup will result in a final price that is not only feasible but optimal, no matter what the level of costs.[7] These conditions are: (1) unit costs are equal for all units within the relevant range, although the level of unit costs may vary among products and over time, and (2) demand is isoelastic (i.e., has the same *elasticity*) with respect to price throughout the relevant range. These two conditions are illustrated in figure 12–2 for an iso-

Figure 12–2   Optimal Markup Conditions

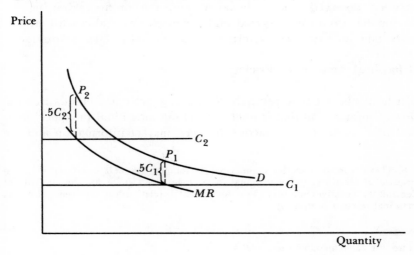

elastic demand curve (D) with a constant elasticity of -3. The corresponding marginal revenue curve (MR) is also drawn, along with two horizontal but different unit (average and marginal) cost levels, C_1 and C_2. It will be evident that optimal prices are in each case 50

7. This argument was originally developed in Preston (1963), pp. 4–8.

percent greater than unit costs. Thus a uniform 50 percent markup rule will yield the profit-maximizing price for every unit cost level, provided those costs are the same for all units, so long as the elasticity of demand does not change.[8] Note also that if the demand curve were to shift, but not change its elasticity as a result, the constant markup rule would continue to hold good.

This model, though highly simplified, seems to suggest some of the real forces underlying the prevalence, and apparent success, of markup pricing in practice. Areas of marketing in which markup rules are routinely applied are principally those in which unit costs of individual items and products are substantially the same over large numbers of units—for example, retailing, wholesaling, and mass production manufacturing. Further, given the fundamental lack of detailed information about actual demand conditions, it may be efficient —and probably not greatly in error—to assume that the responsiveness of sales quantities to price changes is approximately constant, at least over relatively small changes in either direction; that is, to assume that demand is of constant elasticity. It may be that the correspondence between observed pricing behavior and the profit-maximizing behavior that would be expected under these theoretical conditions suggests some important characteristics of the actual pricing environment.

Behavioral Analysis of Pricing

Much of the current research on pricing activities emphasizes the flow of information that is used in reaching individual price decisions, and particularly the interaction between market information and the

---

8. This argument may be summarized as follows. Let MR stand for marginal revenue, P for price, C for marginal (= average) cost, and e for the elasticity of demand (a negative number). The fundamental relationship between price and marginal revenue is given by

$$MR = (1 + \frac{1}{e})P \qquad (1)$$

Since, for profit maximization, $MR = C$, then

$$C = (1 + \frac{1}{e})P \qquad (2)$$

Rearranging, we obtain

$$P = C(1 - \frac{1}{1 + e}) \qquad (3)$$

Since e is a negative number, for all values of e that are numerically greater than one the negative signs cancel out, and the fraction becomes an expression of the percentage markup over cost. Illustrative values for elasticity and markup are -2, 100 percent; -5, 24 percent; -21, 5 percent; and so on.

firm's own information system and decision processes. For example, a recent report described the price-decision process for a single, slightly differentiated product of a large firm (Howard and Morgenroth, 1968). The product is constantly visible in the market; its prices are frequently changed and the price changes are executed rapidly. A record of price decision making was obtained from the observation of executives and study of past records, and a decision flow chart (shown in figure 12–3) was constructed and used as the basis for a computer simulation.

The price analysis begins with the inspection of competitive prices (box 1), and if competitive prices are the same as the firm's own price (box 2), the firm continues to watch the competition and makes no change. However, if prices are different, the firm checks with its district sales offices to gather information from the field on expected market developments. The results of these successive inquiries and responses, with intervening delays, lead to many different reaction paths, each culminating in a decision either (*a*) to hold the price stable and continue watching the market or (*b*) to match the observed competitive price change (box 5). In a replication of thirty-one price decisions by means of the simulation model, the direction of the resultant price change was correctly predicted in all instances.

Models of this type represent an important forward step in price analysis because they formalize the process by which prices are actually set and changed within large sectors of the economy. They also provide a basis for improving and simplifying price administration procedures. Of course, a simple behavioral model, such as this one, does not explain the initial level of prices or the reasons for price changes by competitors. For these purposes, more extensive analysis of cost and demand conditions throughout the market is required. However, behavioral models serve to emphasize the repetitive character of marketing activity and competitive market interactions, an emphasis that is difficult to retain in discussions of basic price-policy determination and cost-and-demand-based decision rules.

Pricing in the Marketing Mix

Throughout this chapter we have noted the important interrelationships between price policies and other marketing mix variables. This connection is worth reemphasizing as a conclusion to this chapter and to Part III. Price and product policies are intimately related through

Figure 12–3   Model of Pricing Decision Process (Howard, 1968)

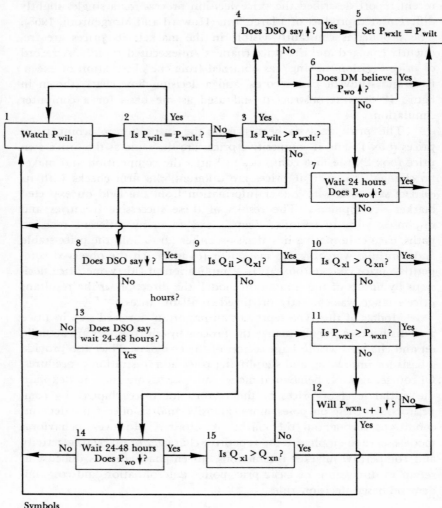

Symbols

P = price
w = wholesale
i = initiator
l = local market
n = nearby market
t = time
DSO = district sales office
DM = decision maker
x = decision maker's company
o = other major competitors (neither i nor x)
Q = expected physical volume of sales

production and procurement costs since actual merchandise and service costs are the base expenditures that, over time, must be recovered through pricing. In addition, prices convey information about product quality, relative to other products on the market, that may not be readily summarized in a more specific description of physical or performance attributes. For example, how would you better describe the broad qualitative differences among the major groups of American automobiles than in terms of lower-price, medium-price, and higher-price lines?

Pricing and distribution channel policy are also closely linked because the basic price range of products broadly determines the types of distribution activity they will justify or require and it limits the amount of distribution costs that can profitably be incurred. For example, high-price products cannot be readily sold through channels that deal primarily in cash sales, nor can low-price products support large expenditures for personal selling. In addition, as was discussed in detail above, distribution margins have an important effect on the size and number of distribution outlets, and therefore on the density and location of marketing facilities throughout the economy. Note that this connection extends far beyond the narrow resale-price-maintenance case. For example, either numerous and scattered small warehouses, or high-cost and rapid transportation modes can be used to keep users supplied with high-value industrial goods on short notice. However, low-value goods must be distributed from a few central locations by relatively slow transit modes since buyers would be unwilling to pay the cost of expensive distribution arrangements.

The connection between pricing and promotional activity, particularly advertising, is very complex. On one hand, it is clear that advertising requires costs that have to be recovered through prices. Further, the differences between the prices of highly advertised and less advertised similar products, and between the profit rates of high-advertising and low-advertising consumer goods marketing firms, strongly suggest that "advertising can be sold at a profit"; that is, advertising expenditures can be more than offset by increased revenues. This observation seems to suggest that advertising typically raises prices. However, it is important not to overlook the possibility that production and distribution costs for individual items may be substantially reduced due to the large and stable sales volumes made possible by mass advertising. Thus the unit costs of these large production volumes, including advertising, may not, in fact, be higher than the unit costs of the smaller volumes that would be sold in the absence of advertising. Promotional activity of all types, of course, is closely related to product quality, particularly the image of product quality held by potential buyers, and to distribution channel policy, since the channel must make the product available to the same group of potential customers reached by the promotional effort—and on a consistent or compatible basis. And all of these marketing mix variables— product, promotion, and distribution—are joined in the determination of total costs, and thus of price and profit alternatives.

Summary

Prices are the terms of exchange among goods and services, and **price policy** is a central element in the marketing program of a business enterprise. Under competitive conditions, prices are determined primarily by **costs**. However, since prices may be varied as part of the marketing policy of a firm, and costs may be varied correspondingly, costs may also be determined primarily by prices.

The relationship between a firm's own prices and the costs and prices of its competitors is an important determinant of its sales success in the market. Moreover, the relationship between a firm's prices and its costs determines the profitability of its sales.

A firm may adopt a single-price or multiple-price policy for its various products and customer groups, and either type of policy may involve **price discrimination.** Discrimination occurs when outputs that have the same costs are sold at different prices, or when outputs that have different costs are sold at the same price. Selling the same product at different prices to buyers with different demand characteristics will result in greater total revenues for a firm than selling to the same group of buyers at a single price. However, the costs of discrimination may outweight the benefits. On the other hand, eliminating discrimination that arises from cost differences on low-value single-price products would often be expensive and inconvenient. Price discrimination is illegal in the United States if it tends to lessen competition in interstate commerce.

A firm pricing multiple products must take account of their potential cost and demand interrelationships. It may adopt price lines that indicate sharp differences among the products, and thereby hope to separate the potential customers into market segments. Conversely, a firm may offer low prices on some of its products to attract customers who will purchase other items as well. This latter practice has been termed **market basket pricing.**

Prices may be systematically varied over time, both in relation to the product life cycle and as a routine practice. During the introductory phase of the life cycle, price policy alternatives range from a (high) **skimming** price, intended to gain profits from those customers who are most willing to pay, to a (low) **penetration** price, intended to gain rapid market acceptance and high-volume production. After the introductory market experience has been completed, prices may be adjusted either downward or upward to appropriate levels for the growth and maturity phase.

Another time-related price policy is **variable price** merchandising, in which selected product prices are varied at regular and frequent intervals in order to draw attention to the firm and its market offering. Supermarkets and many other types of retail outlets typically follow this policy.

Many firms pursue price policies that are designed to establish or control the prices of the resellers of their products. These policies may be informally administered or formally established under resale price maintenance (RPM) agreements. Such policies may be aimed at establishing price-quality relationships in the minds of final buyers, stimulating resellers to provide essential services (including sales effort), and permitting the operation of a larger number of resale outlets than would otherwise be the case—or simply at restraining competition among resellers.

Although RPM has been strong in various parts of the United States at various times, it is constantly under legal attack. In addition, one of the principal results of strong RPM practices has been the growth of reseller brands that allow resellers to circumvent RPM restrictions.

In the routine administration of prices, most firms follow some form of markup pricing rule. Such rules are developed on the basis of market experience, and are changed over time as a result of changes in competitive conditions and costs. The use of a stable markup rule has been shown to be consistent with the implementation of a minimum rate-of-return criterion for investment decisions, and also with an assumption of constant demand elasticity in product markets. Recent studies of actual price administration have shown that price setting is a sequential and adaptive behavioral process rather than a once-and-for-all analytical task, as some simple decision models might suggest.

References

Bureau of Census. *Concentration Ratios in the Manufacturing Industry,* 1963. U.S. Government Printing Office, 1966.

Collins, Norman R., and Lee E. Preston. "Price-Cost Margins and Industry Structure." *Review of Economics and Statistics,* Vol. 51, No. 3, August 1969.

Gould, J. R., and Lee E. Preston. "Resale Price Maintenance and Retail Outlets." *Economica,* Vol. 32, No. 127, August 1965.

Holdren, Bob R. *The Structure of a Retail Market and the Market Behavior of Retail Units.* Prentice-Hall, 1960.

Holton, R. H. "Price Discrimination at Retail: The Supermarket's Case." *Journal of Industrial Economics,* Vol. 6, October 1957.

Howard, J. A., and W. M. Morgenroth. "Information Processing Model of Executive Decision." *Management Science,* Vol. 14, March 1968.

Machlup, Fritz. "Characteristics and Types of Price Discrimination." In *Business Concentration and Price Policy,* National Bureau of Economic Research. Princeton University Press, 1955.

Nelson, Paul E., and Lee E. Preston. *Price Merchandising in Food Retailing: A Case Study.* University of California Institute of Business and Economic Research, 1966.

Phillips, Almarin, and Oliver E. Williamson, eds. *Prices: Issues in Theory, Practice, and Public Policy.* University of Pennsylvania Press, 1967.

Preston, Lee E. *Profits, Competition, and Rules of Thumb in Retail Food Pricing.* University of California, Berkeley, Institute of Business and Economic Research, 1963.

Progressive Grocer. *Super Valu Study,* 1958.

Stigler, G. J. *The Theory of Price,* 3rd ed. Macmillan, 1966.

Telser, Lester G. "Why Should Manufacturers Want Fair Trade?" *Journal of Law and Economics,* Vol. 3, 1960.

Index

1 2 3 4 5 6 7 8 9 10 11 12 13 14 15 16 17 18 19 20 21 22 23 24 25   78 77 76 75 74 73 72 71 70